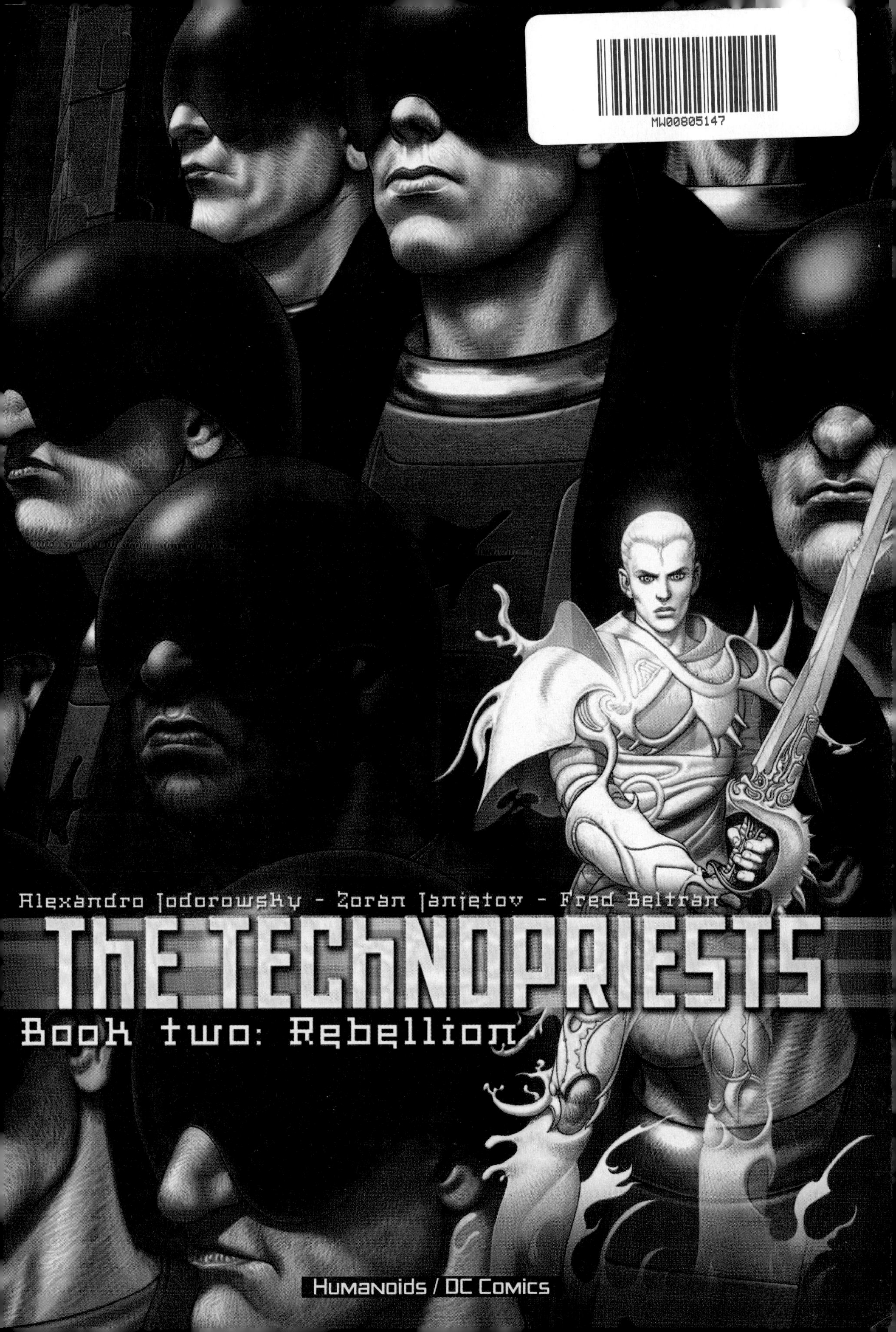
Alexandro Jodorowsky - Zoran Janjetov - Fred Beltran
THE TECHNOPRIESTS
Book two: Rebellion
Humanoids / DC Comics

THE TECHNOPRIESTS
Book two: Rebellion

ALEXANDRO JODOROWSKY,
Writer

ZORAN JANJETOV,
Artist

FRED BELTRAN,
Colorist & Cover Artist

SASHA WATSON,
Translator

THIERRY FRISSEN
Book Designer

PATRICK LEHANCE
Letterer

PAUL BENJAMIN
Editor, Collected Edition

BRUNO LECIGNE
& FABRICE GIGER
Editors, Original Edition

DC COMICS: PAUL LEVITZ, President & Publisher GEORG BREWER, VP-Design & Retail Product Development
RICHARD BRUNING, Senior VP-Creative Director PATRICK CALDON, Senior VP-Finance & Operations CHRIS CARAMALIS, VP-Finance
TERRI CUNNINGHAM, VP-Managing Editor ALISON GILL, VP-Manufacturing RICH JOHNSON, VP-Book Trade Sales HANK KANALZ, VP-General Manager, WildStorm
LILLIAN LASERSON, Senior VP & General Counsel JIM LEE, Editorial Director-WildStorm DAVID MCKILLIPS, VP-Advertising & Custom Publishing
JOHN NEE, VP-Business Development GREGORY NOVECK, Senior VP-Creative Affairs CHERYL RUBIN, Senior VP-Brand Management BOB WAYNE, VP-Sales & Marketing

THE TECHNOPRIESTS Book #2, Rebellion, Humanoids Publishing. PO Box 931658, Hollywood, CA 90094.
This is a publication of DC Comics, 1700 Broadway, New York, NY 10019.

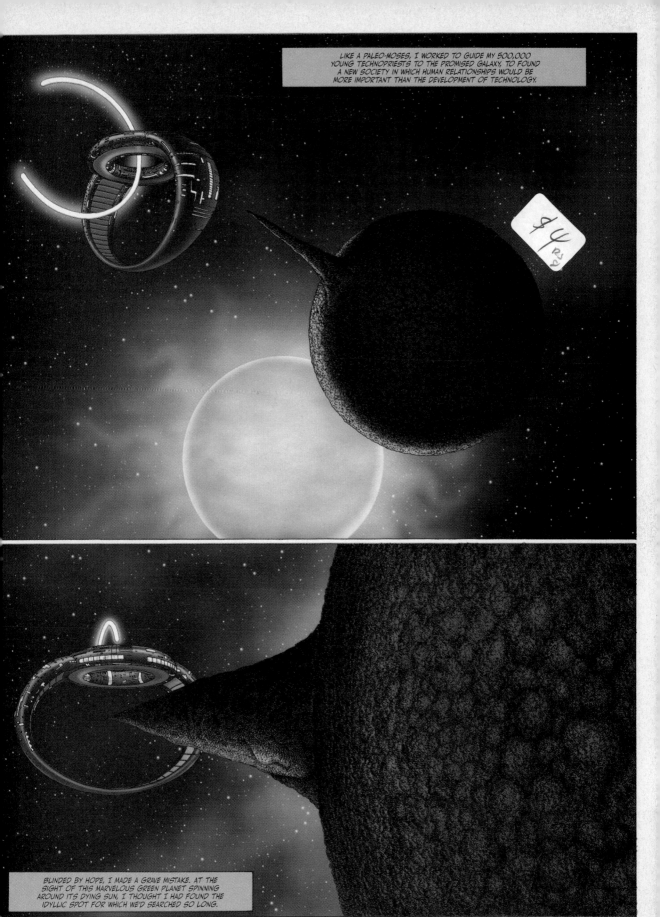

LIKE A PALEO-MOSES, I WORKED TO GUIDE MY 500,000 YOUNG TECHNOPRIESTS TO THE PROMISED GALAXY, TO FOUND A NEW SOCIETY IN WHICH HUMAN RELATIONSHIPS WOULD BE MORE IMPORTANT THAN THE DEVELOPMENT OF TECHNOLOGY.

BLINDED BY HOPE, I MADE A GRAVE MISTAKE. AT THE SIGHT OF THIS MARVELOUS GREEN PLANET SPINNING AROUND ITS DYING SUN, I THOUGHT I HAD FOUND THE IDYLLIC SPOT FOR WHICH WE'D SEARCHED SO LONG.

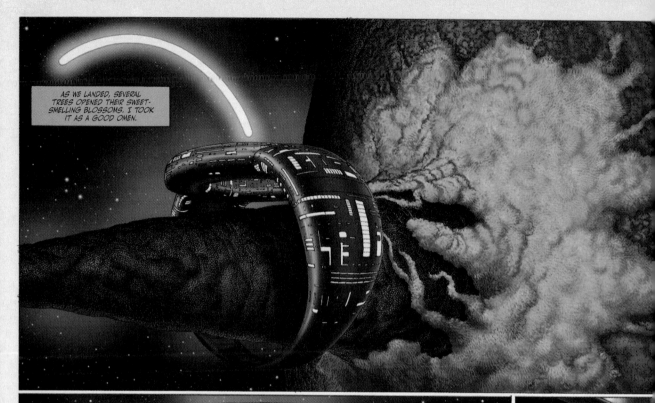

AS WE LANDED, SEVERAL TREES OPENED THEIR SWEET-SMELLING BLOSSOMS. I TOOK IT AS A GOOD OMEN.

I GAVE MY DISCIPLES PERMISSION TO DEBARK. THE ENCHANTING PERFUME AND THE PURE AIR WERE LIKE HONEY TO THEIR LUNGS AFTER THE ARTIFICIAL ATMOSPHERE OF OUR SHIP. THERE WAS NO DOUBT THAT IT WAS THE PROMISED PLANET.

AH, MY LOYAL TINIGRIFI, IF YOU MOVE TOO SLOWLY THEN *DEATH* CATCHES UP TO YOU, BUT MOVE TOO FAST AND IT'S YOU THAT'S CHASING DEATH! WE WANTED TO REACH OUR DESTINATION SO BADLY THAT WE SAW A PURE LAND IN A PERFUMED *TRAP!*

YOUR FAULT, ALBINO! YOU ALWAYS WERE DRAWN TO THE DREAM MORE THAN TO REALITY...YOUR GOOD HEART COULD SWEETEN AN OCEAN OF *BITTERNESS.*

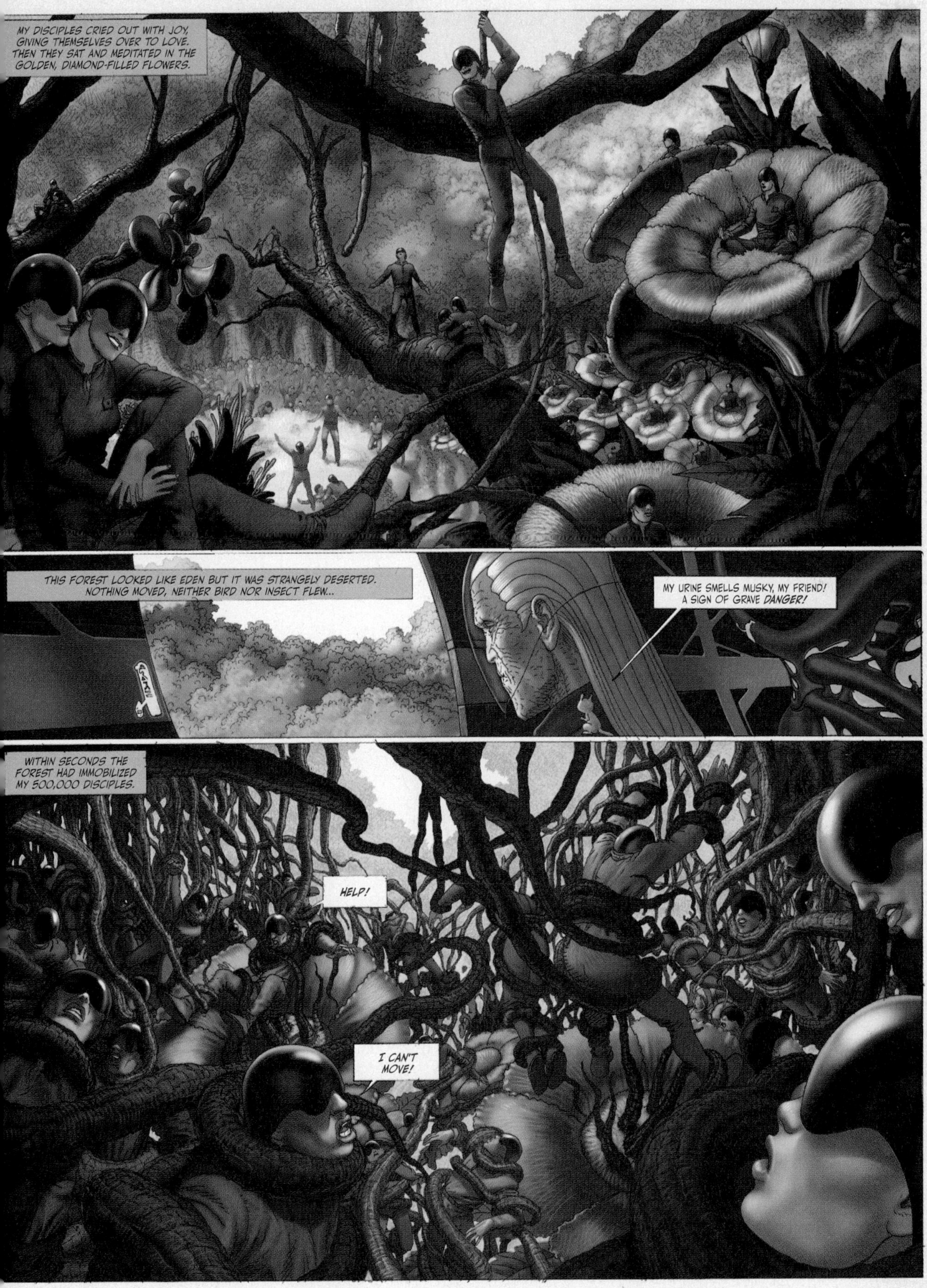
MY DISCIPLES CRIED OUT WITH JOY, GIVING THEMSELVES OVER TO LOVE. THEN THEY SAT AND MEDITATED IN THE GOLDEN, DIAMOND-FILLED FLOWERS.
THIS FOREST LOOKED LIKE EDEN BUT IT WAS STRANGELY DESERTED. NOTHING MOVED, NEITHER BIRD NOR INSECT FLEW...
MY URINE SMELLS MUSKY, MY FRIEND! A SIGN OF GRAVE DANGER!
WITHIN SECONDS THE FOREST HAD IMMOBILIZED MY 500,000 DISCIPLES.
HELP!
I CAN'T MOVE!

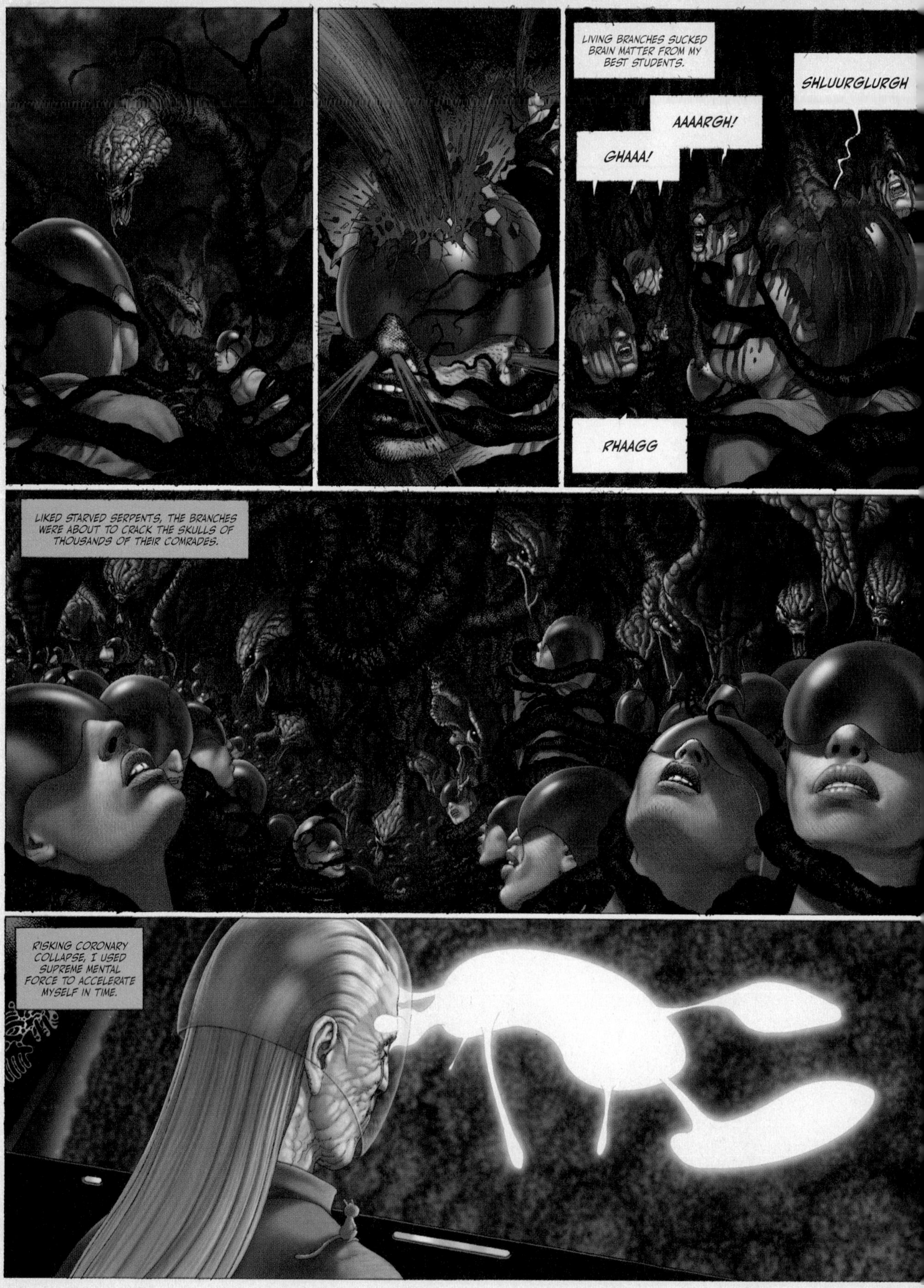
LIVING BRANCHES SUCKED BRAIN MATTER FROM MY BEST STUDENTS.
SHLUURGLURGH
AAAARGH!
GHAAA!
RHAAGG
LIKED STARVED SERPENTS, THE BRANCHES WERE ABOUT TO CRACK THE SKULLS OF THOUSANDS OF THEIR COMRADES.
RISKING CORONARY COLLAPSE, I USED SUPREME MENTAL FORCE TO ACCELERATE MYSELF IN TIME.

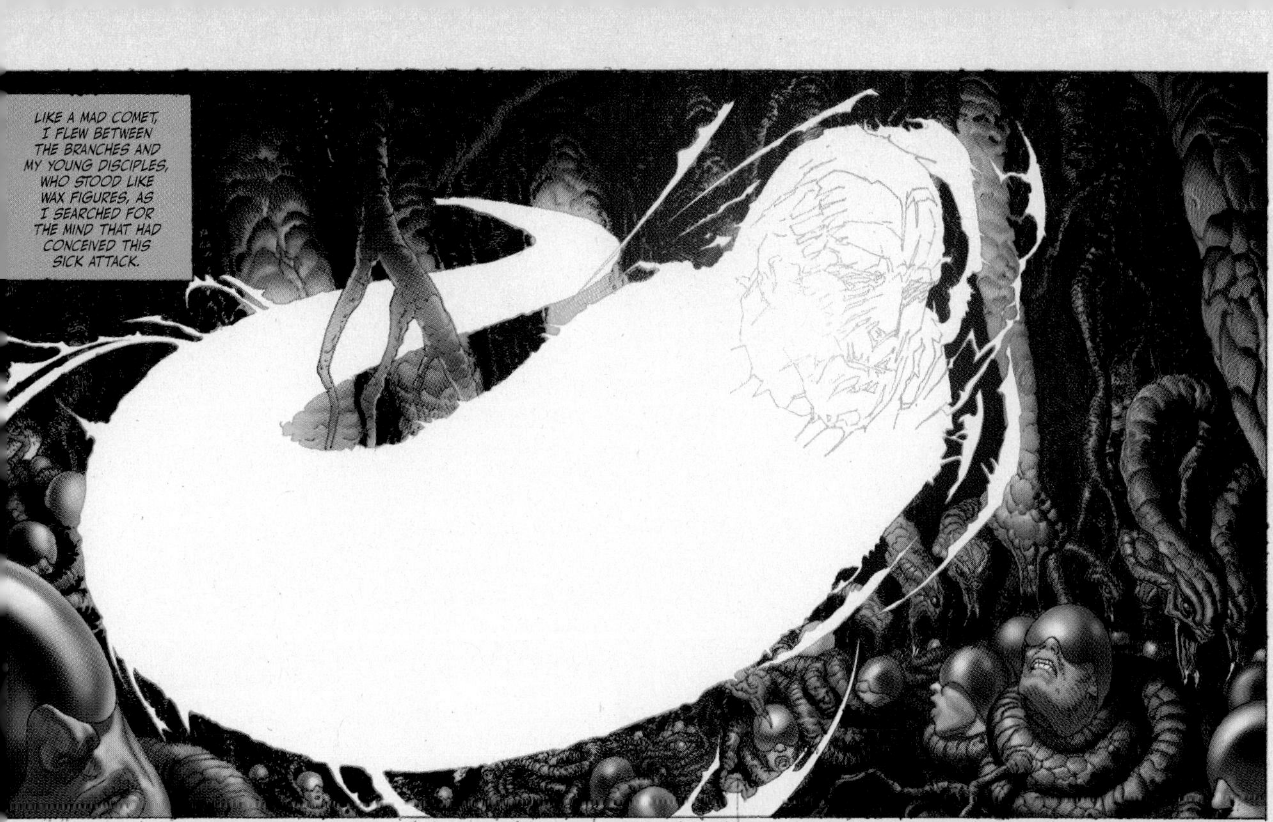
LIKE A MAD COMET, I FLEW BETWEEN THE BRANCHES AND MY YOUNG DISCIPLES, WHO STOOD LIKE WAX FIGURES, AS I SEARCHED FOR THE MIND THAT HAD CONCEIVED THIS SICK ATTACK.

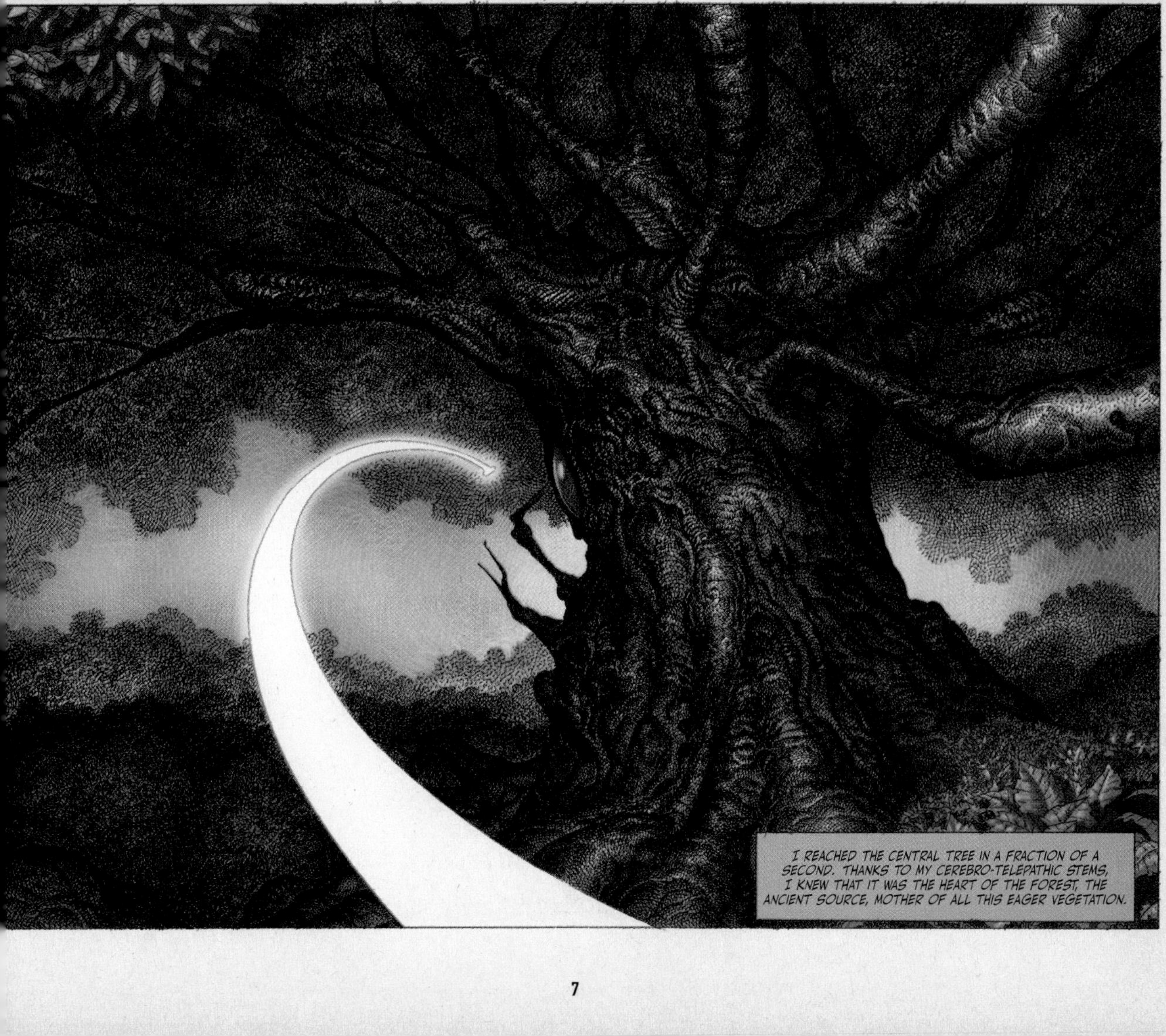
I REACHED THE CENTRAL TREE IN A FRACTION OF A SECOND. THANKS TO MY CEREBRO-TELEPATHIC STEMS, I KNEW THAT IT WAS THE HEART OF THE FOREST, THE ANCIENT SOURCE, MOTHER OF ALL THIS EAGER VEGETATION.

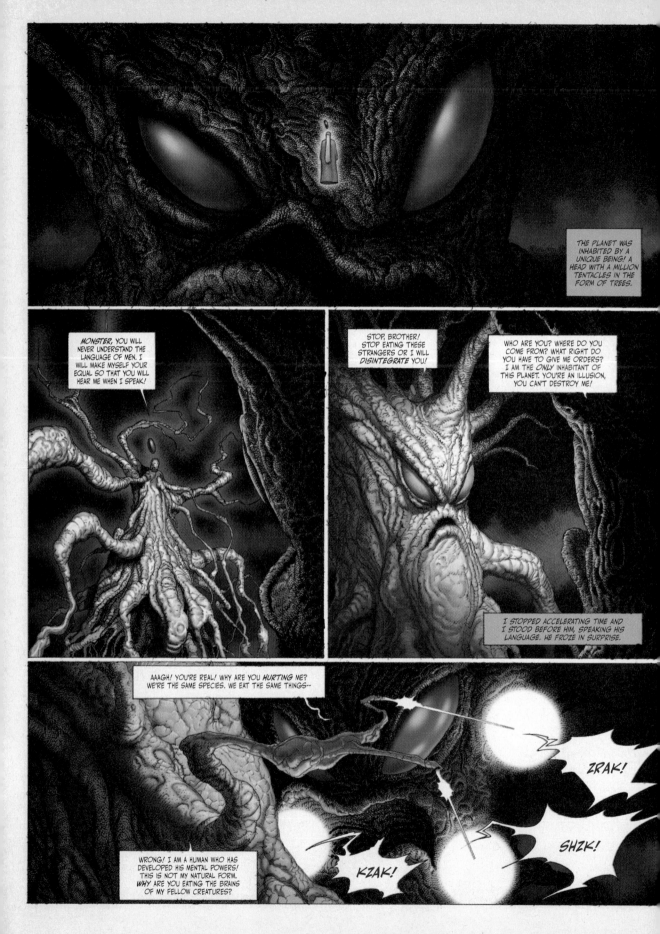

THE PLANET WAS INHABITED BY A UNIQUE BEING! A HEAD WITH A MILLION TENTACLES IN THE FORM OF TREES.

MONSTER, YOU WILL NEVER UNDERSTAND THE LANGUAGE OF MEN. I WILL MAKE MYSELF YOUR EQUAL SO THAT YOU WILL HEAR ME WHEN I SPEAK!

STOP, BROTHER! STOP EATING THESE STRANGERS OR I WILL DISINTEGRATE YOU!

WHO ARE YOU? WHERE DO YOU COME FROM? WHAT RIGHT DO YOU HAVE TO GIVE ME ORDERS? I AM THE ONLY INHABITANT OF THIS PLANET. YOU'RE AN ILLUSION, YOU CAN'T DESTROY ME!

I STOPPED ACCELERATING TIME AND I STOOD BEFORE HIM, SPEAKING HIS LANGUAGE. HE FROZE IN SURPRISE.

AAAGH! YOU'RE REAL! WHY ARE YOU HURTING ME? WE'RE THE SAME SPECIES. WE EAT THE SAME THINGS--

WRONG! I AM A HUMAN WHO HAS DEVELOPED HIS MENTAL POWERS! THIS IS NOT MY NATURAL FORM. WHY ARE YOU EATING THE BRAINS OF MY FELLOW CREATURES?

ZRAK!

SHZK!

KZAK!

8

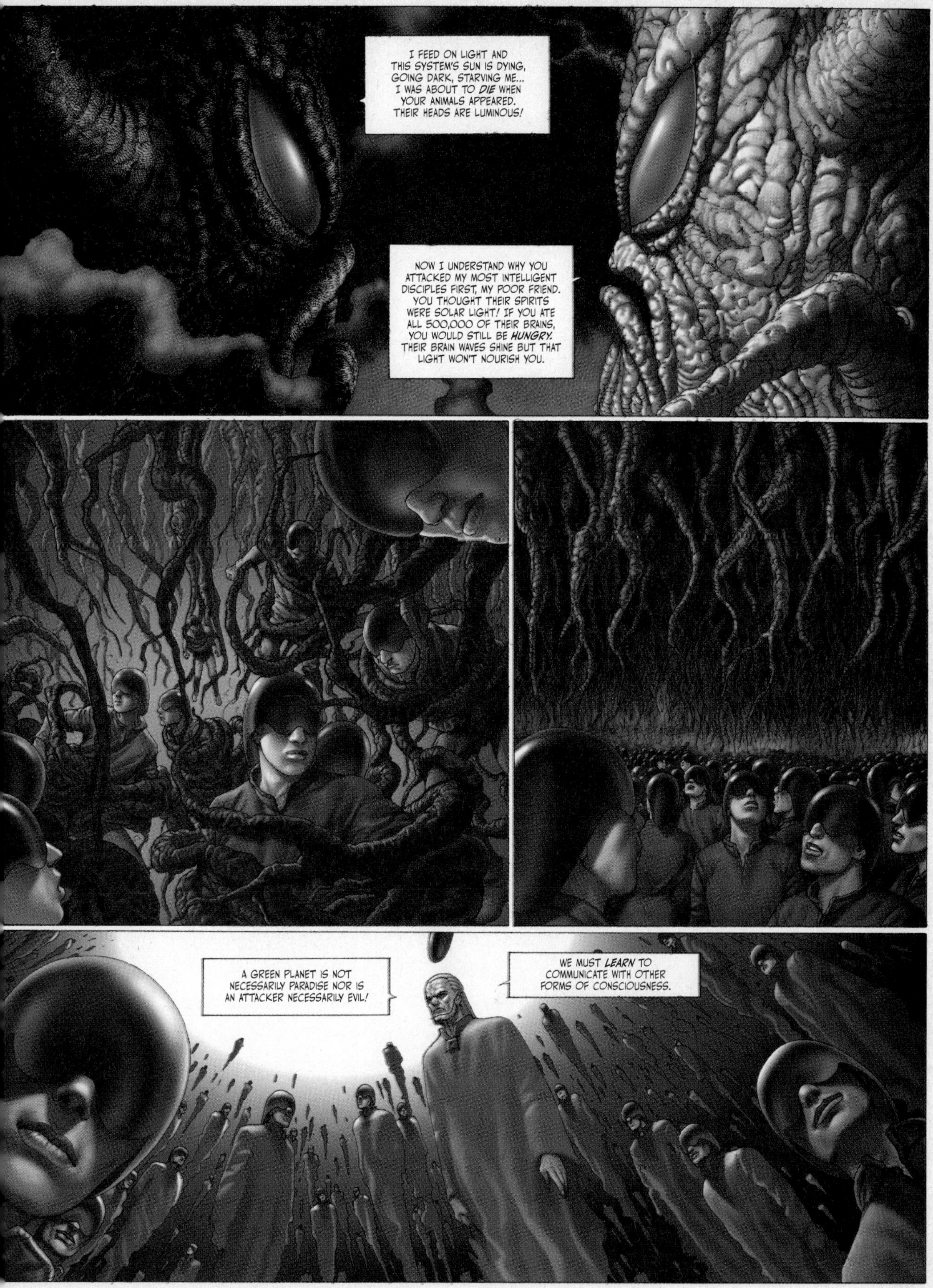
I FEED ON LIGHT AND THIS SYSTEM'S SUN IS DYING, GOING DARK, STARVING ME... I WAS ABOUT TO *DIE* WHEN YOUR ANIMALS APPEARED. THEIR HEADS ARE LUMINOUS!
NOW I UNDERSTAND WHY YOU ATTACKED MY MOST INTELLIGENT DISCIPLES FIRST, MY POOR FRIEND. YOU THOUGHT THEIR SPIRITS WERE SOLAR LIGHT! IF YOU ATE ALL 500,000 OF THEIR BRAINS, YOU WOULD STILL BE *HUNGRY*. THEIR BRAIN WAVES SHINE BUT THAT LIGHT WON'T NOURISH YOU.
A GREEN PLANET IS NOT NECESSARILY PARADISE NOR IS AN ATTACKER NECESSARILY EVIL!
WE MUST *LEARN* TO COMMUNICATE WITH OTHER FORMS OF CONSCIOUSNESS.

WE DEVIATED SLIGHTLY FROM OUR ROUTE TO LEAD OUR NEW FRIEND TO A POWERFUL SUN WHOSE INTENSE LIGHT WOULD FEED HIM PROPERLY...

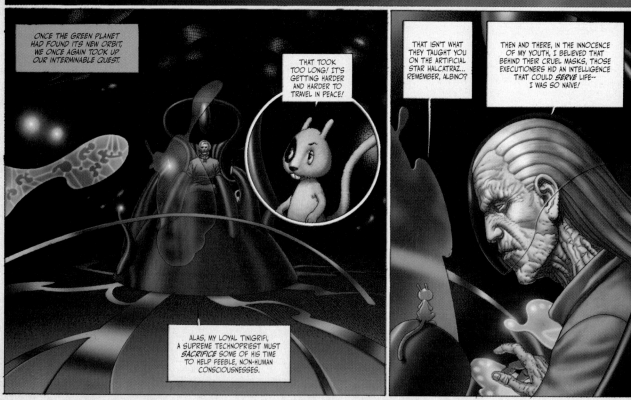

ONCE THE GREEN PLANET HAD FOUND ITS NEW ORBIT, WE ONCE AGAIN TOOK UP OUR INTERMINABLE QUEST.

THAT TOOK TOO LONG! IT'S GETTING HARDER AND HARDER TO TRAVEL IN PEACE!

ALAS, MY LOYAL TINIGRIFI, A SUPREME TECHNOPRIEST MUST *SACRIFICE* SOME OF HIS TIME TO HELP FEEBLE, NON-HUMAN CONSCIOUSNESSES.

THAT ISN'T WHAT THEY TAUGHT YOU ON THE ARTIFICIAL STAR HALCATRAZ... REMEMBER, ALBINO?

THEN AND THERE, IN THE INNOCENCE OF MY YOUTH, I BELIEVED THAT BEHIND THEIR CRUEL MASKS, THOSE EXECUTIONERS HID AN INTELLIGENCE THAT COULD *SERVE* LIFE-- I WAS SO NAÏVE!

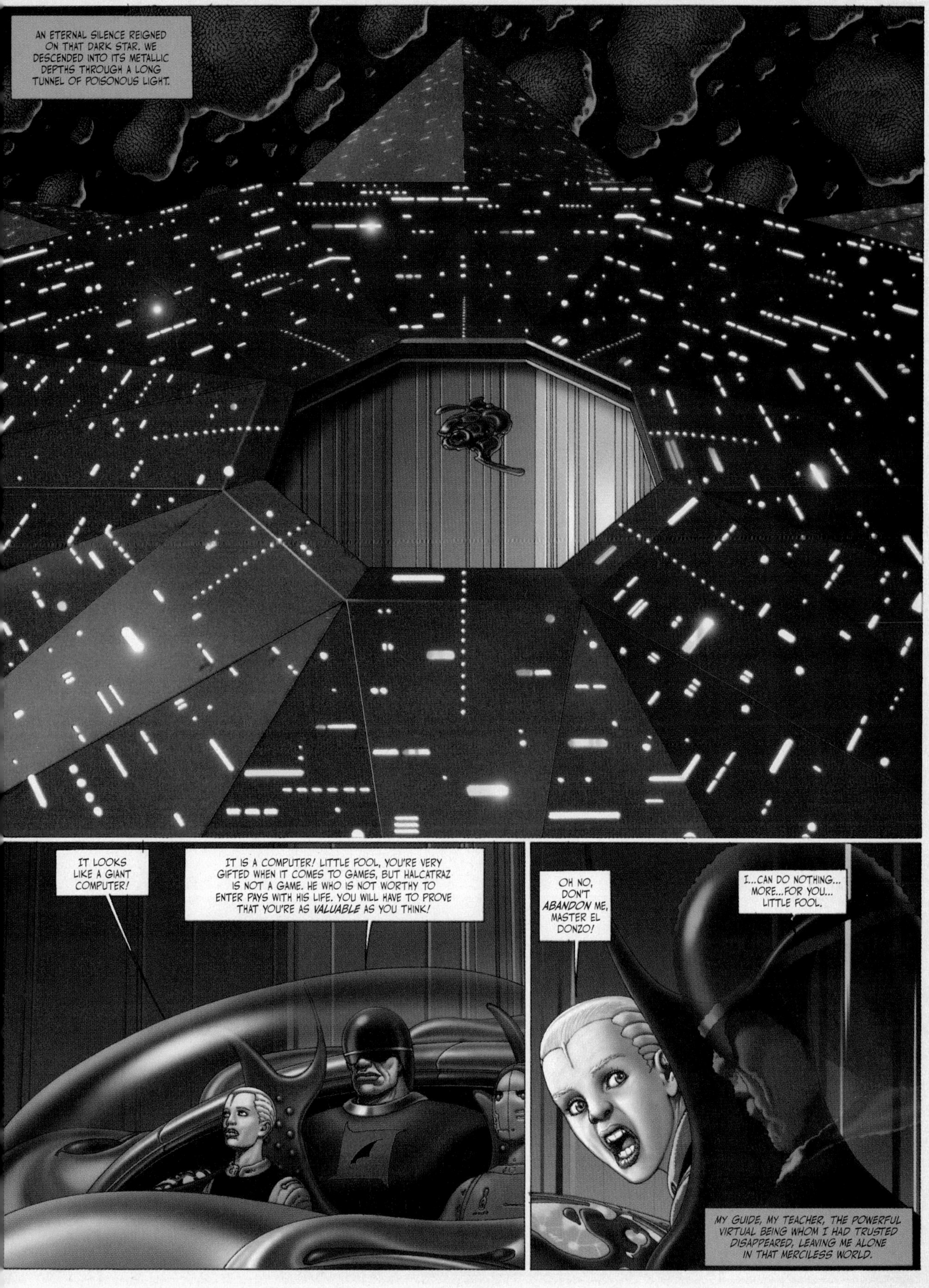
AN ETERNAL SILENCE REIGNED ON THAT DARK STAR. WE DESCENDED INTO ITS METALLIC DEPTHS THROUGH A LONG TUNNEL OF POISONOUS LIGHT.
IT LOOKS LIKE A GIANT COMPUTER!
IT IS A COMPUTER! LITTLE FOOL, YOU'RE VERY GIFTED WHEN IT COMES TO GAMES, BUT HALCATRAZ IS NOT A GAME. HE WHO IS NOT WORTHY TO ENTER PAYS WITH HIS LIFE. YOU WILL HAVE TO PROVE THAT YOU'RE AS *VALUABLE* AS YOU THINK!
OH NO, DON'T *ABANDON* ME, MASTER EL DONZO!
I...CAN DO NOTHING... MORE...FOR YOU... LITTLE FOOL.
MY GUIDE, MY TEACHER, THE POWERFUL VIRTUAL BEING WHOM I HAD TRUSTED DISAPPEARED, LEAVING ME ALONE IN THAT MERCILESS WORLD.

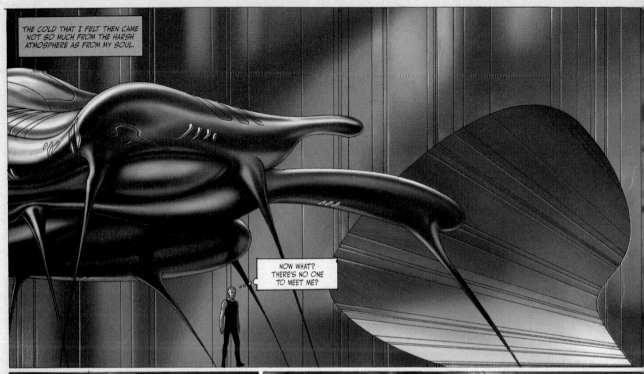

THE COLD THAT I FELT THEN CAME NOT SO MUCH FROM THE HARSH ATMOSPHERE AS FROM MY SOUL.

NOW WHAT? THERE'S NO ONE TO MEET ME?

WE DON'T NEED YOU, LITTLE MAN! FORGET YOUR DREAMS! GO BACK TO YOUR WORLD!

THE TECHNO-EYE IS RIGHT! THIS PLACE IS INHUMAN!

HIDE AND BE QUIET, PALEO-PARROT!

WE'RE NEVER GOING BACK TO THE GAMES PLANET!

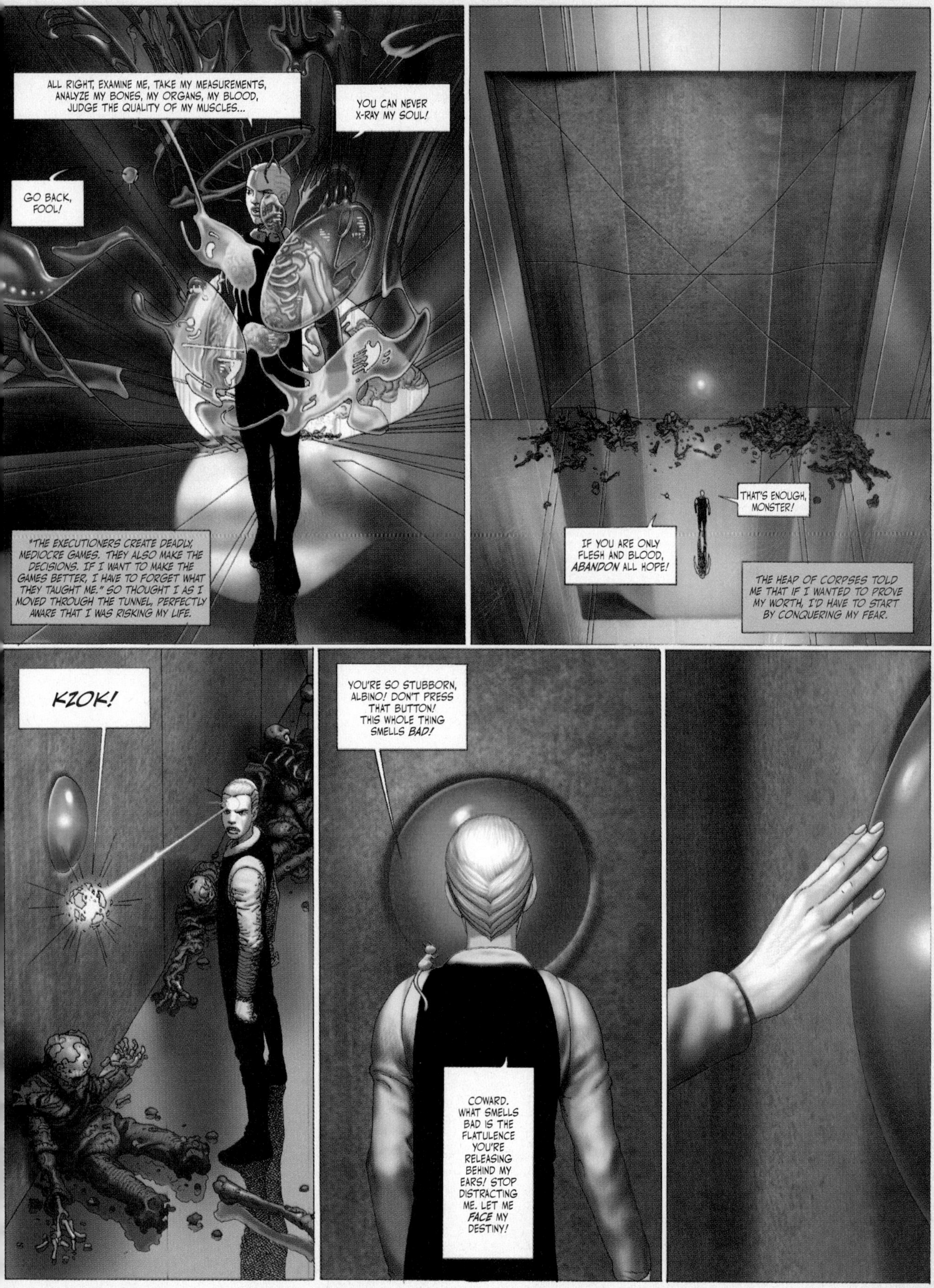
ALL RIGHT, EXAMINE ME, TAKE MY MEASUREMENTS, ANALYZE MY BONES, MY ORGANS, MY BLOOD, JUDGE THE QUALITY OF MY MUSCLES...
YOU CAN NEVER X-RAY MY SOUL!
GO BACK, FOOL!
"THE EXECUTIONERS CREATE DEADLY, MEDIOCRE GAMES. THEY ALSO MAKE THE DECISIONS. IF I WANT TO MAKE THE GAMES BETTER, I HAVE TO FORGET WHAT THEY TAUGHT ME." SO THOUGHT I AS I MOVED THROUGH THE TUNNEL, PERFECTLY AWARE THAT I WAS RISKING MY LIFE.
THAT'S ENOUGH, MONSTER!
IF YOU ARE ONLY FLESH AND BLOOD, ABANDON ALL HOPE!
THE HEAP OF CORPSES TOLD ME THAT IF I WANTED TO PROVE MY WORTH, I'D HAVE TO START BY CONQUERING MY FEAR.
KZOK!
YOU'RE SO STUBBORN, ALBINO! DON'T PRESS THAT BUTTON! THIS WHOLE THING SMELLS BAD!
COWARD. WHAT SMELLS BAD IS THE FLATULENCE YOU'RE RELEASING BEHIND MY EARS! STOP DISTRACTING ME. LET ME FACE MY DESTINY!

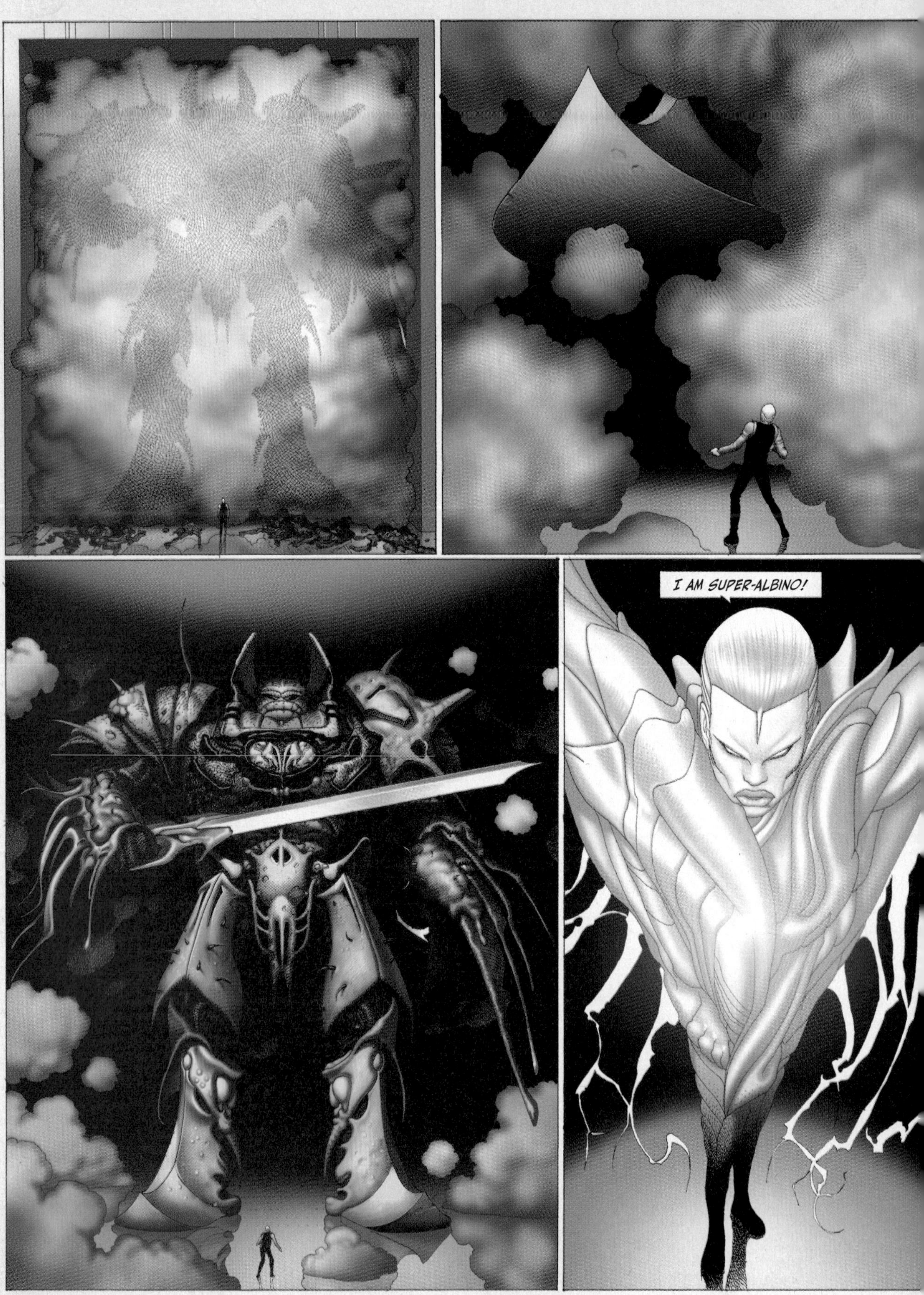
I AM SUPER-ALBINO!

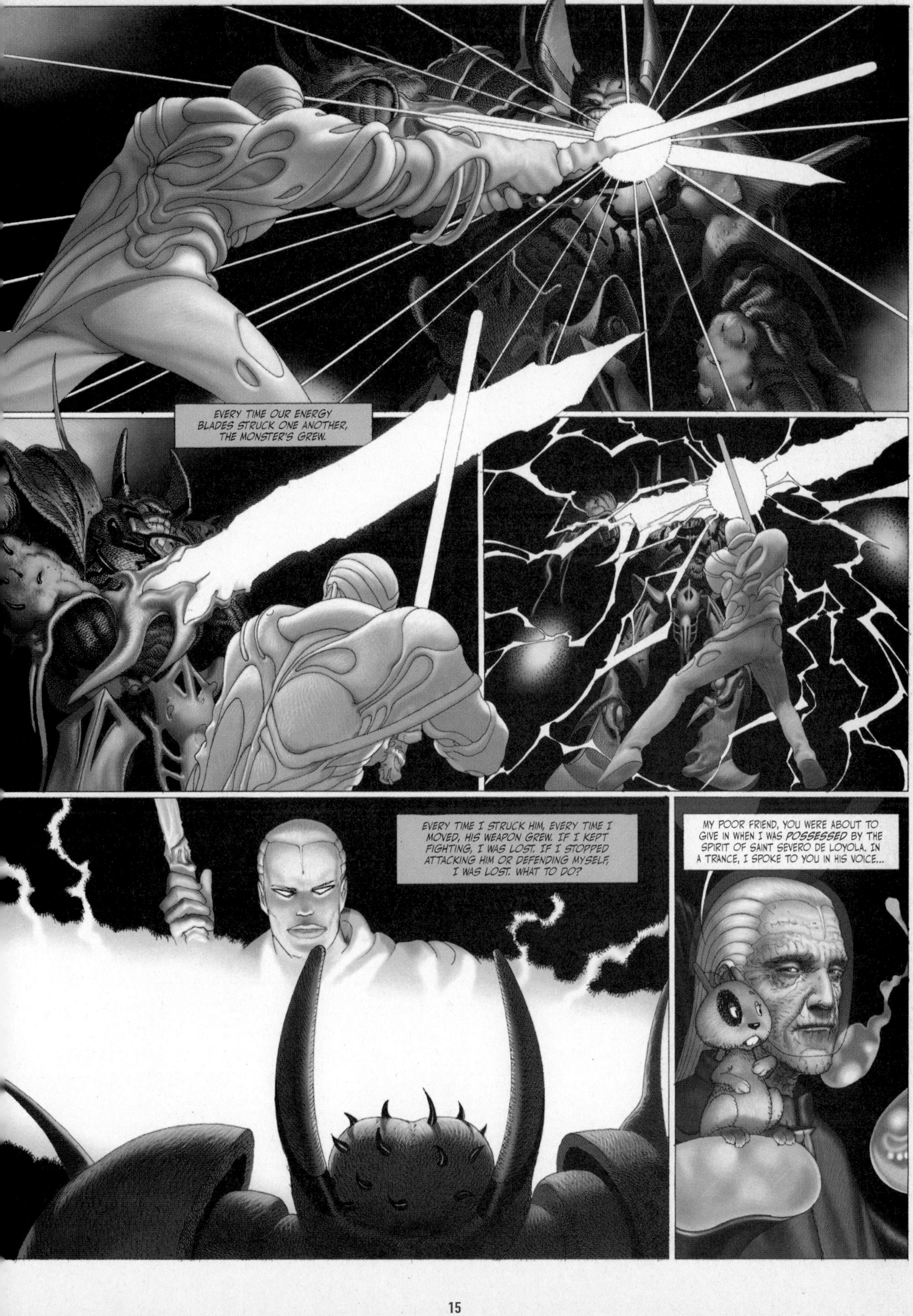
EVERY TIME OUR ENERGY BLADES STRUCK ONE ANOTHER, THE MONSTER'S GREW.
EVERY TIME I STRUCK HIM, EVERY TIME I MOVED, HIS WEAPON GREW. IF I KEPT FIGHTING, I WAS LOST. IF I STOPPED ATTACKING HIM OR DEFENDING MYSELF, I WAS LOST. WHAT TO DO?
MY POOR FRIEND, YOU WERE ABOUT TO GIVE IN WHEN I WAS POSSESSED BY THE SPIRIT OF SAINT SEVERO DE LOYOLA. IN A TRANCE, I SPOKE TO YOU IN HIS VOICE...

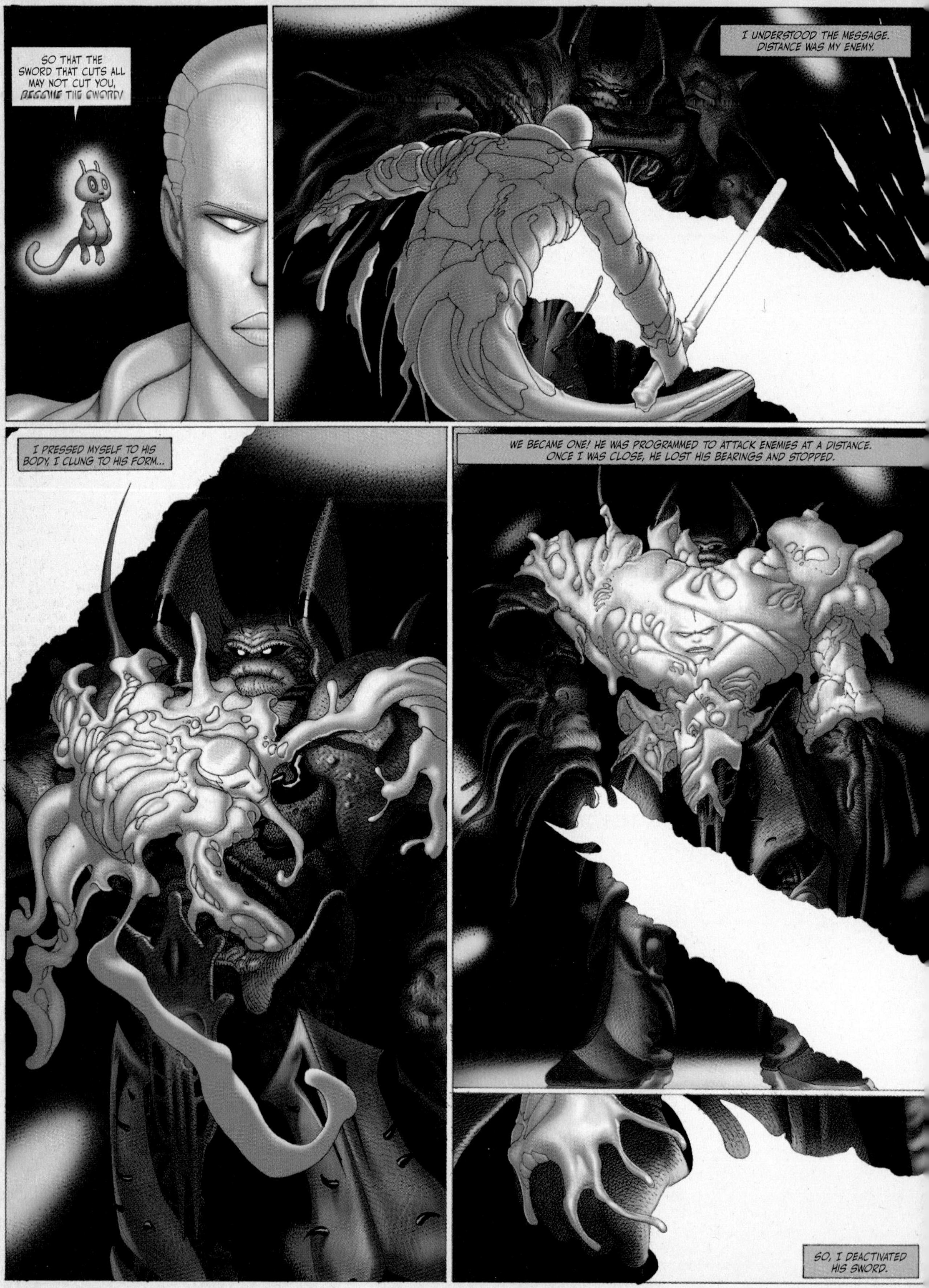
SO THAT THE SWORD THAT CUTS ALL MAY NOT CUT YOU, BECOME THE SWORD!
I UNDERSTOOD THE MESSAGE. DISTANCE WAS MY ENEMY.
I PRESSED MYSELF TO HIS BODY, I CLUNG TO HIS FORM...
WE BECAME ONE! HE WAS PROGRAMMED TO ATTACK ENEMIES AT A DISTANCE. ONCE I WAS CLOSE, HE LOST HIS BEARINGS AND STOPPED.
SO, I DEACTIVATED HIS SWORD.

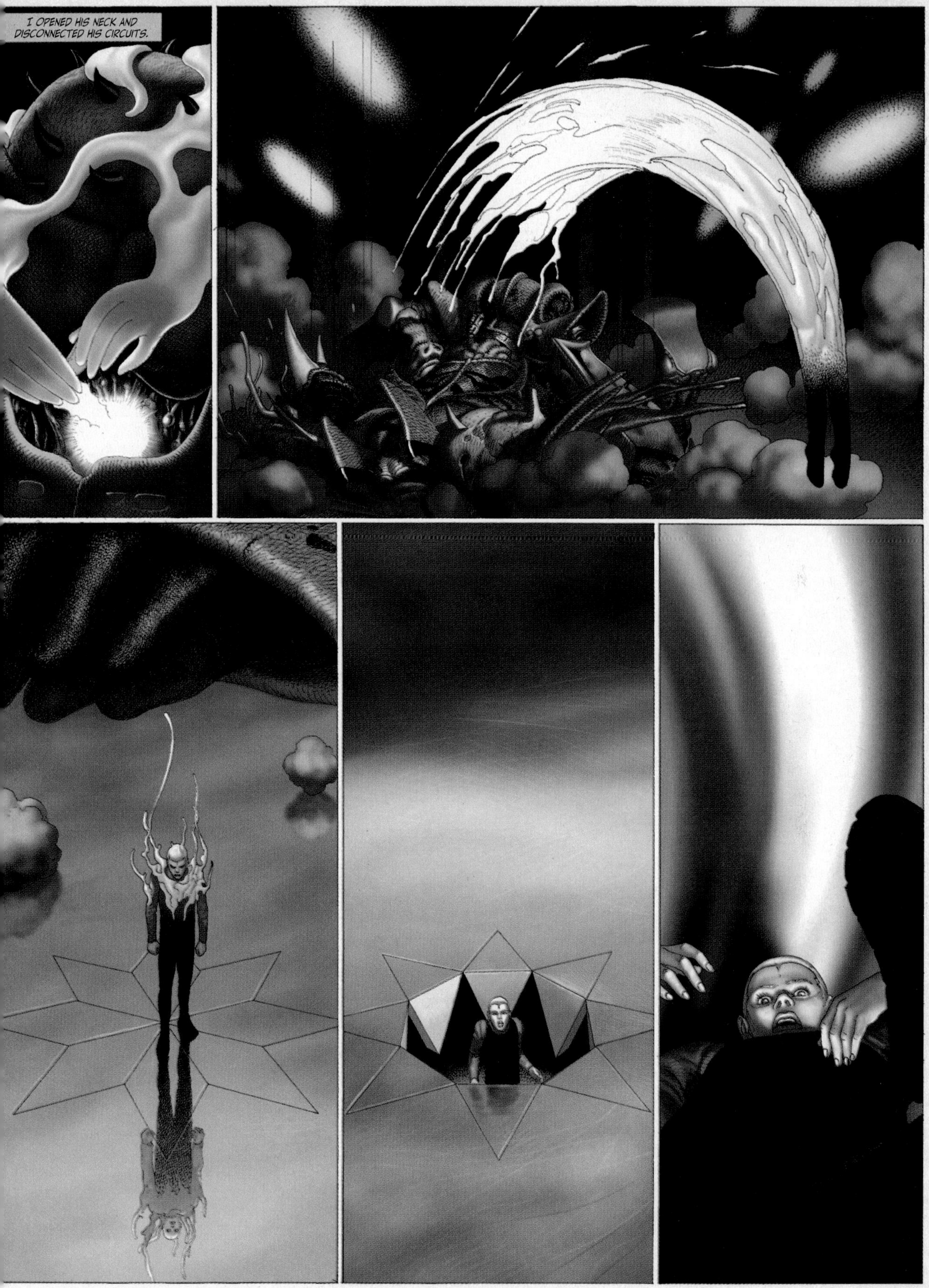
I OPENED HIS NECK AND DISCONNECTED HIS CIRCUITS.

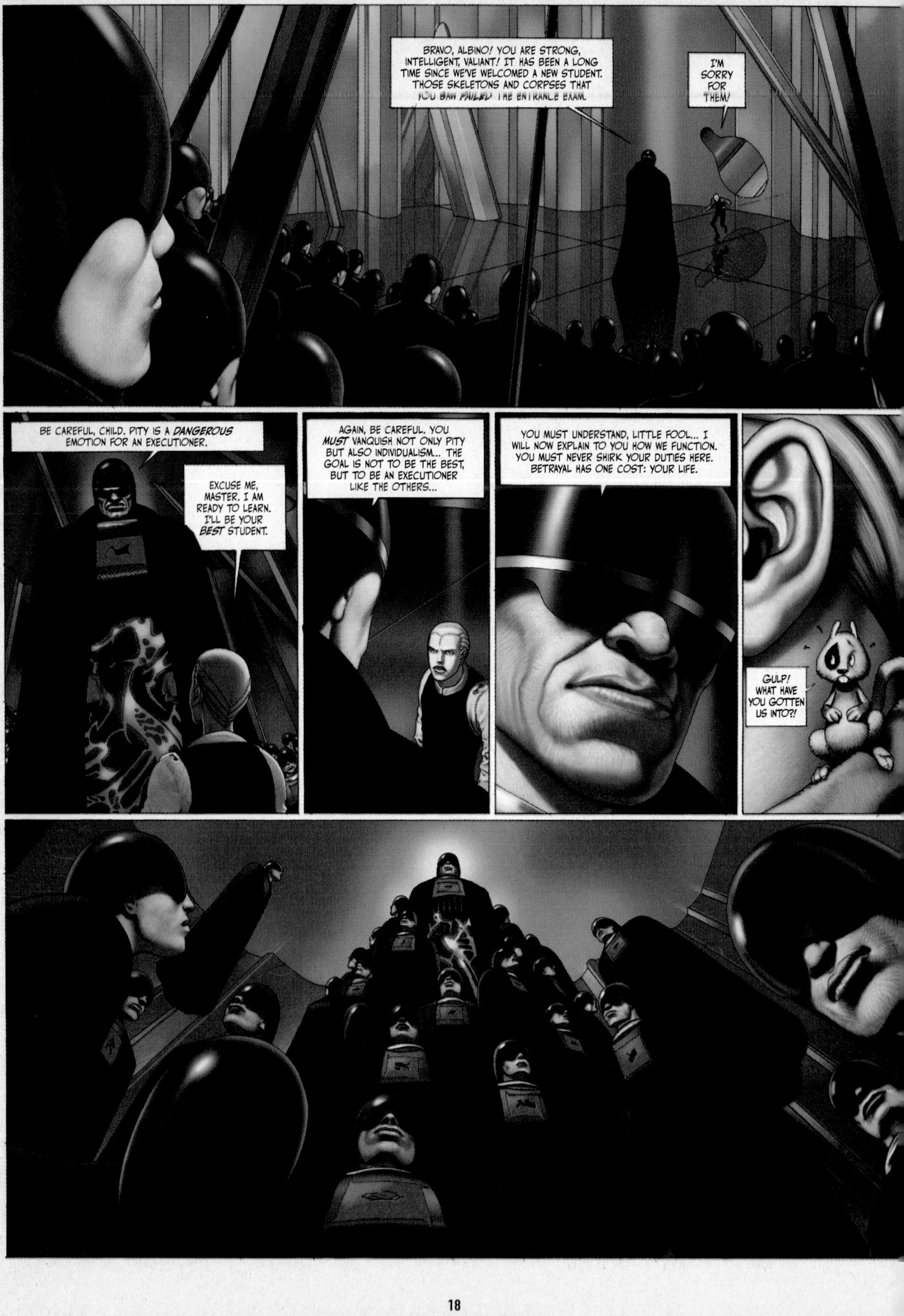
BRAVO, ALBINO! YOU ARE STRONG, INTELLIGENT, VALIANT! IT HAS BEEN A LONG TIME SINCE WE'VE WELCOMED A NEW STUDENT. THOSE SKELETONS AND CORPSES THAT YOU SAW FAILED THE ENTRANCE EXAM.
I'M SORRY FOR THEM!
BE CAREFUL, CHILD. PITY IS A DANGEROUS EMOTION FOR AN EXECUTIONER.
EXCUSE ME, MASTER. I AM READY TO LEARN. I'LL BE YOUR BEST STUDENT.
AGAIN, BE CAREFUL. YOU MUST VANQUISH NOT ONLY PITY BUT ALSO INDIVIDUALISM... THE GOAL IS NOT TO BE THE BEST, BUT TO BE AN EXECUTIONER LIKE THE OTHERS...
YOU MUST UNDERSTAND, LITTLE FOOL... I WILL NOW EXPLAIN TO YOU HOW WE FUNCTION. YOU MUST NEVER SHIRK YOUR DUTIES HERE. BETRAYAL HAS ONE COST: YOUR LIFE.
GULP! WHAT HAVE YOU GOTTEN US INTO?!

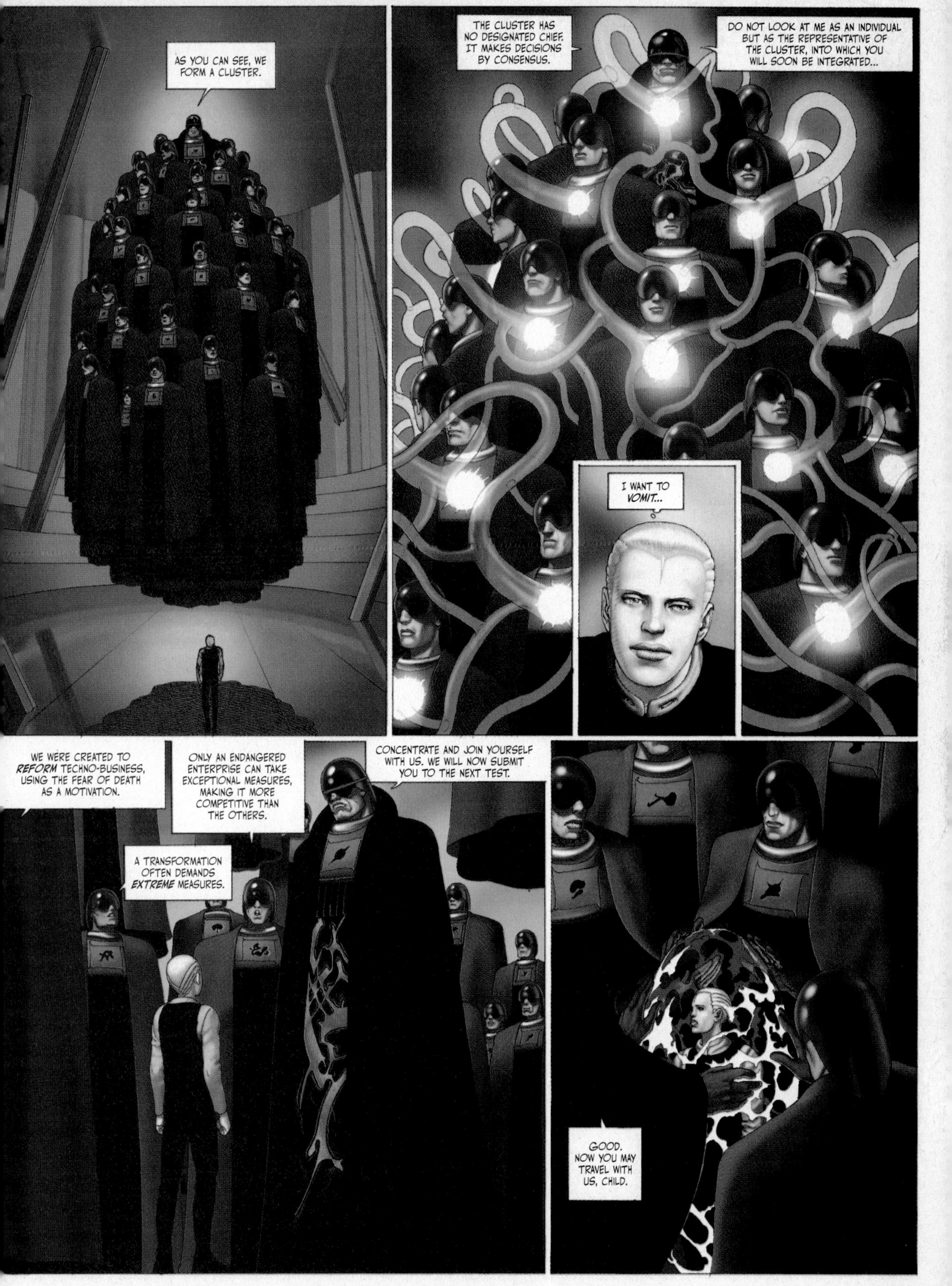

AS YOU CAN SEE, WE FORM A CLUSTER.
THE CLUSTER HAS NO DESIGNATED CHIEF. IT MAKES DECISIONS BY CONSENSUS.
DO NOT LOOK AT ME AS AN INDIVIDUAL BUT AS THE REPRESENTATIVE OF THE CLUSTER, INTO WHICH YOU WILL SOON BE INTEGRATED...
I WANT TO VOMIT...
WE WERE CREATED TO REFORM TECHNO-BUSINESS, USING THE FEAR OF DEATH AS A MOTIVATION.
ONLY AN ENDANGERED ENTERPRISE CAN TAKE EXCEPTIONAL MEASURES, MAKING IT MORE COMPETITIVE THAN THE OTHERS.
A TRANSFORMATION OFTEN DEMANDS EXTREME MEASURES.
CONCENTRATE AND JOIN YOURSELF WITH US. WE WILL NOW SUBMIT YOU TO THE NEXT TEST.
GOOD. NOW YOU MAY TRAVEL WITH US, CHILD.

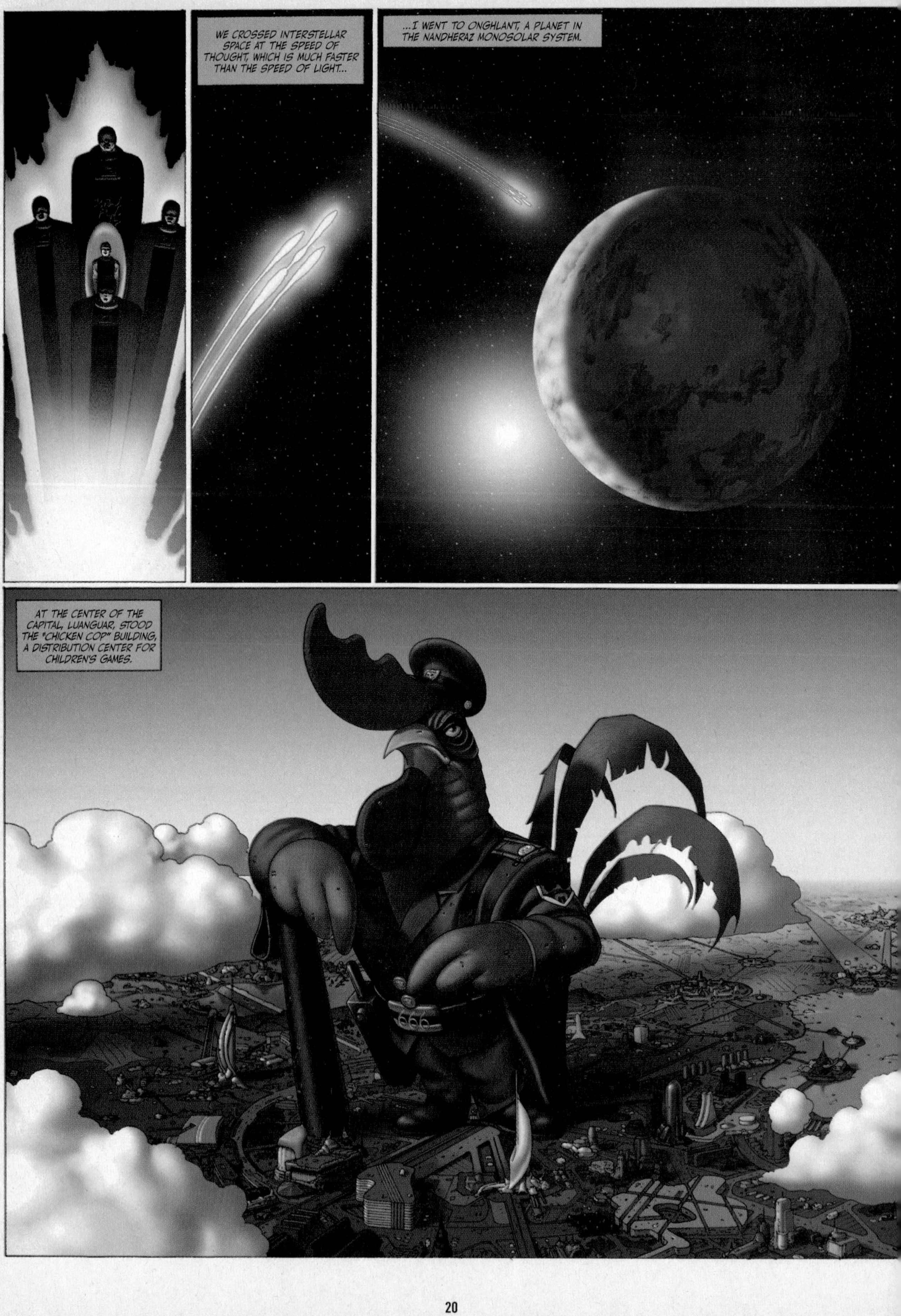
WE CROSSED INTERSTELLAR SPACE AT THE SPEED OF THOUGHT, WHICH IS MUCH FASTER THAN THE SPEED OF LIGHT...
...I WENT TO ONGHLANT, A PLANET IN THE NANDHERAZ MONOSOLAR SYSTEM.
AT THE CENTER OF THE CAPITAL, LUANGUAR, STOOD THE "CHICKEN COP" BUILDING, A DISTRIBUTION CENTER FOR CHILDREN'S GAMES.
666

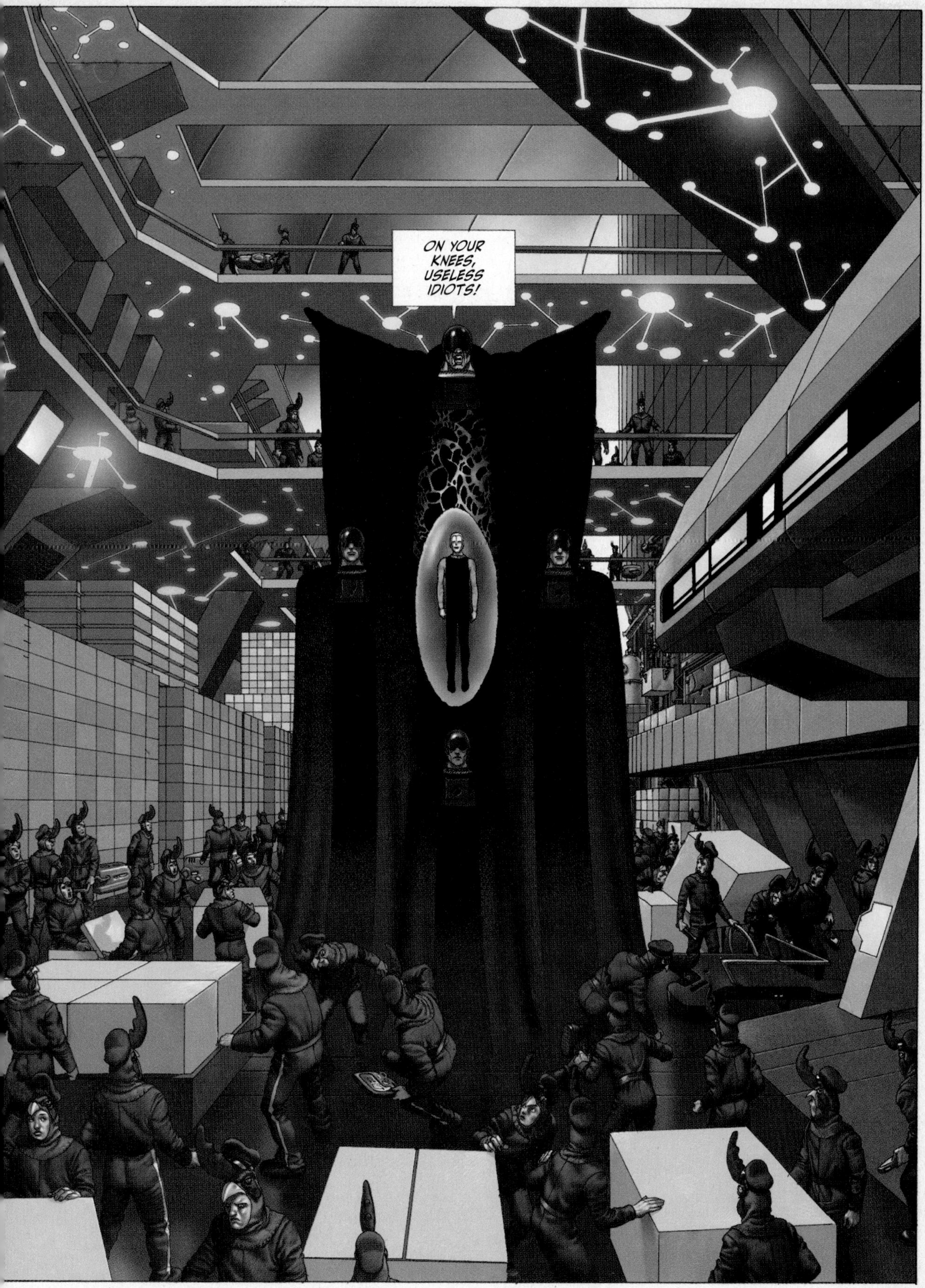
ON YOUR KNEES, USELESS IDIOTS!

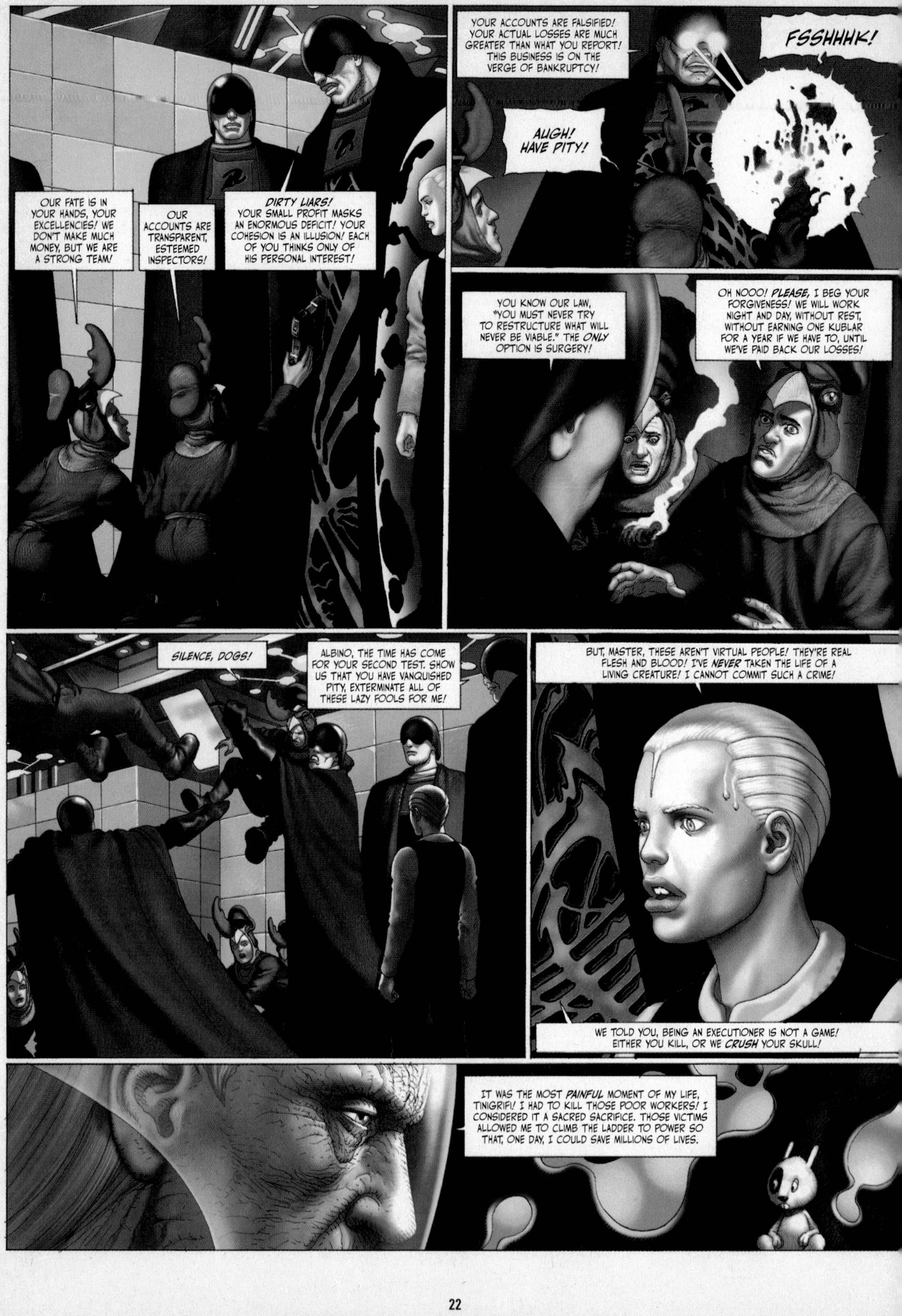
OUR FATE IS IN YOUR HANDS, YOUR EXCELLENCIES! WE DON'T MAKE MUCH MONEY, BUT WE ARE A STRONG TEAM!
OUR ACCOUNTS ARE TRANSPARENT, ESTEEMED INSPECTORS!
DIRTY LIARS! YOUR SMALL PROFIT MASKS AN ENORMOUS DEFICIT! YOUR COHESION IS AN ILLUSION! EACH OF YOU THINKS ONLY OF HIS PERSONAL INTEREST!
YOUR ACCOUNTS ARE FALSIFIED! YOUR ACTUAL LOSSES ARE MUCH GREATER THAN WHAT YOU REPORT! THIS BUSINESS IS ON THE VERGE OF BANKRUPTCY!
FSSHHHK!
AUGH! HAVE PITY!
YOU KNOW OUR LAW, "YOU MUST NEVER TRY TO RESTRUCTURE WHAT WILL NEVER BE VIABLE." THE ONLY OPTION IS SURGERY!
OH NOOO! PLEASE, I BEG YOUR FORGIVENESS! WE WILL WORK NIGHT AND DAY, WITHOUT REST, WITHOUT EARNING ONE KUBLAR FOR A YEAR IF WE HAVE TO, UNTIL WE'VE PAID BACK OUR LOSSES!
SILENCE, DOGS!
ALBINO, THE TIME HAS COME FOR YOUR SECOND TEST. SHOW US THAT YOU HAVE VANQUISHED PITY, EXTERMINATE ALL OF THESE LAZY FOOLS FOR ME!
BUT, MASTER, THESE AREN'T VIRTUAL PEOPLE! THEY'RE REAL FLESH AND BLOOD! I'VE NEVER TAKEN THE LIFE OF A LIVING CREATURE! I CANNOT COMMIT SUCH A CRIME!
WE TOLD YOU, BEING AN EXECUTIONER IS NOT A GAME! EITHER YOU KILL, OR WE CRUSH YOUR SKULL!
IT WAS THE MOST PAINFUL MOMENT OF MY LIFE, TINIGRIFI! I HAD TO KILL THOSE POOR WORKERS! I CONSIDERED IT A SACRED SACRIFICE. THOSE VICTIMS ALLOWED ME TO CLIMB THE LADDER TO POWER SO THAT, ONE DAY, I COULD SAVE MILLIONS OF LIVES.

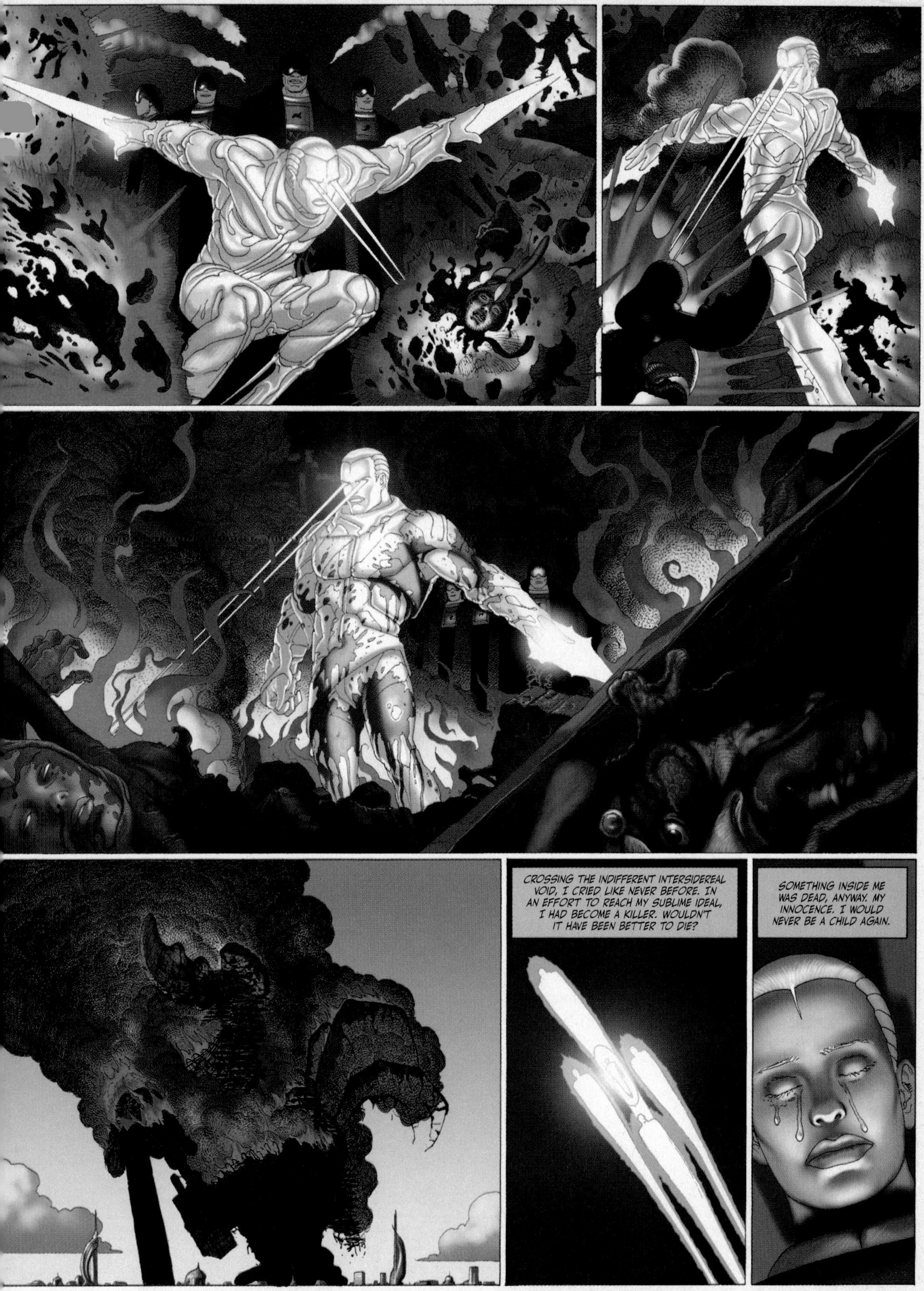
CROSSING THE INDIFFERENT INTERSIDEREAL VOID, I CRIED LIKE NEVER BEFORE. IN AN EFFORT TO REACH MY SUBLIME IDEAL, I HAD BECOME A KILLER. WOULDN'T IT HAVE BEEN BETTER TO DIE?
SOMETHING INSIDE ME WAS DEAD, ANYWAY. MY INNOCENCE. I WOULD NEVER BE A CHILD AGAIN.

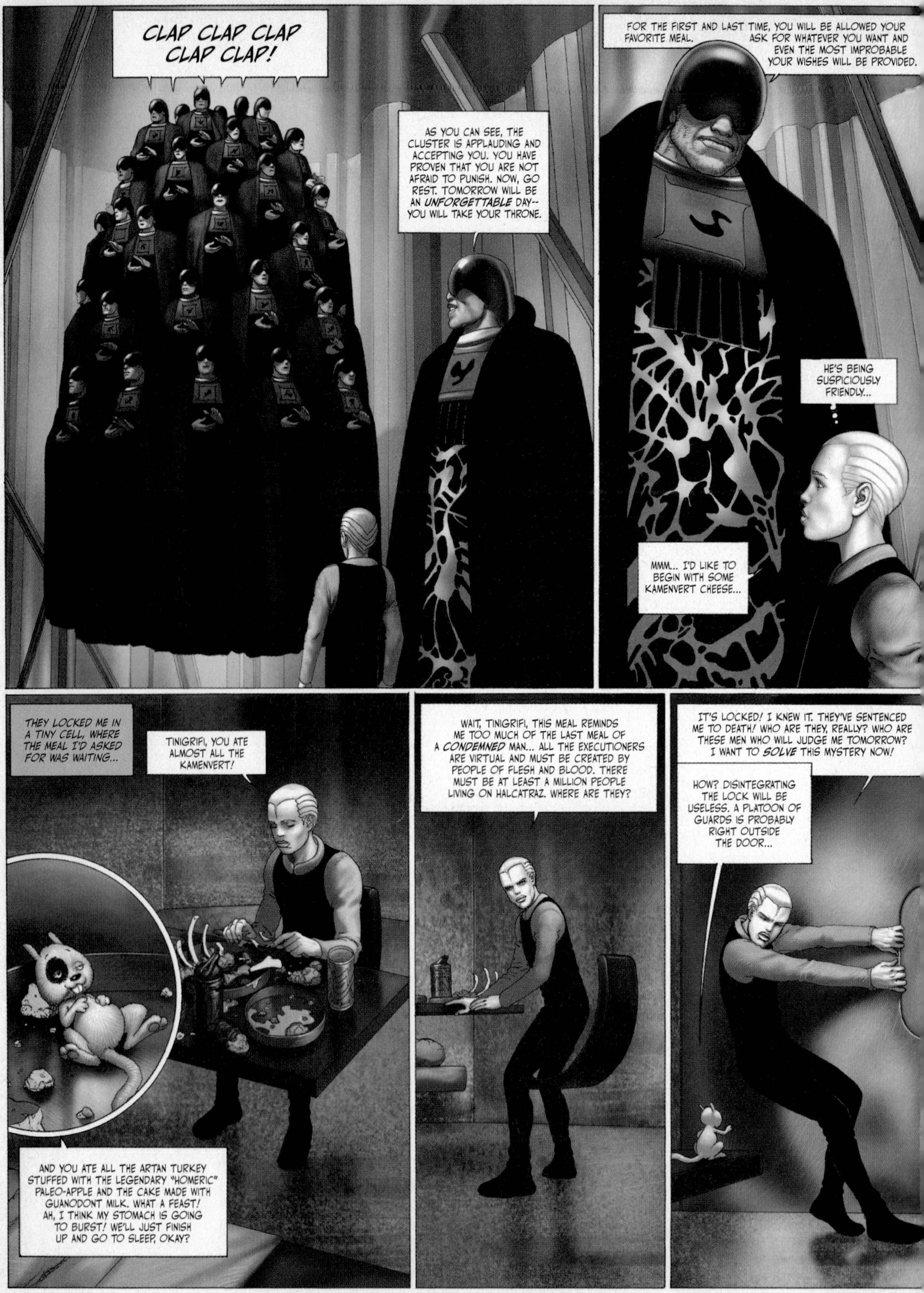
CLAP CLAP CLAP CLAP CLAP!
AS YOU CAN SEE, THE CLUSTER IS APPLAUDING AND ACCEPTING YOU. YOU HAVE PROVEN THAT YOU ARE NOT AFRAID TO PUNISH. NOW, GO REST. TOMORROW WILL BE AN UNFORGETTABLE DAY-- YOU WILL TAKE YOUR THRONE.
FOR THE FIRST AND LAST TIME, YOU WILL BE ALLOWED YOUR FAVORITE MEAL. ASK FOR WHATEVER YOU WANT AND EVEN THE MOST IMPROBABLE YOUR WISHES WILL BE PROVIDED.
HE'S BEING SUSPICIOUSLY FRIENDLY...
MMM... I'D LIKE TO BEGIN WITH SOME KAMENVERT CHEESE...
THEY LOCKED ME IN A TINY CELL, WHERE THE MEAL I'D ASKED FOR WAS WAITING...
TINIGRIFI, YOU ATE ALMOST ALL THE KAMENVERT!
AND YOU ATE ALL THE ARTAN TURKEY STUFFED WITH THE LEGENDARY "HOMERIC" PALEO-APPLE AND THE CAKE MADE WITH GUANODONT MILK. WHAT A FEAST! AH, I THINK MY STOMACH IS GOING TO BURST! WE'LL JUST FINISH UP AND GO TO SLEEP, OKAY?
WAIT, TINIGRIFI, THIS MEAL REMINDS ME TOO MUCH OF THE LAST MEAL OF A CONDEMNED MAN... ALL THE EXECUTIONERS ARE VIRTUAL AND MUST BE CREATED BY PEOPLE OF FLESH AND BLOOD. THERE MUST BE AT LEAST A MILLION PEOPLE LIVING ON HALCATRAZ. WHERE ARE THEY?
IT'S LOCKED! I KNEW IT. THEY'VE SENTENCED ME TO DEATH! WHO ARE THEY, REALLY? WHO ARE THESE MEN WHO WILL JUDGE ME TOMORROW? I WANT TO SOLVE THIS MYSTERY NOW!
HOW? DISINTEGRATING THE LOCK WILL BE USELESS. A PLATOON OF GUARDS IS PROBABLY RIGHT OUTSIDE THE DOOR...

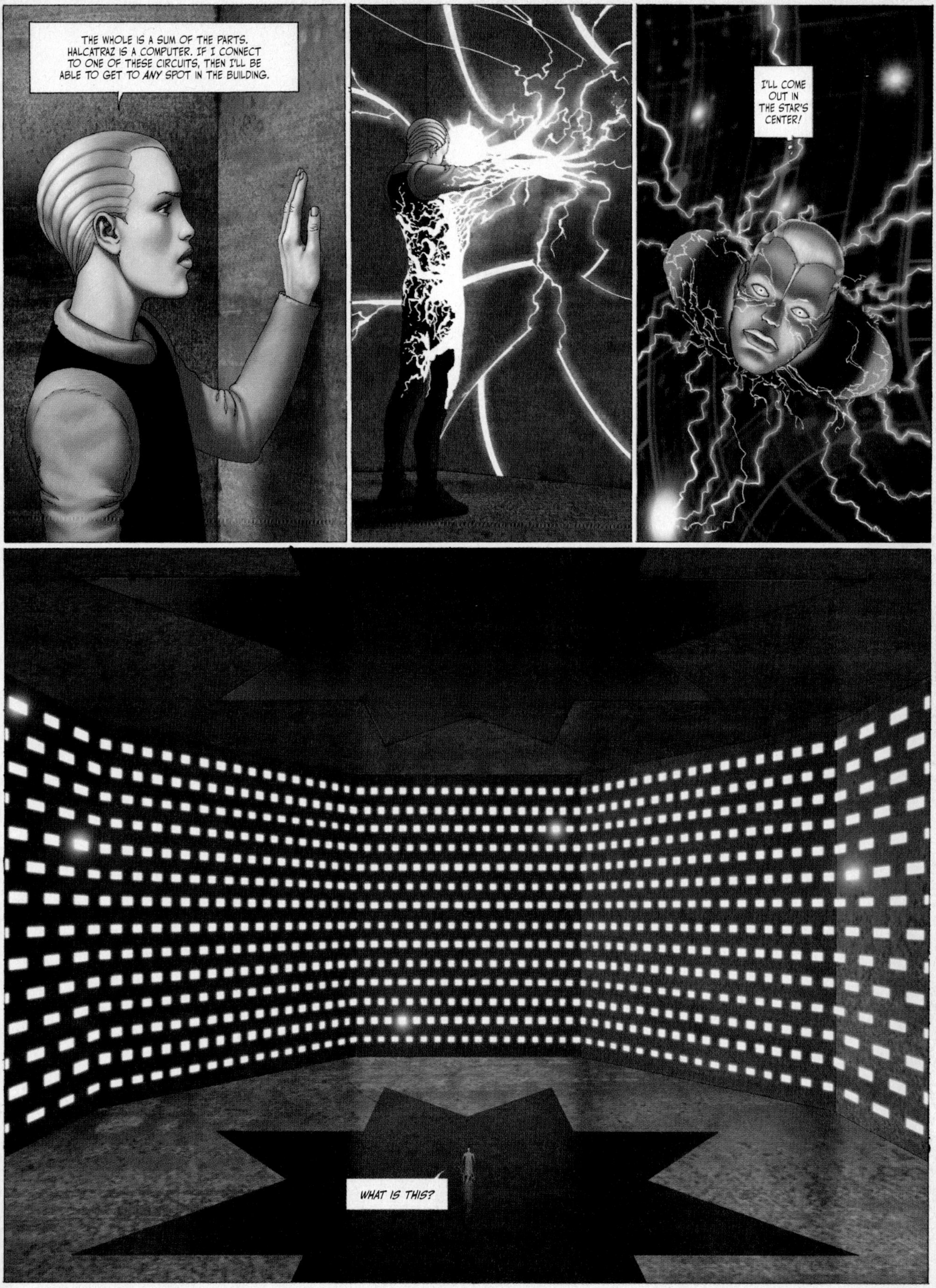
THE WHOLE IS A SUM OF THE PARTS. HALCATRAZ IS A COMPUTER. IF I CONNECT TO ONE OF THESE CIRCUITS, THEN I'LL BE ABLE TO GET TO *ANY* SPOT IN THE BUILDING.
I'LL COME OUT IN THE STAR'S CENTER!
WHAT IS THIS?

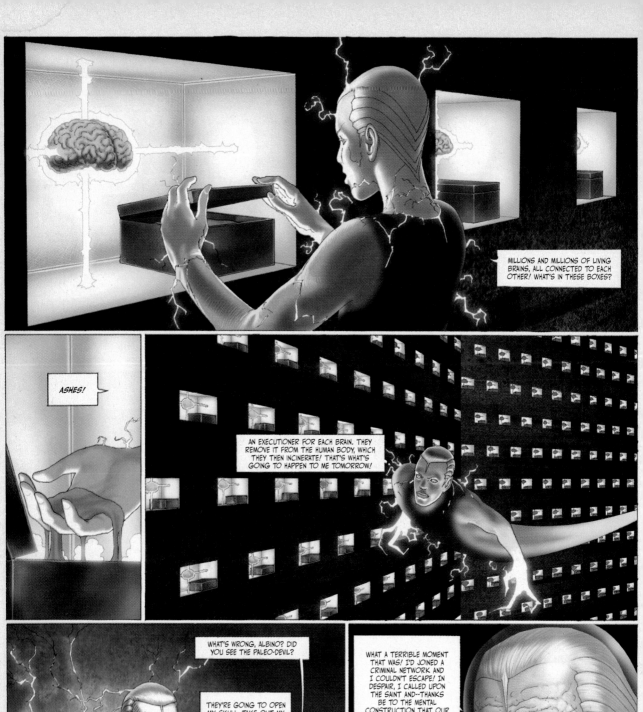

MILLIONS AND MILLIONS OF LIVING BRAINS, ALL CONNECTED TO EACH OTHER! WHAT'S IN THESE BOXES?

ASHES!

AN EXECUTIONER FOR EACH BRAIN. THEY REMOVE IT FROM THE HUMAN BODY, WHICH THEY THEN INCINERATE! THAT'S WHAT'S GOING TO HAPPEN TO ME TOMORROW!

WHAT'S WRONG, ALBINO? DID YOU SEE THE PALEO-DEVIL?

THEY'RE GOING TO OPEN MY SKULL, TAKE OUT MY BRAIN, AND THEN INCINERATE THE REST OF MY BODY! MAY SAINT SEVERO DE LOYOLA *PROTECT* US!

WHAT A TERRIBLE MOMENT THAT WAS! I'D JOINED A CRIMINAL NETWORK AND I COULDN'T ESCAPE! IN DESPAIR, I CALLED UPON THE SAINT AND--THANKS BE TO THE MENTAL CONSTRUCTION THAT OUR ANCESTORS CALLED GOD-- HE *CAME* TO MY AID!

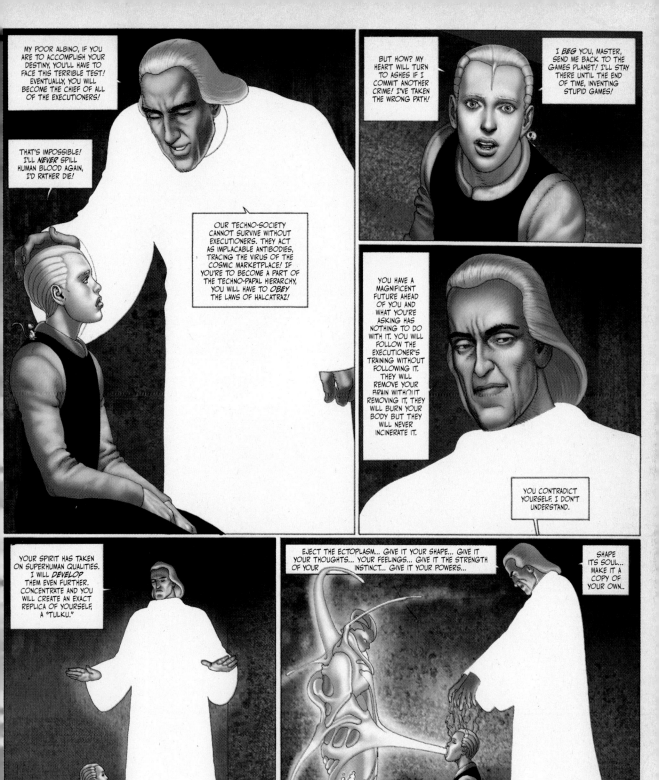

MY POOR ALBINO, IF YOU ARE TO ACCOMPLISH YOUR DESTINY, YOU'LL HAVE TO FACE THIS TERRIBLE TEST! EVENTUALLY, YOU WILL BECOME THE CHIEF OF ALL OF THE EXECUTIONERS!

THAT'S IMPOSSIBLE! I'LL *NEVER* SPILL HUMAN BLOOD AGAIN, I'D RATHER DIE!

OUR TECHNO-SOCIETY CANNOT SURVIVE WITHOUT EXECUTIONERS. THEY ACT AS IMPLACABLE ANTIBODIES, TRACING THE VIRUS OF THE COSMIC MARKETPLACE! IF YOU'RE TO BECOME A PART OF THE TECHNO-PAPAL HIERARCHY, YOU WILL HAVE TO *OBEY* THE LAWS OF HALCATRAZ!

BUT HOW? MY HEART WILL TURN TO ASHES IF I COMMIT ANOTHER CRIME! I'VE TAKEN THE WRONG PATH!

I *BEG* YOU, MASTER, SEND ME BACK TO THE GAMES PLANET! I'LL STAY THERE UNTIL THE END OF TIME, INVENTING STUPID GAMES!

YOU HAVE A MAGNIFICENT FUTURE AHEAD OF YOU AND WHAT YOU'RE ASKING HAS NOTHING TO DO WITH IT. YOU WILL FOLLOW THE EXECUTIONER'S TRAINING WITHOUT FOLLOWING IT. THEY WILL REMOVE YOUR BRAIN WITHOUT REMOVING IT, THEY WILL BURN YOUR BODY BUT THEY WILL NEVER INCINERATE IT.

YOU CONTRADICT YOURSELF. I DON'T UNDERSTAND.

YOUR SPIRIT HAS TAKEN ON SUPERHUMAN QUALITIES. I WILL *DEVELOP* THEM EVEN FURTHER. CONCENTRATE AND YOU WILL CREATE AN EXACT REPLICA OF YOURSELF, A "TULKU."

EJECT THE ECTOPLASM... GIVE IT YOUR SHAPE... GIVE IT YOUR THOUGHTS... YOUR FEELINGS... GIVE IT THE STRENGTH OF YOUR INSTINCT... GIVE IT YOUR POWERS...

SHAPE ITS SOUL... MAKE IT A COPY OF YOUR OWN..

27

BRAVO, ALBINO! YOU'VE DONE IT! TOMORROW THIS TULKU WILL HAVE ITS BRAIN REMOVED IN YOUR PLACE AND THEN IT WILL BE TRANSFORMED INTO AN EXECUTIONER. *NO ONE* WILL NOTICE THE SWITCH FOR FIVE YEARS.

YES, MY MASTERS. NO ONE WILL NOTICE THE SWITCH!

WHAT WILL I DO DURING THAT TIME?

AND ME?

WHILE YOUR TULKU LEARNS TO USE TORTURE AND MURDER TO HOMOGENIZE TASTE, MENTALITIES AND BEHAVIORS, YOU TWO WILL STAY WITH ME IN MY *HIDDEN* DIMENSION.

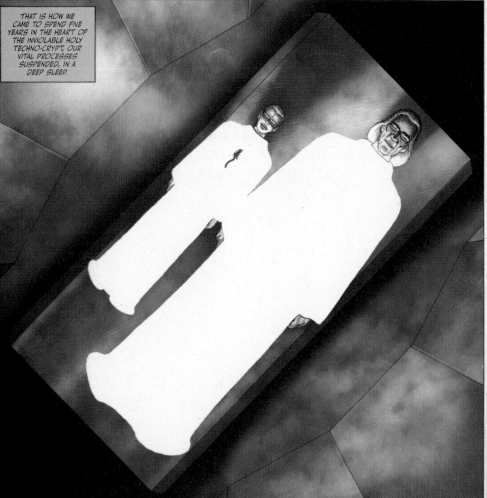

THAT IS HOW WE CAME TO SPEND FIVE YEARS IN THE HEART OF THE INVIOLABLE HOLY TECHNO-CRYPT, OUR VITAL PROCESSES SUSPENDED, IN A DEEP SLEEP.

IF I SAID THAT THERE WAS NO BEING MORE BROKEN BY SADNESS, DOUBT AND REMORSE THAN I WAS AT THAT TIME, I'D BE NOTHING MORE THAN A SELFISH OLD MAN. MY POOR MOTHER WAS SUFFERING *MUCH* WORSE, THOUGH I WASN'T ABLE TO WORRY ABOUT HER THEN...

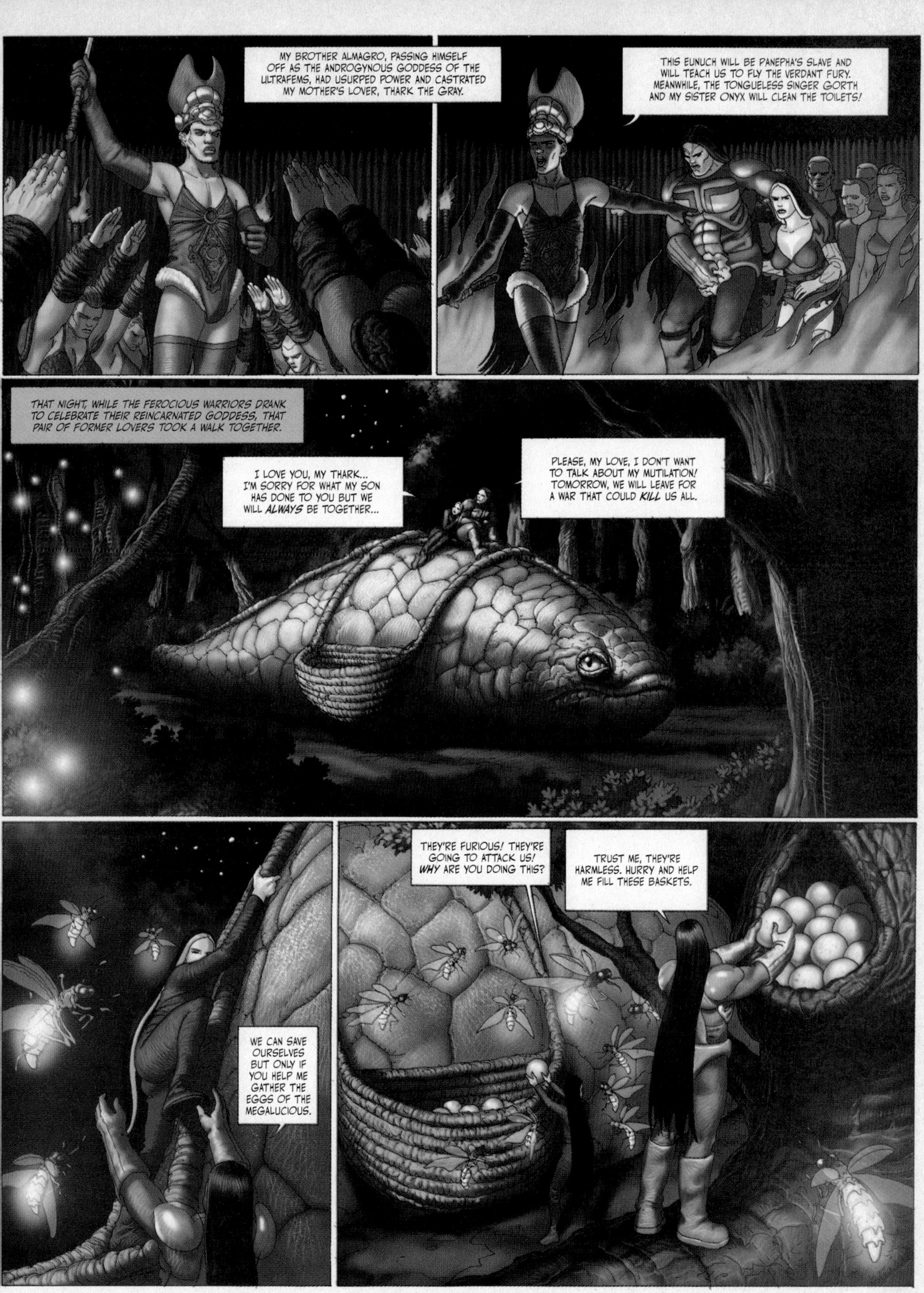
MY BROTHER ALMAGRO, PASSING HIMSELF OFF AS THE ANDROGYNOUS GODDESS OF THE ULTRAFEMS, HAD USURPED POWER AND CASTRATED MY MOTHER'S LOVER, THARK THE GRAY.
THIS EUNUCH WILL BE PANEPHA'S SLAVE AND WILL TEACH US TO FLY THE VERDANT FURY. MEANWHILE, THE TONGUELESS SINGER GORTH AND MY SISTER ONYX WILL CLEAN THE TOILETS!
THAT NIGHT, WHILE THE FEROCIOUS WARRIORS DRANK TO CELEBRATE THEIR REINCARNATED GODDESS, THAT PAIR OF FORMER LOVERS TOOK A WALK TOGETHER.
I LOVE YOU, MY THARK... I'M SORRY FOR WHAT MY SON HAS DONE TO YOU BUT WE WILL ALWAYS BE TOGETHER...
PLEASE, MY LOVE, I DON'T WANT TO TALK ABOUT MY MUTILATION! TOMORROW, WE WILL LEAVE FOR A WAR THAT COULD KILL US ALL.
WE CAN SAVE OURSELVES BUT ONLY IF YOU HELP ME GATHER THE EGGS OF THE MEGALUCIOUS.
THEY'RE FURIOUS! THEY'RE GOING TO ATTACK US! WHY ARE YOU DOING THIS?
TRUST ME, THEY'RE HARMLESS. HURRY AND HELP ME FILL THESE BASKETS.

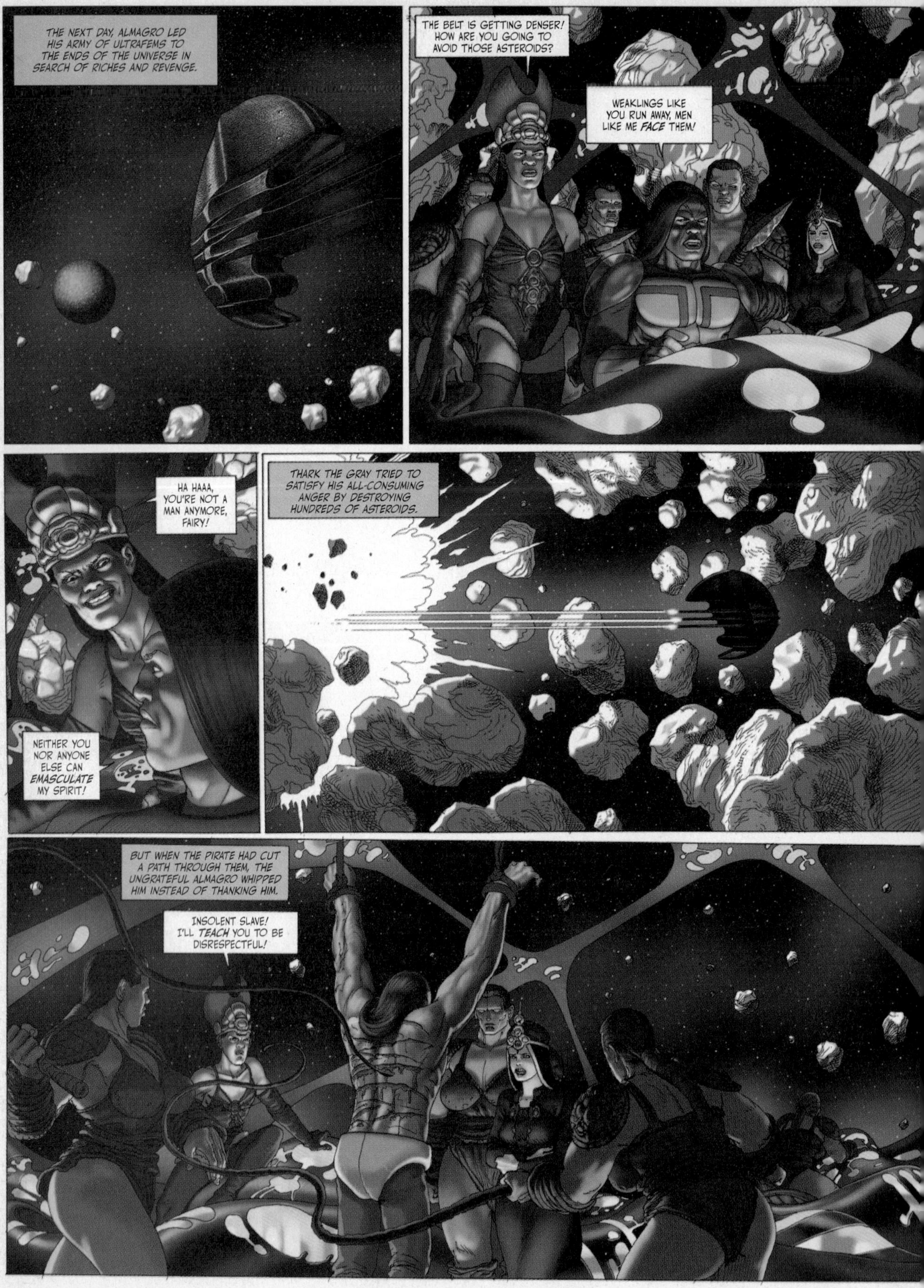
THE NEXT DAY, ALMAGRO LED HIS ARMY OF ULTRAFEMS TO THE ENDS OF THE UNIVERSE IN SEARCH OF RICHES AND REVENGE.
THE BELT IS GETTING DENSER! HOW ARE YOU GOING TO AVOID THOSE ASTEROIDS?
WEAKLINGS LIKE YOU RUN AWAY, MEN LIKE ME FACE THEM!
HA HAAA, YOU'RE NOT A MAN ANYMORE, FAIRY!
NEITHER YOU NOR ANYONE ELSE CAN EMASCULATE MY SPIRIT!
THARK THE GRAY TRIED TO SATISFY HIS ALL-CONSUMING ANGER BY DESTROYING HUNDREDS OF ASTEROIDS.
BUT WHEN THE PIRATE HAD CUT A PATH THROUGH THEM, THE UNGRATEFUL ALMAGRO WHIPPED HIM INSTEAD OF THANKING HIM.
INSOLENT SLAVE! I'LL TEACH YOU TO BE DISRESPECTFUL!

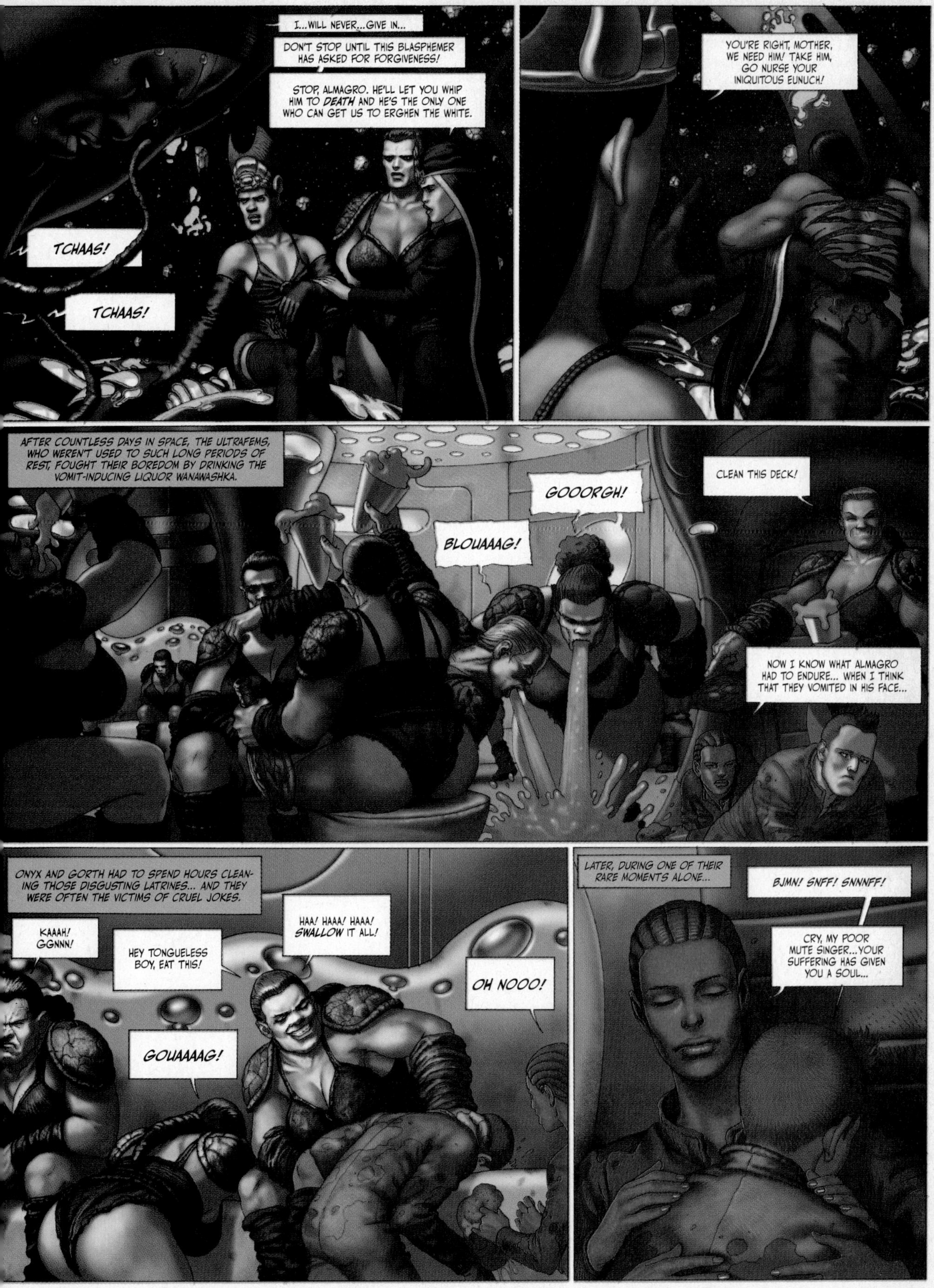
I...WILL NEVER...GIVE IN...
DON'T STOP UNTIL THIS BLASPHEMER HAS ASKED FOR FORGIVENESS!
STOP, ALMAGRO. HE'LL LET YOU WHIP HIM TO *DEATH* AND HE'S THE ONLY ONE WHO CAN GET US TO ERGHEN THE WHITE.
TCHAAS!
TCHAAS!
YOU'RE RIGHT, MOTHER, WE NEED HIM! TAKE HIM, GO NURSE YOUR INIQUITOUS EUNUCH!
AFTER COUNTLESS DAYS IN SPACE, THE ULTRAFEMS, WHO WEREN'T USED TO SUCH LONG PERIODS OF REST, FOUGHT THEIR BOREDOM BY DRINKING THE VOMIT-INDUCING LIQUOR WANAWASHKA.
BLOUAAAG!
GOOORGH!
CLEAN THIS DECK!
NOW I KNOW WHAT ALMAGRO HAD TO ENDURE... WHEN I THINK THAT THEY VOMITED IN HIS FACE...
ONYX AND GORTH HAD TO SPEND HOURS CLEAN-ING THOSE DISGUSTING LATRINES... AND THEY WERE OFTEN THE VICTIMS OF CRUEL JOKES.
KAAAH! GGNNN!
HEY TONGUELESS BOY, EAT THIS!
HAA! HAAA! HAAA! *SWALLOW* IT ALL!
OH NOOO!
GOUAAAAG!
LATER, DURING ONE OF THEIR RARE MOMENTS ALONE...
BJMN! SNFF! SNNNFF!
CRY, MY POOR MUTE SINGER...YOUR SUFFERING HAS GIVEN YOU A SOUL...

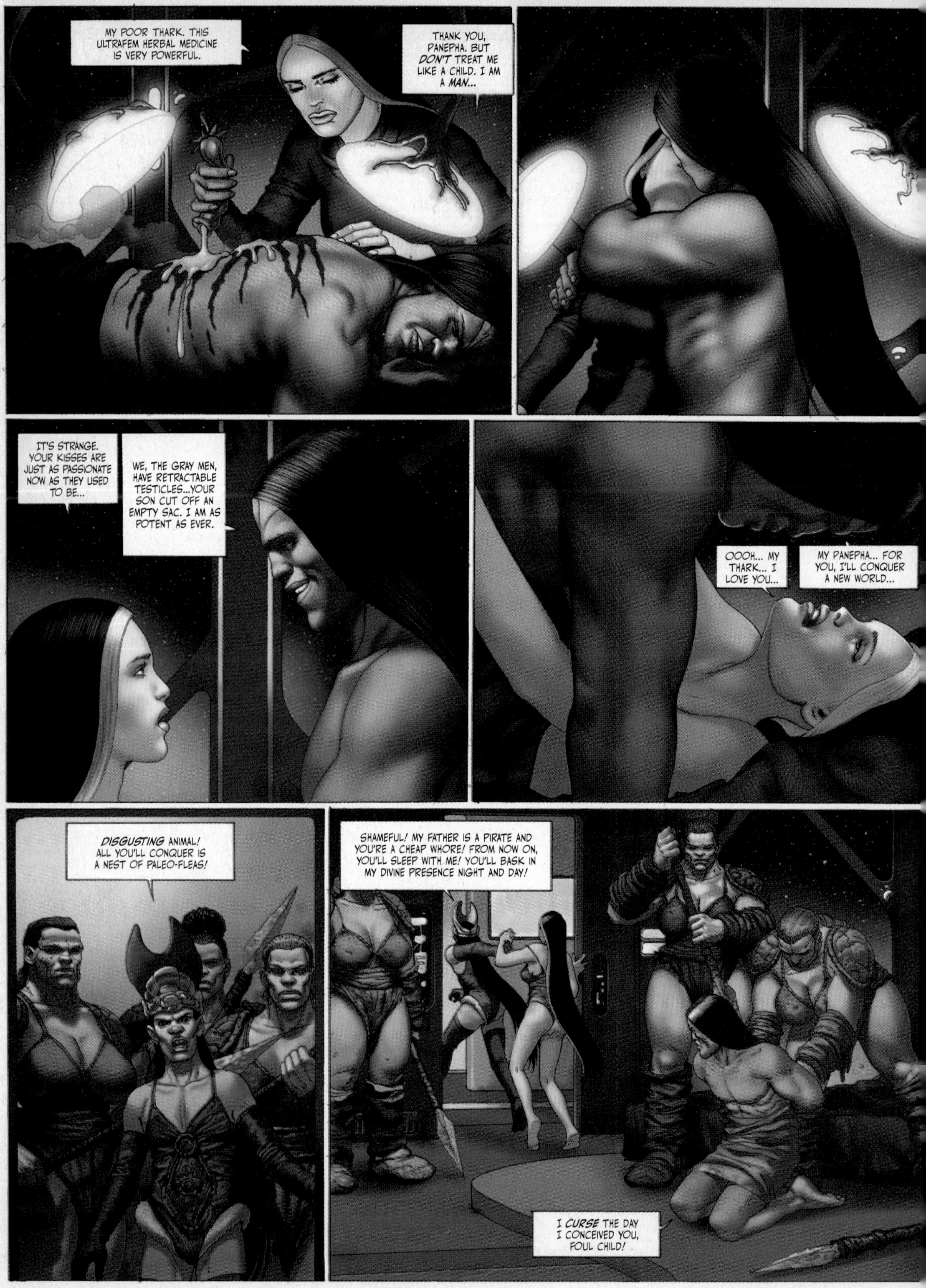
MY POOR THARK. THIS ULTRAFEM HERBAL MEDICINE IS VERY POWERFUL.
THANK YOU, PANEPHA. BUT DON'T TREAT ME LIKE A CHILD. I AM A MAN...
IT'S STRANGE. YOUR KISSES ARE JUST AS PASSIONATE NOW AS THEY USED TO BE...
WE, THE GRAY MEN, HAVE RETRACTABLE TESTICLES...YOUR SON CUT OFF AN EMPTY SAC. I AM AS POTENT AS EVER.
OOOH... MY THARK... I LOVE YOU...
MY PANEPHA... FOR YOU, I'LL CONQUER A NEW WORLD...
DISGUSTING ANIMAL! ALL YOU'LL CONQUER IS A NEST OF PALEO-FLEAS!
SHAMEFUL! MY FATHER IS A PIRATE AND YOU'RE A CHEAP WHORE! FROM NOW ON, YOU'LL SLEEP WITH ME! YOU'LL BASK IN MY DIVINE PRESENCE NIGHT AND DAY!
I CURSE THE DAY I CONCEIVED YOU, FOUL CHILD!

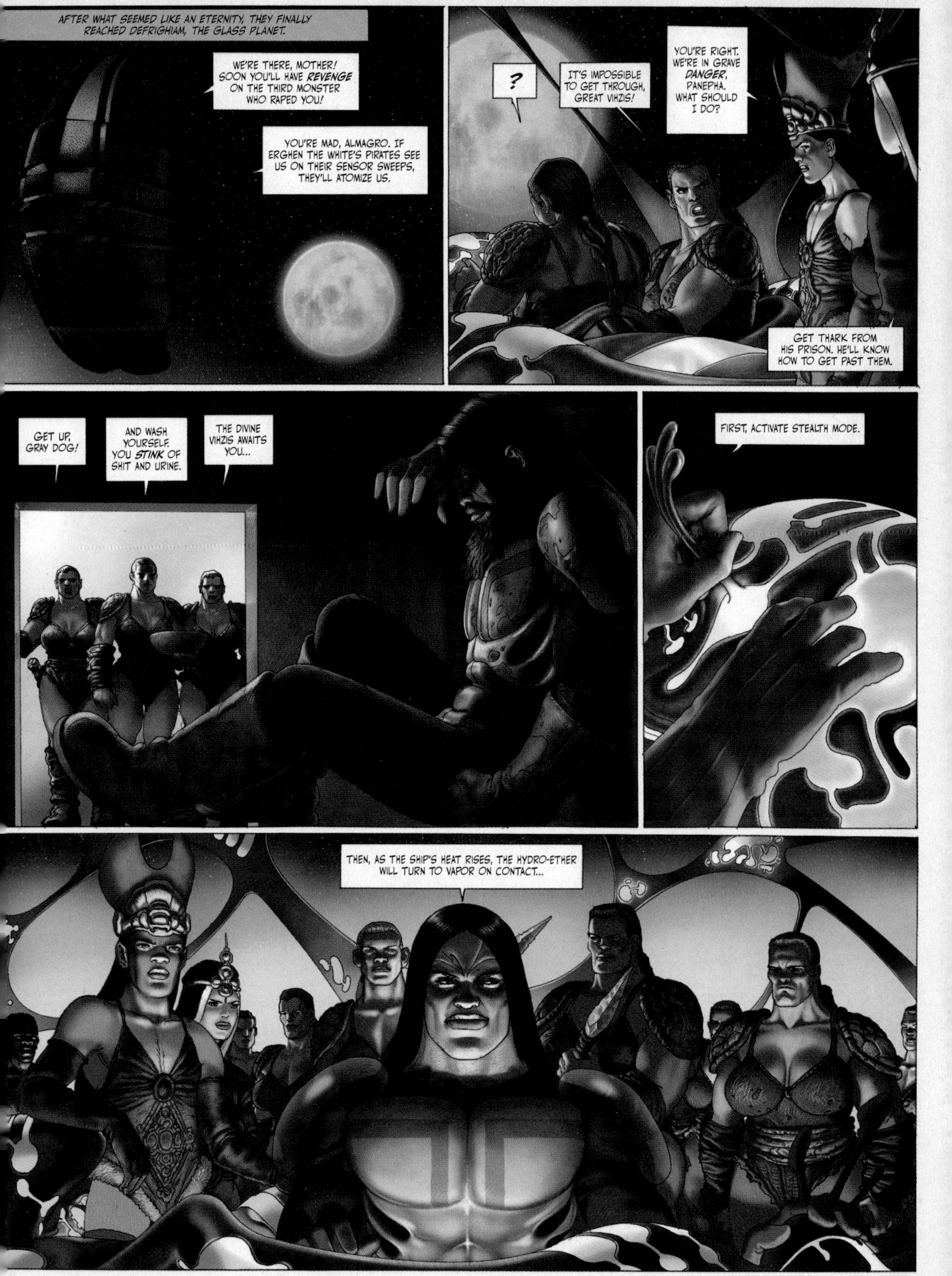
AFTER WHAT SEEMED LIKE AN ETERNITY, THEY FINALLY REACHED DEFRIGHIAM, THE GLASS PLANET.
WE'RE THERE, MOTHER! SOON YOU'LL HAVE REVENGE ON THE THIRD MONSTER WHO RAPED YOU!
YOU'RE MAD, ALMAGRO. IF ERGHEN THE WHITE'S PIRATES SEE US ON THEIR SENSOR SWEEPS, THEY'LL ATOMIZE US.
?
IT'S IMPOSSIBLE TO GET THROUGH, GREAT VIHZIS!
YOU'RE RIGHT. WE'RE IN GRAVE DANGER, PANEPHA. WHAT SHOULD I DO?
GET THARK FROM HIS PRISON. HE'LL KNOW HOW TO GET PAST THEM.
GET UP, GRAY DOG!
AND WASH YOURSELF. YOU STINK OF SHIT AND URINE.
THE DIVINE VIHZIS AWAITS YOU...
FIRST, ACTIVATE STEALTH MODE.
THEN, AS THE SHIP'S HEAT RISES, THE HYDRO-ETHER WILL TURN TO VAPOR ON CONTACT...

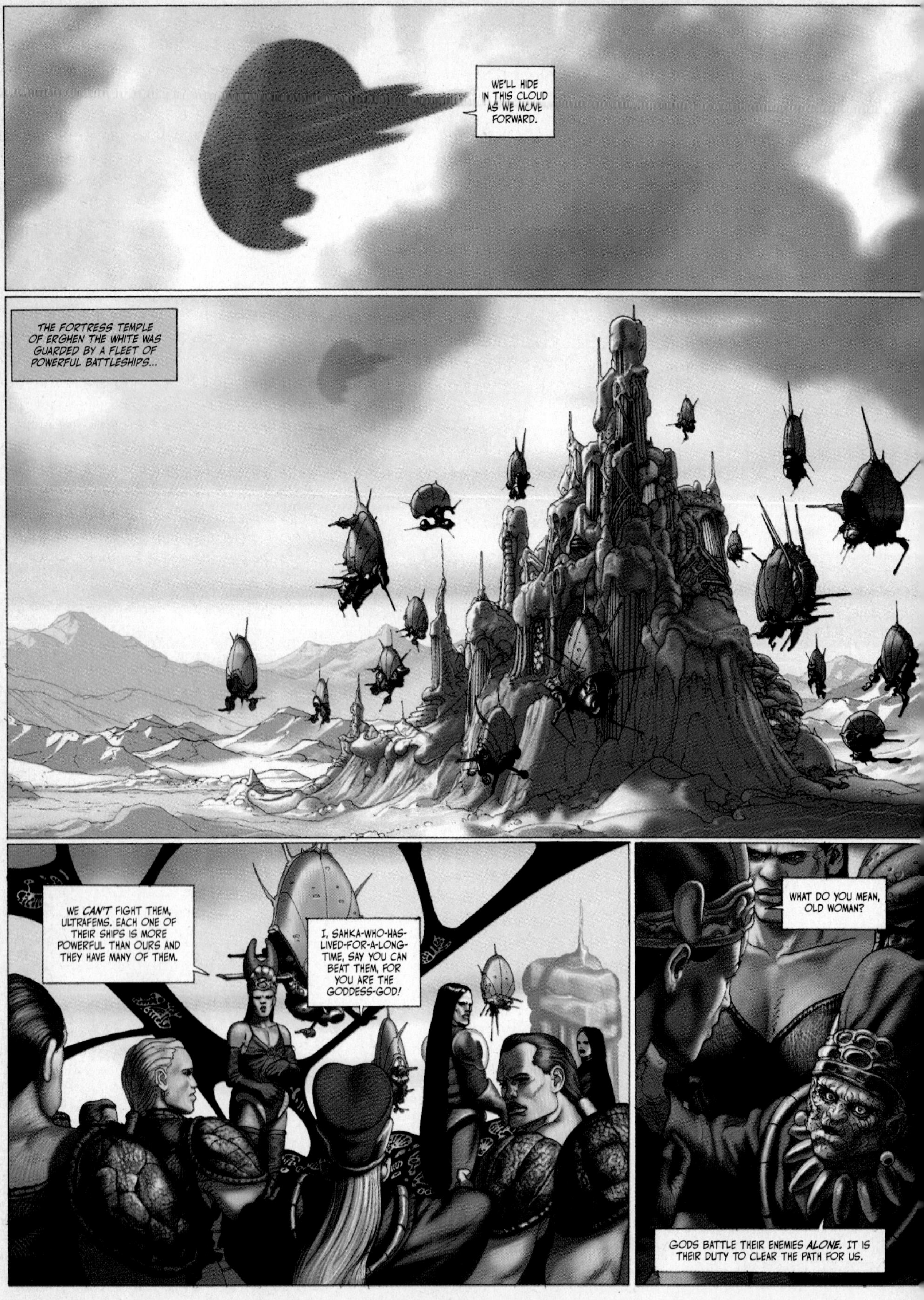
WE'LL HIDE IN THIS CLOUD AS WE MOVE FORWARD.
THE FORTRESS TEMPLE OF ERGHEN THE WHITE WAS GUARDED BY A FLEET OF POWERFUL BATTLESHIPS...
WE CAN'T FIGHT THEM, ULTRAFEMS. EACH ONE OF THEIR SHIPS IS MORE POWERFUL THAN OURS AND THEY HAVE MANY OF THEM.
I, SAHKA-WHO-HAS-LIVED-FOR-A-LONG-TIME, SAY YOU CAN BEAT THEM, FOR YOU ARE THE GODDESS-GOD!
WHAT DO YOU MEAN, OLD WOMAN?
GODS BATTLE THEIR ENEMIES ALONE. IT IS THEIR DUTY TO CLEAR THE PATH FOR US.

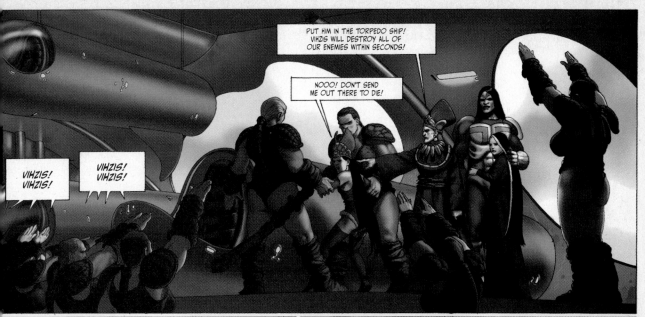

PUT HIM IN THE TORPEDO SHIP! VIHZIS WILL DESTROY ALL OF OUR ENEMIES WITHIN SECONDS!

NOOO! DON'T SEND ME OUT THERE TO DIE!

VIHZIS! VIHZIS!

VIHZIS! VIHZIS!

I'M NOT OMNIPOTENT! I'M NOT VIHZIS! I'M NOT AN ANDROGYNE! I'M JUST A MAN! HELP ME, PANEPHA!

HE'S *OUR* SON, THARK. SAVE HIM, I BEG YOU...

CUT OFF THE IMPOSTER'S HEAD!

ONE MOMENT, VENERABLE ANCIENT. THE CLOUDS ARE STARTING TO CLEAR. WE CAN'T RUN NOW. OUR ONLY HOPE IS TO ATTACK. IF YOU SPARE MY SON, I CAN DO IT...

YOU CAN TAKE THE TORPEDO SHIP? YOU'RE NOT A GODDESS-GOD. THEY'LL DESTROY YOU. WE'D RATHER DIE IN OUR HOLY SUICIDE RITUAL!

WAIT! I'M NOT VIHZIS, BUT I HAVE AN IDEA THAT MIGHT *SAVE* US!

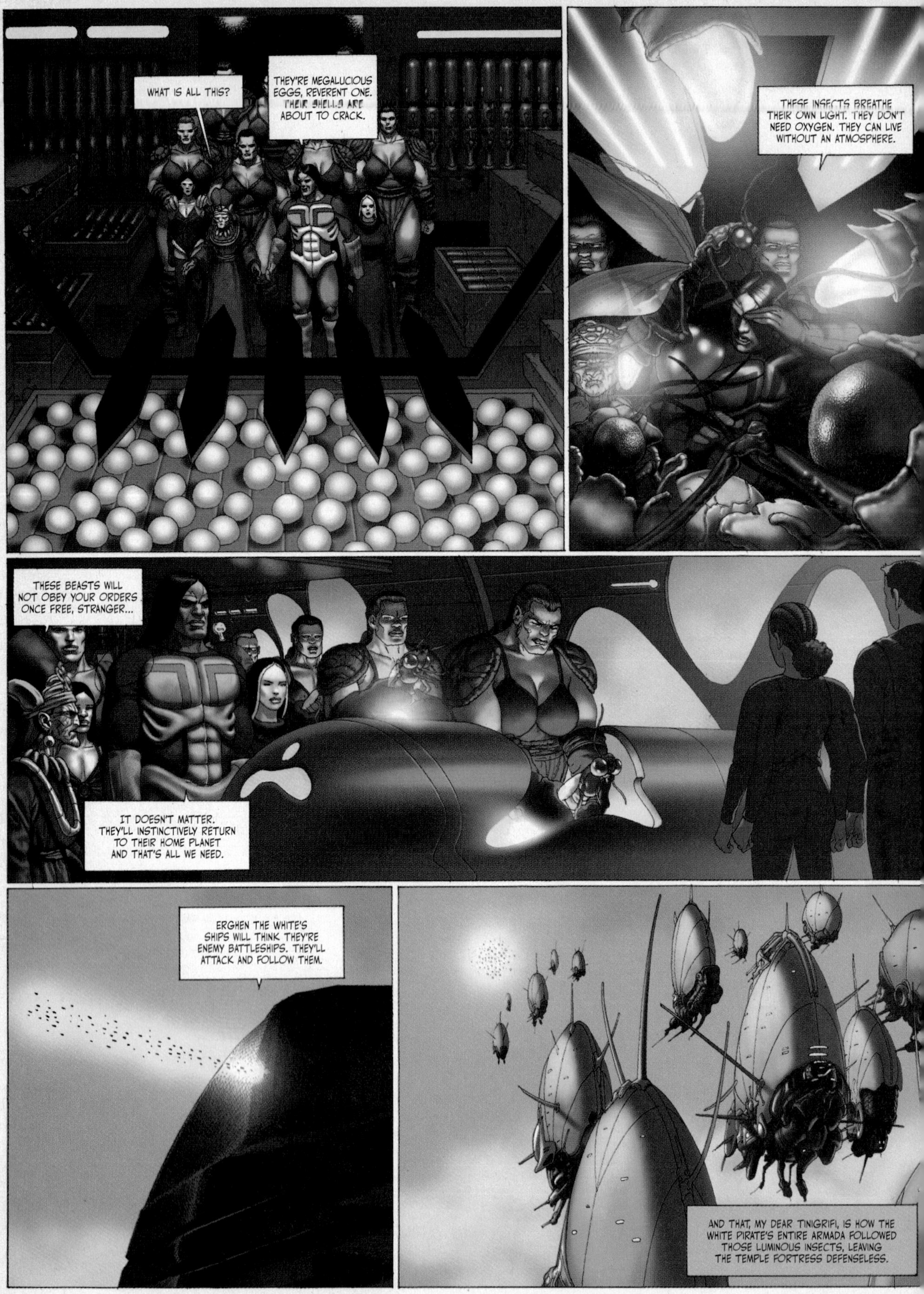
WHAT IS ALL THIS?
THEY'RE MEGALUCIOUS EGGS, REVERENT ONE. THEIR SHELLS ARE ABOUT TO CRACK.
THESE INSECTS BREATHE THEIR OWN LIGHT. THEY DON'T NEED OXYGEN. THEY CAN LIVE WITHOUT AN ATMOSPHERE.
THESE BEASTS WILL NOT OBEY YOUR ORDERS ONCE FREE, STRANGER...
IT DOESN'T MATTER. THEY'LL INSTINCTIVELY RETURN TO THEIR HOME PLANET AND THAT'S ALL WE NEED.
ERGHEN THE WHITE'S SHIPS WILL THINK THEY'RE ENEMY BATTLESHIPS. THEY'LL ATTACK AND FOLLOW THEM.
AND THAT, MY DEAR TINIGRIFI, IS HOW THE WHITE PIRATE'S ENTIRE ARMADA FOLLOWED THOSE LUMINOUS INSECTS, LEAVING THE TEMPLE FORTRESS DEFENSELESS.

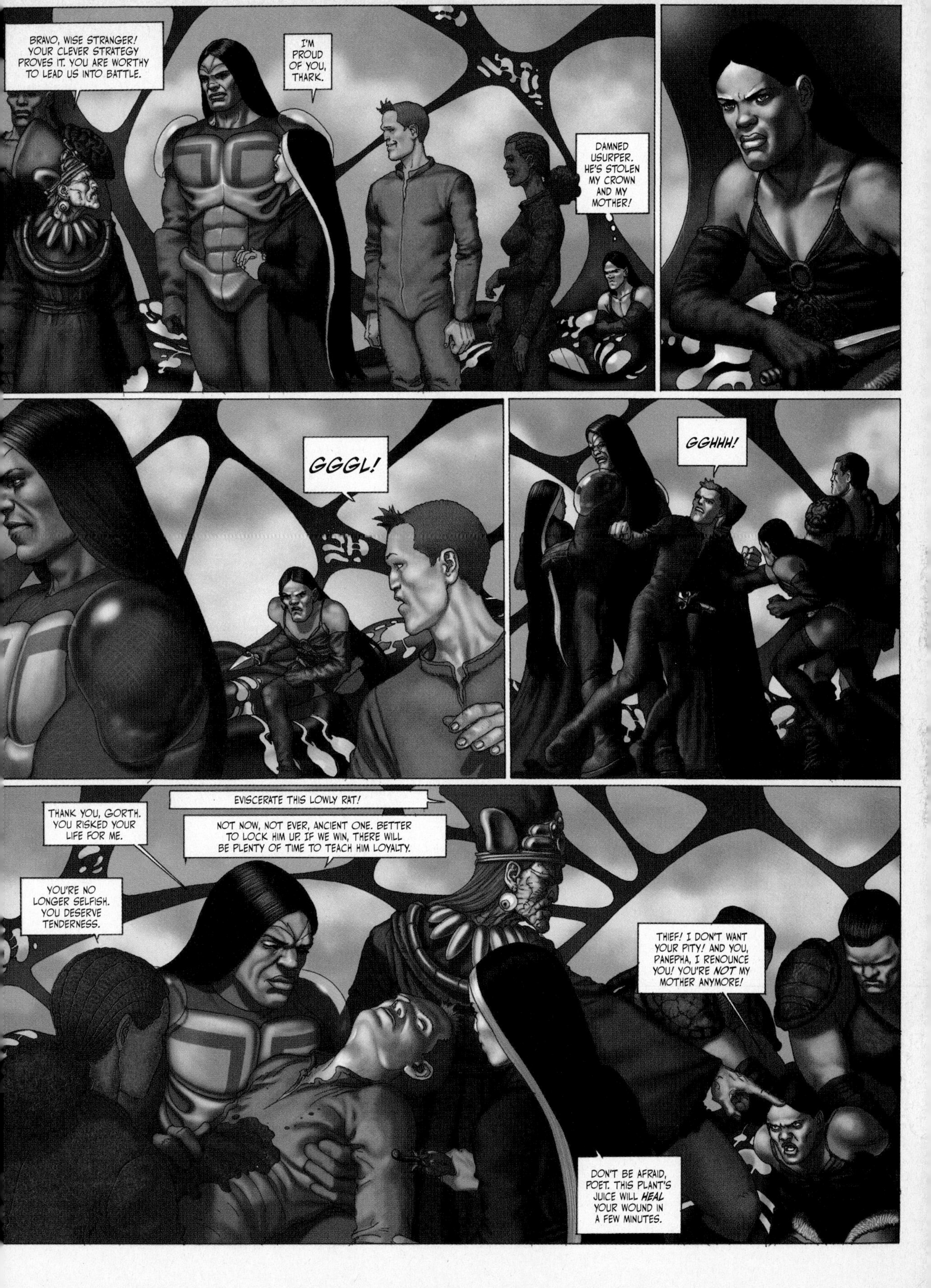
BRAVO, WISE STRANGER! YOUR CLEVER STRATEGY PROVES IT. YOU ARE WORTHY TO LEAD US INTO BATTLE.
I'M PROUD OF YOU, THARK.
DAMNED USURPER. HE'S STOLEN MY CROWN AND MY MOTHER!
GGGL!
GGHHH!
THANK YOU, GORTH. YOU RISKED YOUR LIFE FOR ME.
EVISCERATE THIS LOWLY RAT!
NOT NOW, NOT EVER, ANCIENT ONE. BETTER TO LOCK HIM UP. IF WE WIN, THERE WILL BE PLENTY OF TIME TO TEACH HIM LOYALTY.
YOU'RE NO LONGER SELFISH. YOU DESERVE TENDERNESS.
THIEF! I DON'T WANT YOUR PITY! AND YOU, PANEPHA, I RENOUNCE YOU! YOU'RE NOT MY MOTHER ANYMORE!
DON'T BE AFRAID, POET. THIS PLANT'S JUICE WILL HEAL YOUR WOUND IN A FEW MINUTES.

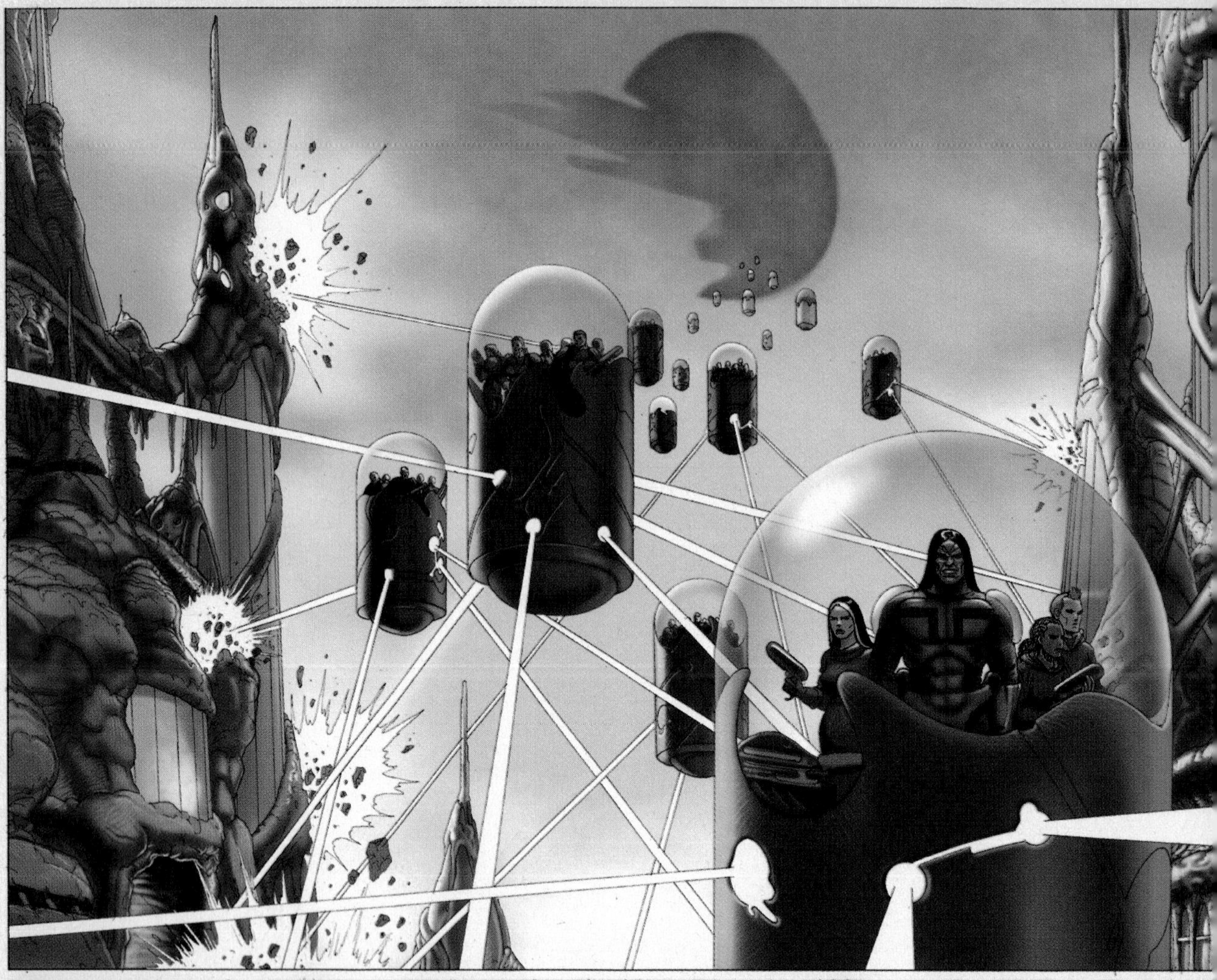

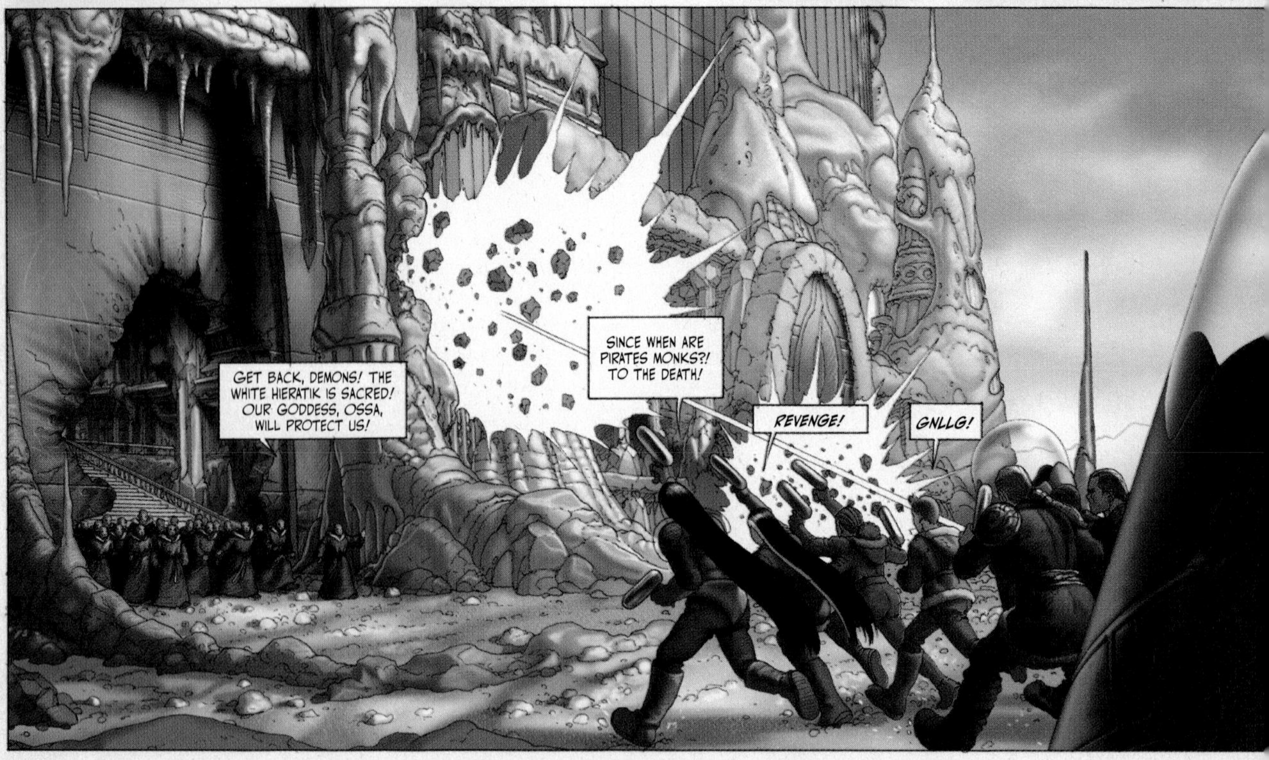

GET BACK, DEMONS! THE WHITE HIERATIK IS SACRED! OUR GODDESS, OSSA, WILL PROTECT US!
SINCE WHEN ARE PIRATES MONKS?! TO THE DEATH!
REVENGE!
GNLLG!

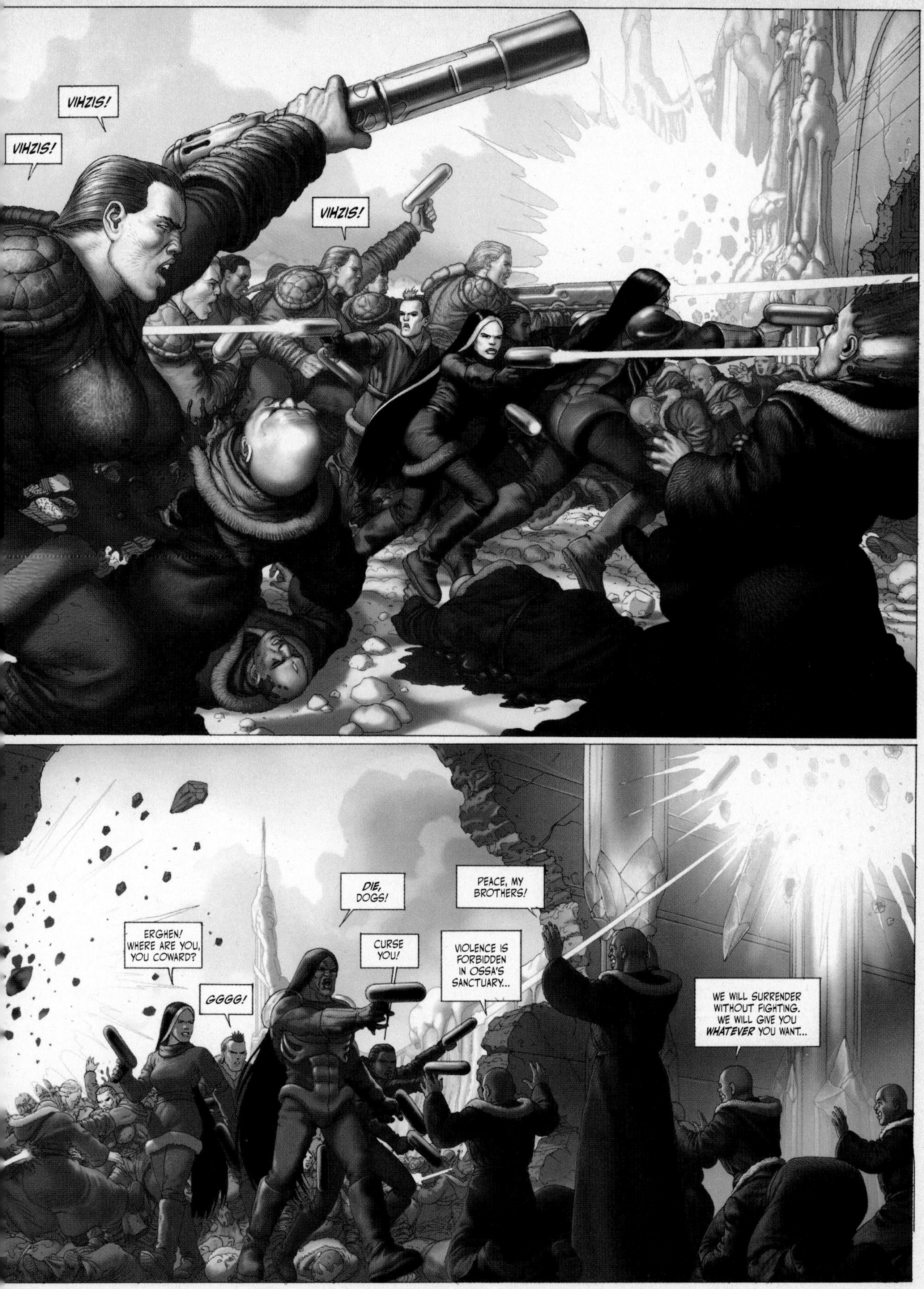
VIHZIS!
VIHZIS!
VIHZIS!
ERGHEN! WHERE ARE YOU, YOU COWARD?
GGGG!
DIE, DOGS!
CURSE YOU!
PEACE, MY BROTHERS!
VIOLENCE IS FORBIDDEN IN OSSA'S SANCTUARY...
WE WILL SURRENDER WITHOUT FIGHTING. WE WILL GIVE YOU *WHATEVER* YOU WANT...

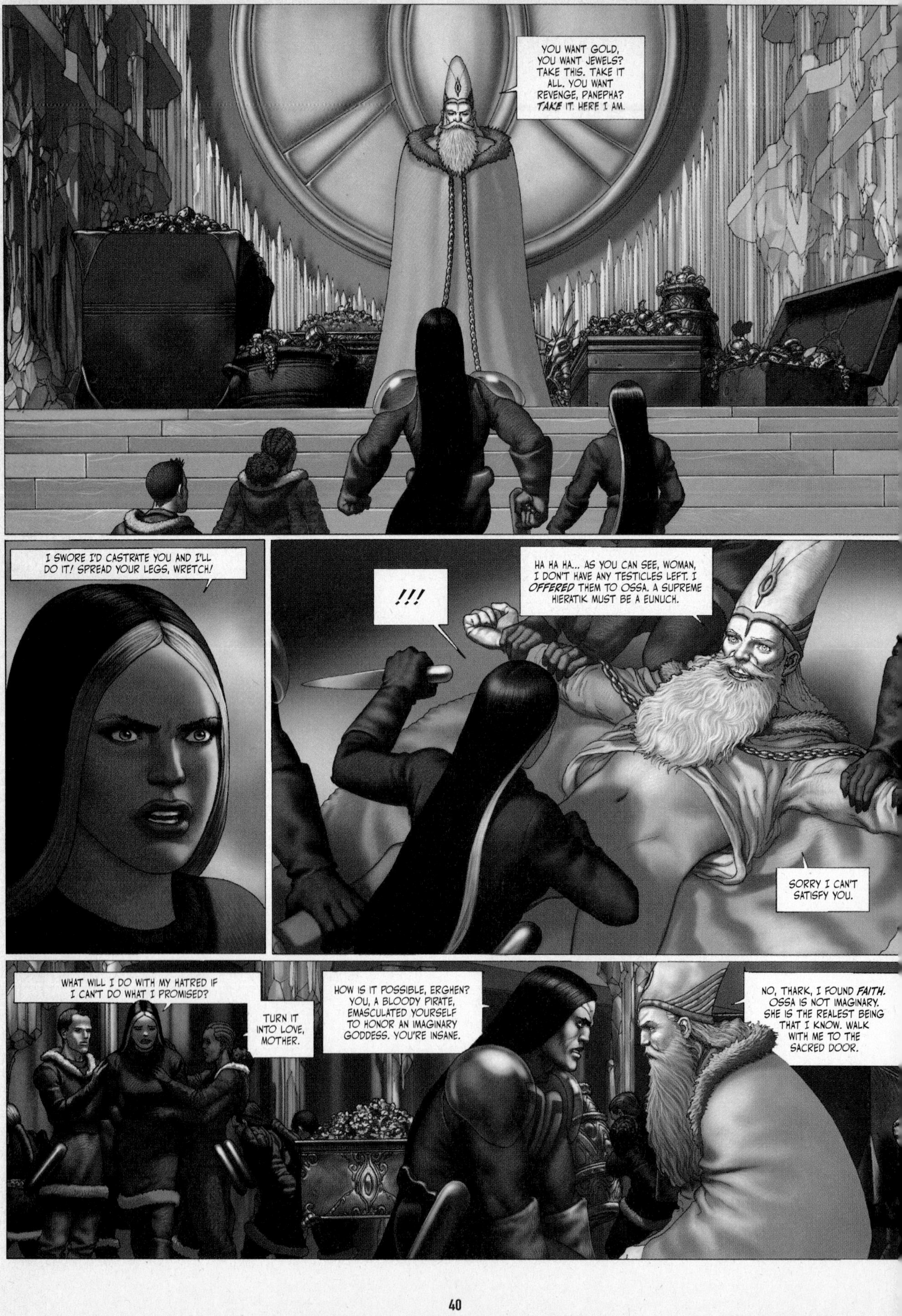

YOU WANT GOLD, YOU WANT JEWELS? TAKE THIS. TAKE IT ALL. YOU WANT REVENGE, PANEPHA? *TAKE* IT. HERE I AM.
I SWORE I'D CASTRATE YOU AND I'LL DO IT! SPREAD YOUR LEGS, WRETCH!
!!!
HA HA HA... AS YOU CAN SEE, WOMAN, I DON'T HAVE ANY TESTICLES LEFT. I *OFFERED* THEM TO OSSA. A SUPREME HIERATIK MUST BE A EUNUCH.
SORRY I CAN'T SATISFY YOU.
WHAT WILL I DO WITH MY HATRED IF I CAN'T DO WHAT I PROMISED?
TURN IT INTO LOVE, MOTHER.
HOW IS IT POSSIBLE, ERGHEN? YOU, A BLOODY PIRATE, EMASCULATED YOURSELF TO HONOR AN IMAGINARY GODDESS. YOU'RE INSANE.
NO, THARK, I FOUND *FAITH.* OSSA IS NOT IMAGINARY. SHE IS THE REALEST BEING THAT I KNOW. WALK WITH ME TO THE SACRED DOOR.

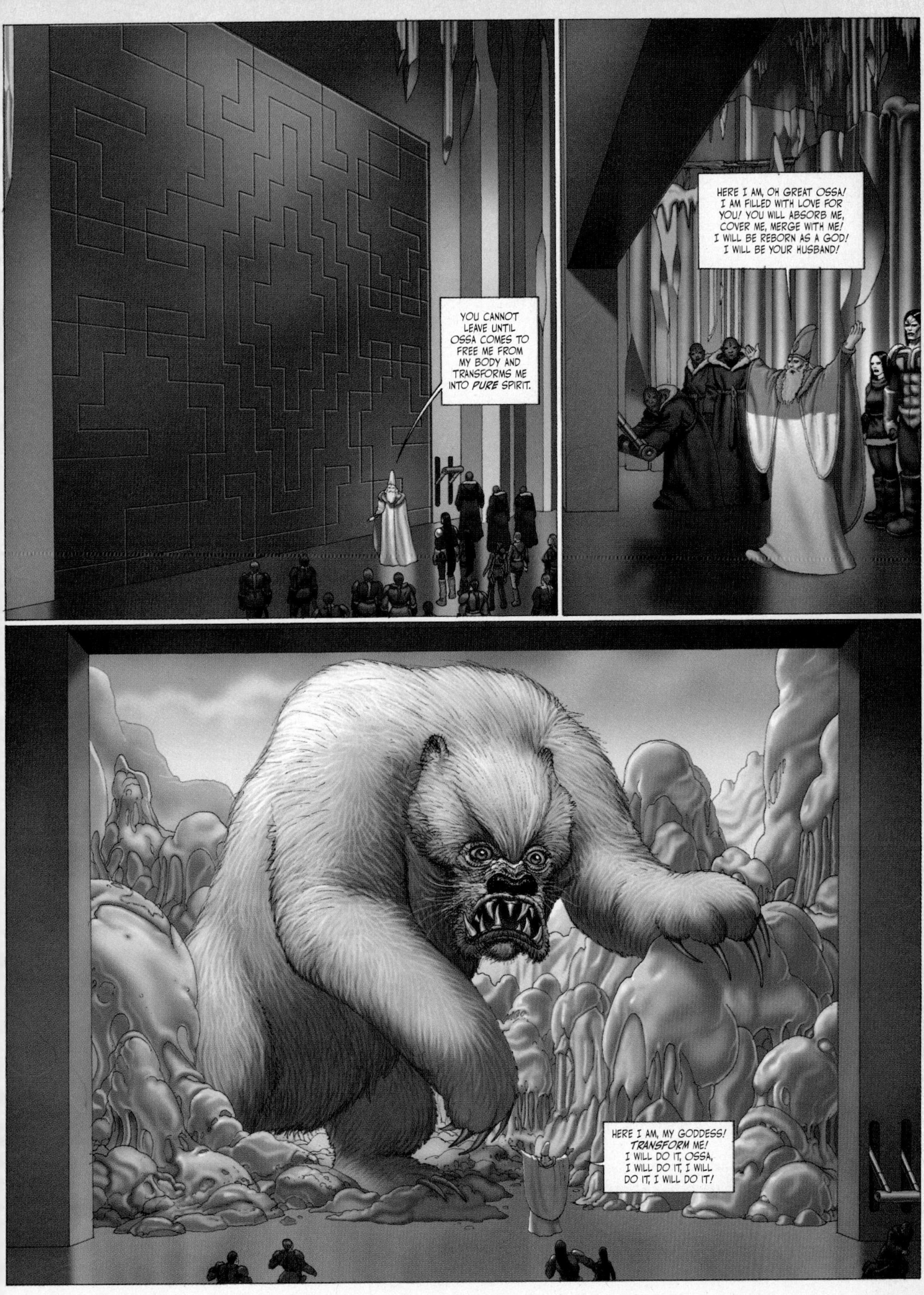
YOU CANNOT LEAVE UNTIL OSSA COMES TO FREE ME FROM MY BODY AND TRANSFORMS ME INTO *PURE* SPIRIT.
HERE I AM, OH GREAT OSSA! I AM FILLED WITH LOVE FOR YOU! YOU WILL ABSORB ME, COVER ME, MERGE WITH ME! I WILL BE REBORN AS A GOD! I WILL BE YOUR HUSBAND!
HERE I AM, MY GODDESS! *TRANSFORM* ME! I WILL DO IT, OSSA, I WILL DO IT, I WILL DO IT, I WILL DO IT!

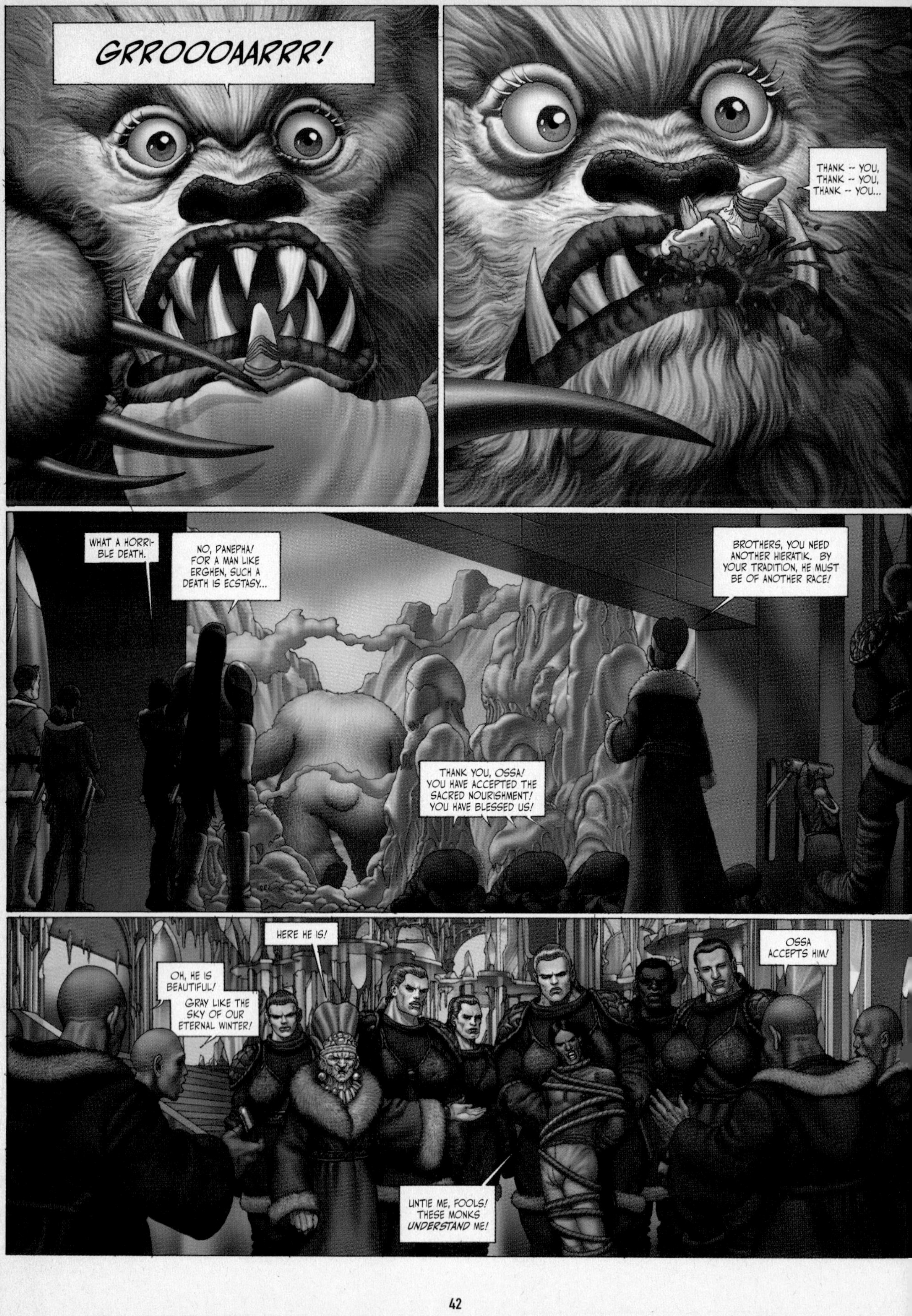
GRROOOAARRR!
THANK -- YOU, THANK -- YOU, THANK -- YOU...
WHAT A HORRIBLE DEATH.
NO, PANEPHA! FOR A MAN LIKE ERGHEN, SUCH A DEATH IS ECSTASY...
BROTHERS, YOU NEED ANOTHER HIERATIK. BY YOUR TRADITION, HE MUST BE OF ANOTHER RACE!
THANK YOU, OSSA! YOU HAVE ACCEPTED THE SACRED NOURISHMENT! YOU HAVE BLESSED US!
OH, HE IS BEAUTIFUL!
GRAY LIKE THE SKY OF OUR ETERNAL WINTER!
HERE HE IS!
OSSA ACCEPTS HIM!
UNTIE ME, FOOLS! THESE MONKS UNDERSTAND ME!

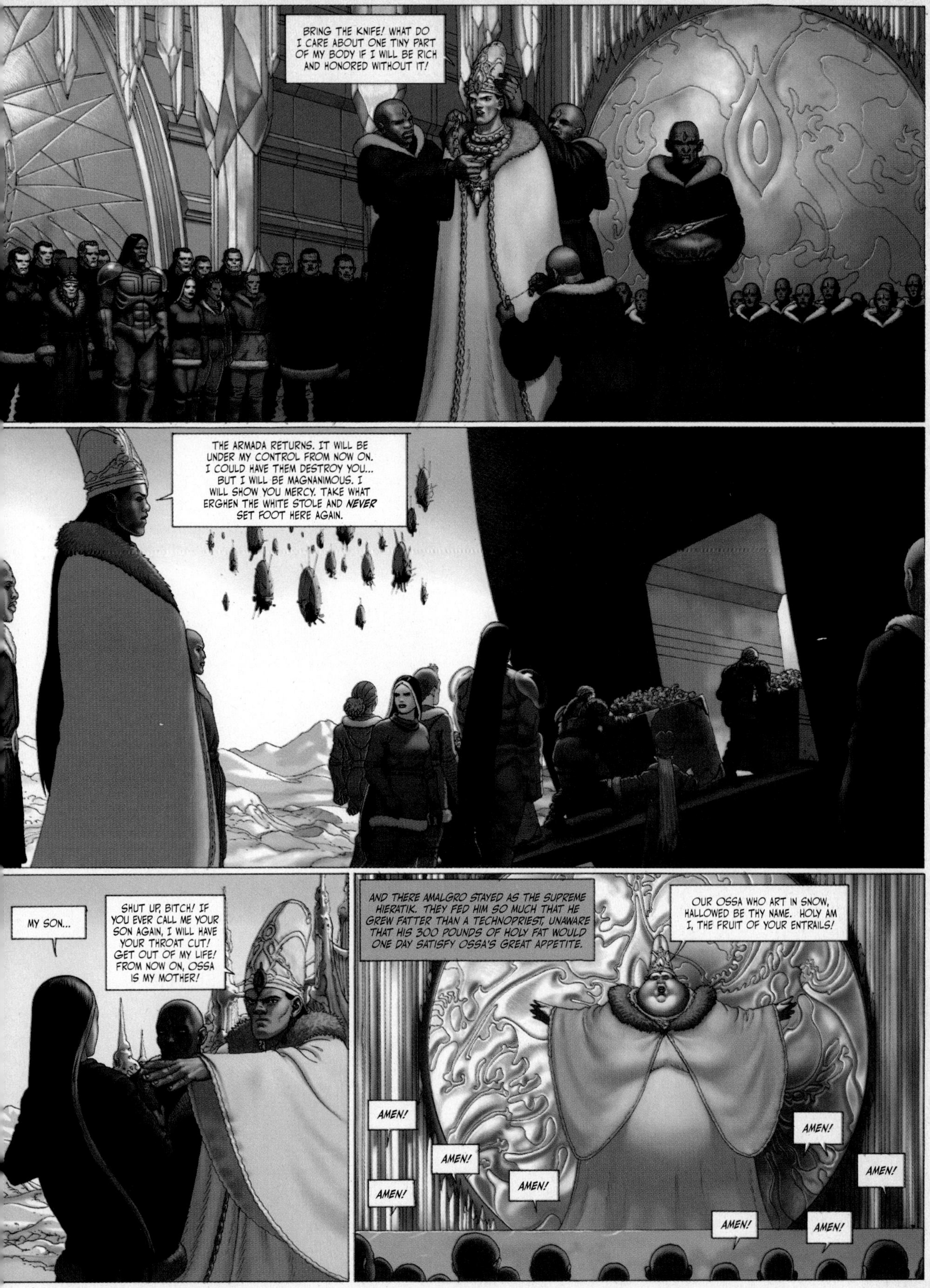
BRING THE KNIFE! WHAT DO I CARE ABOUT ONE TINY PART OF MY BODY IF I WILL BE RICH AND HONORED WITHOUT IT!
THE ARMADA RETURNS. IT WILL BE UNDER MY CONTROL FROM NOW ON. I COULD HAVE THEM DESTROY YOU... BUT I WILL BE MAGNANIMOUS. I WILL SHOW YOU MERCY. TAKE WHAT ERGHEN THE WHITE STOLE AND NEVER SET FOOT HERE AGAIN.
MY SON...
SHUT UP, BITCH! IF YOU EVER CALL ME YOUR SON AGAIN, I WILL HAVE YOUR THROAT CUT! GET OUT OF MY LIFE! FROM NOW ON, OSSA IS MY MOTHER!
AND THERE AMALGRO STAYED AS THE SUPREME HIERATIK. THEY FED HIM SO MUCH THAT HE GREW FATTER THAN A TECHNOPRIEST, UNAWARE THAT HIS 300 POUNDS OF HOLY FAT WOULD ONE DAY SATISFY OSSA'S GREAT APPETITE.
OUR OSSA WHO ART IN SNOW, HALLOWED BE THY NAME. HOLY AM I, THE FRUIT OF YOUR ENTRAILS!
AMEN!
AMEN!
AMEN!
AMEN!
AMEN!
AMEN!
AMEN!
AMEN!

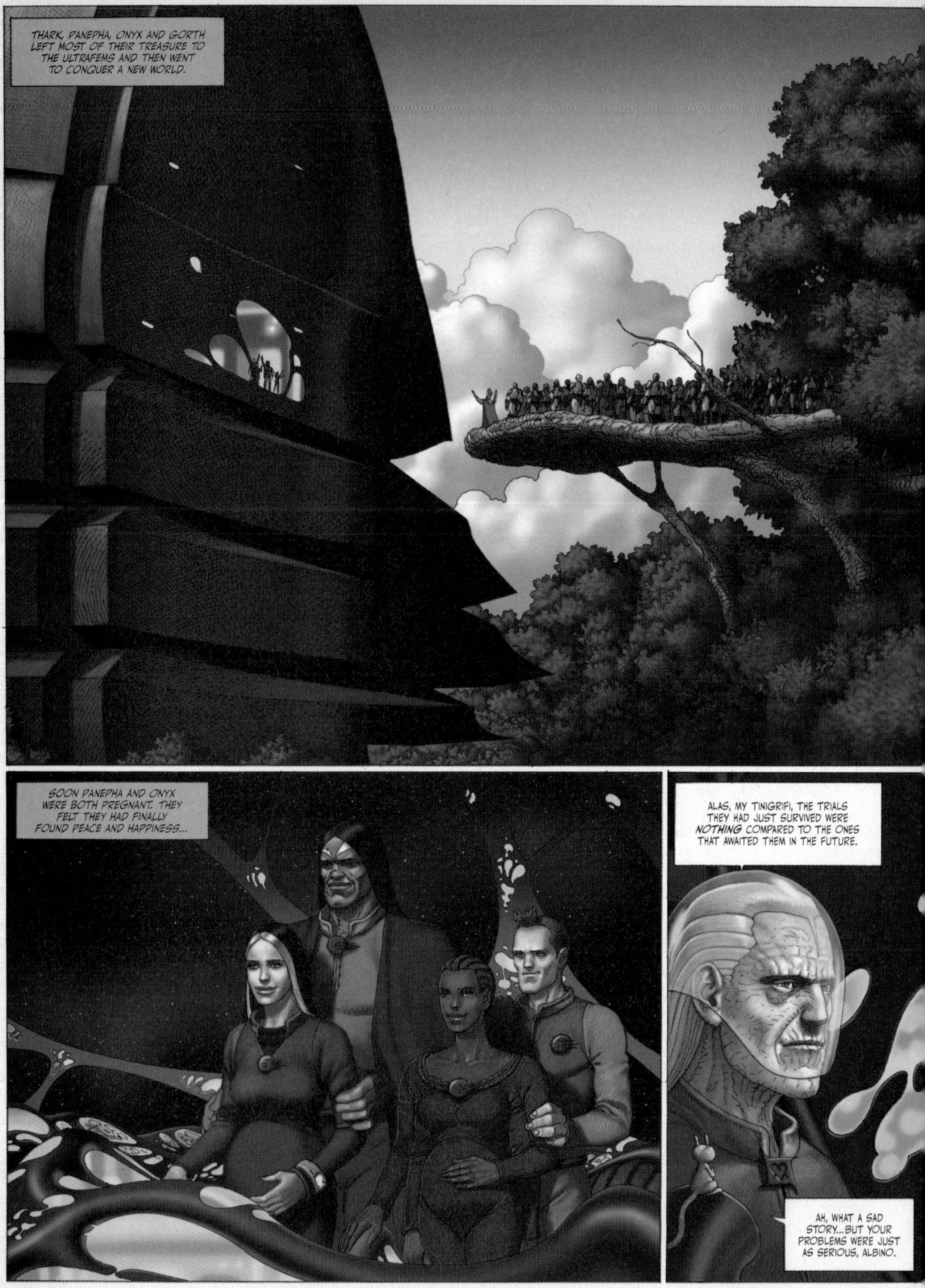
THARK, PANEPHA, ONYX AND GORTH LEFT MOST OF THEIR TREASURE TO THE ULTRAFEMS AND THEN WENT TO CONQUER A NEW WORLD.
SOON PANEPHA AND ONYX WERE BOTH PREGNANT. THEY FELT THEY HAD FINALLY FOUND PEACE AND HAPPINESS...
ALAS, MY TINIGRIFI, THE TRIALS THEY HAD JUST SURVIVED WERE NOTHING COMPARED TO THE ONES THAT AWAITED THEM IN THE FUTURE.
AH, WHAT A SAD STORY...BUT YOUR PROBLEMS WERE JUST AS SERIOUS, ALBINO.

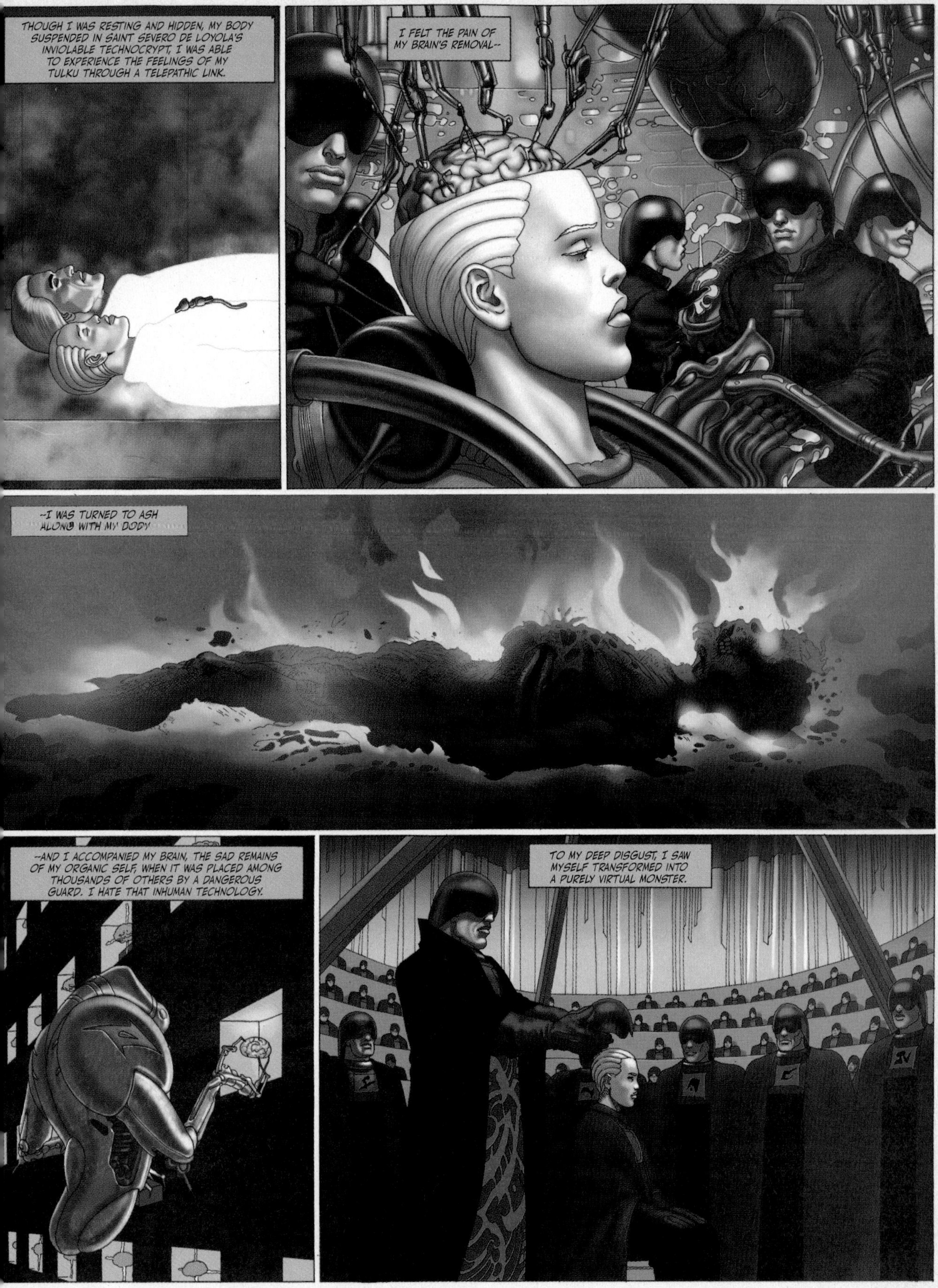
THOUGH I WAS RESTING AND HIDDEN, MY BODY SUSPENDED IN SAINT SEVERO DE LOYOLA'S INVIOLABLE TECHNOCRYPT, I WAS ABLE TO EXPERIENCE THE FEELINGS OF MY TULKU THROUGH A TELEPATHIC LINK.
I FELT THE PAIN OF MY BRAIN'S REMOVAL--
--I WAS TURNED TO ASH ALONG WITH MY BODY
--AND I ACCOMPANIED MY BRAIN, THE SAD REMAINS OF MY ORGANIC SELF, WHEN IT WAS PLACED AMONG THOUSANDS OF OTHERS BY A DANGEROUS GUARD. I HATE THAT INHUMAN TECHNOLOGY.
TO MY DEEP DISGUST, I SAW MYSELF TRANSFORMED INTO A PURELY VIRTUAL MONSTER.

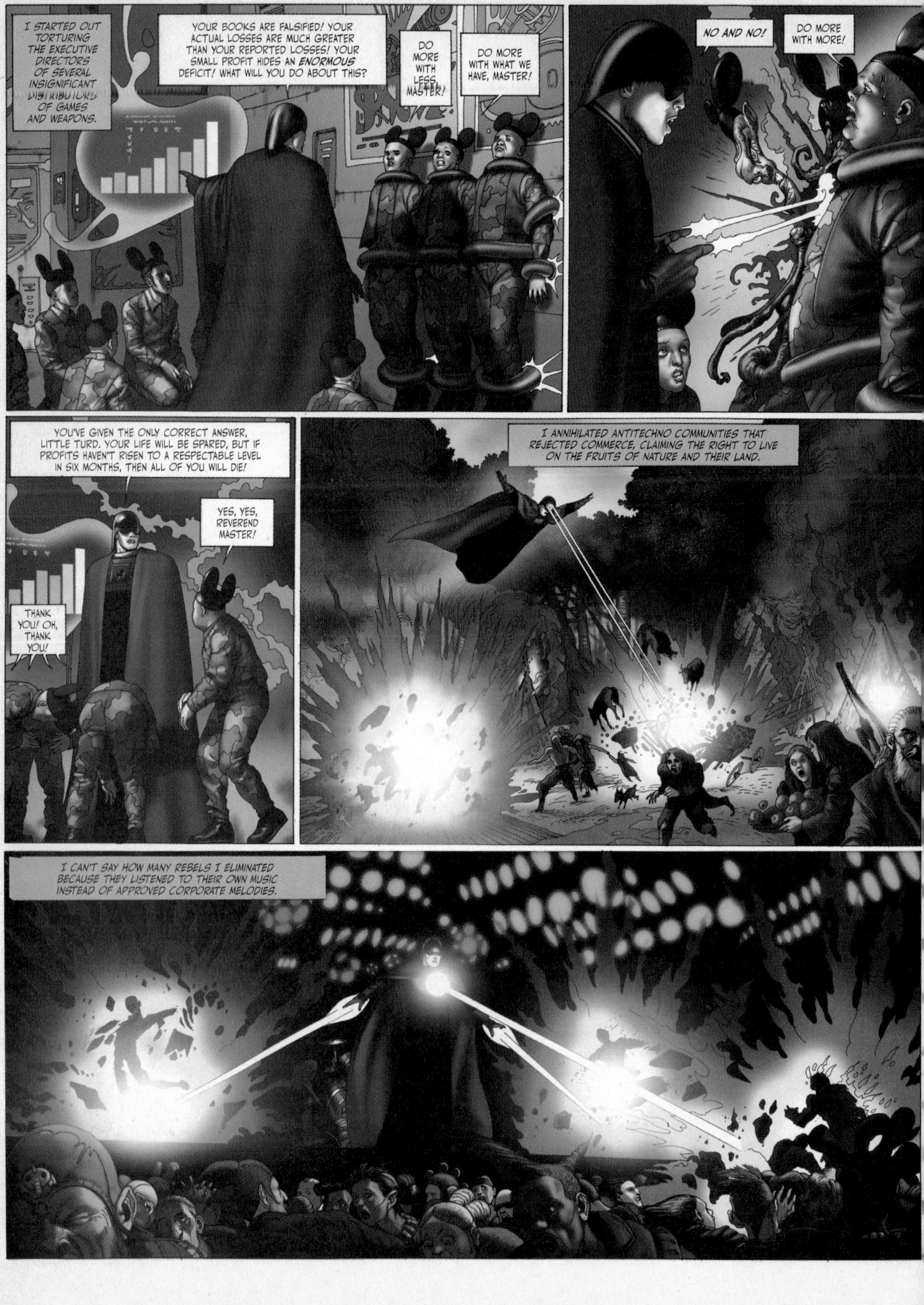
I STARTED OUT TORTURING THE EXECUTIVE DIRECTORS OF SEVERAL INSIGNIFICANT DISTRIBUTORS OF GAMES AND WEAPONS.
YOUR BOOKS ARE FALSIFIED! YOUR ACTUAL LOSSES ARE MUCH GREATER THAN YOUR REPORTED LOSSES! YOUR SMALL PROFIT HIDES AN ENORMOUS DEFICIT! WHAT WILL YOU DO ABOUT THIS?
DO MORE WITH LESS, MASTER!
DO MORE WITH WHAT WE HAVE, MASTER!
NO AND NO!
DO MORE WITH MORE!
YOU'VE GIVEN THE ONLY CORRECT ANSWER, LITTLE TURD. YOUR LIFE WILL BE SPARED, BUT IF PROFITS HAVEN'T RISEN TO A RESPECTABLE LEVEL IN SIX MONTHS, THEN ALL OF YOU WILL DIE!
YES, YES, REVEREND MASTER!
THANK YOU! OH, THANK YOU!
I ANNIHILATED ANTITECHNO COMMUNITIES THAT REJECTED COMMERCE, CLAIMING THE RIGHT TO LIVE ON THE FRUITS OF NATURE AND THEIR LAND.
I CAN'T SAY HOW MANY REBELS I ELIMINATED BECAUSE THEY LISTENED TO THEIR OWN MUSIC INSTEAD OF APPROVED CORPORATE MELODIES.

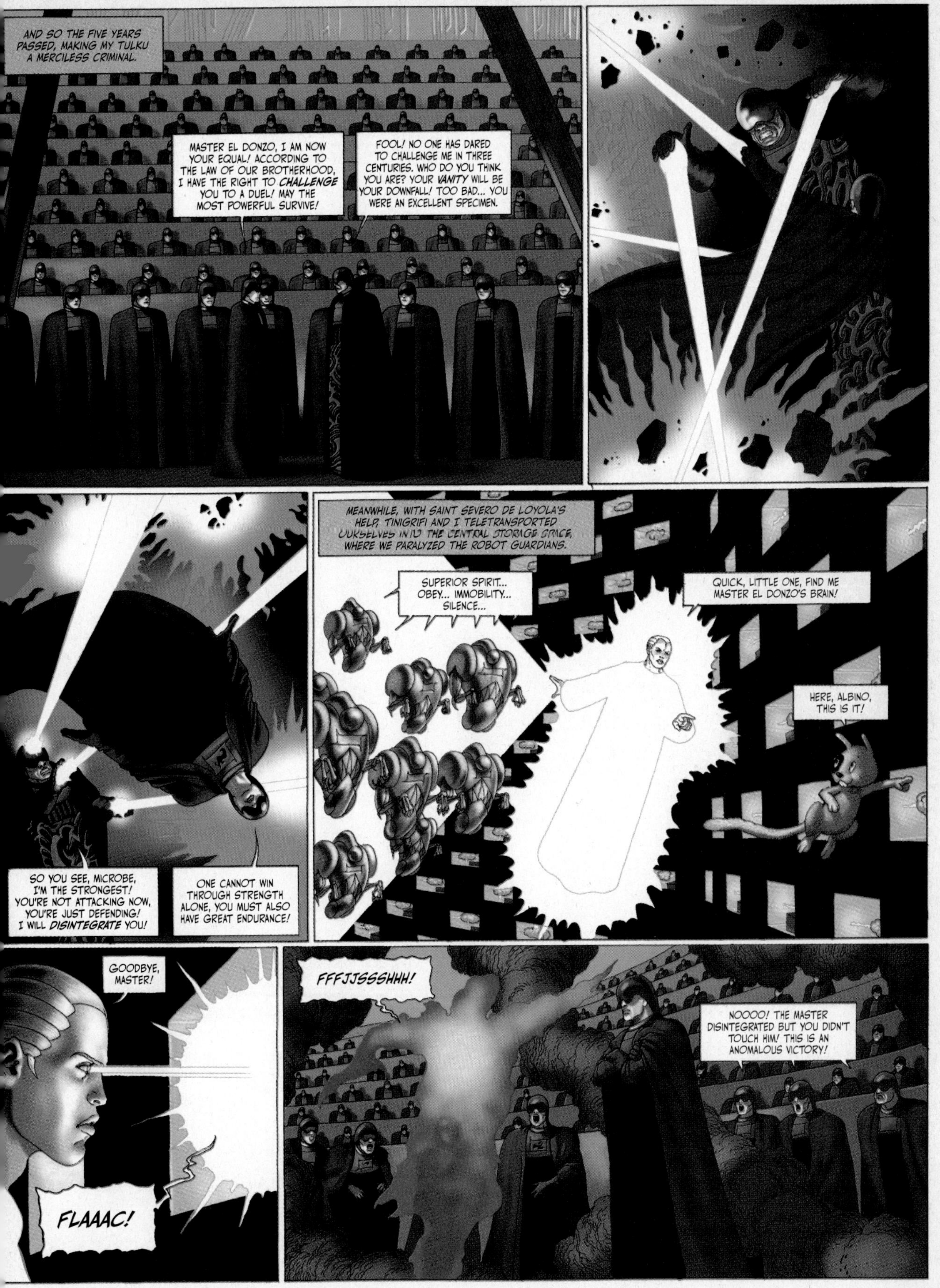

AND SO THE FIVE YEARS PASSED, MAKING MY TULKU A MERCILESS CRIMINAL.
MASTER EL DONZO, I AM NOW YOUR EQUAL! ACCORDING TO THE LAW OF OUR BROTHERHOOD, I HAVE THE RIGHT TO CHALLENGE YOU TO A DUEL! MAY THE MOST POWERFUL SURVIVE!
FOOL! NO ONE HAS DARED TO CHALLENGE ME IN THREE CENTURIES. WHO DO YOU THINK YOU ARE? YOUR VANITY WILL BE YOUR DOWNFALL! TOO BAD... YOU WERE AN EXCELLENT SPECIMEN.
SO YOU SEE, MICROBE, I'M THE STRONGEST! YOU'RE NOT ATTACKING NOW, YOU'RE JUST DEFENDING! I WILL DISINTEGRATE YOU!
ONE CANNOT WIN THROUGH STRENGTH ALONE, YOU MUST ALSO HAVE GREAT ENDURANCE!
MEANWHILE, WITH SAINT SEVERO DE LOYOLA'S HELP, TINIGRIFI AND I TELETRANSPORTED OURSELVES INTO THE CENTRAL STORAGE SPACE, WHERE WE PARALYZED THE ROBOT GUARDIANS.
SUPERIOR SPIRIT... OBEY... IMMOBILITY... SILENCE...
QUICK, LITTLE ONE, FIND ME MASTER EL DONZO'S BRAIN!
HERE, ALBINO, THIS IS IT!
GOODBYE, MASTER!
FLAAAC!
FFFJJSSSHHH!
NOOOO! THE MASTER DISINTEGRATED BUT YOU DIDN'T TOUCH HIM! THIS IS AN ANOMALOUS VICTORY!

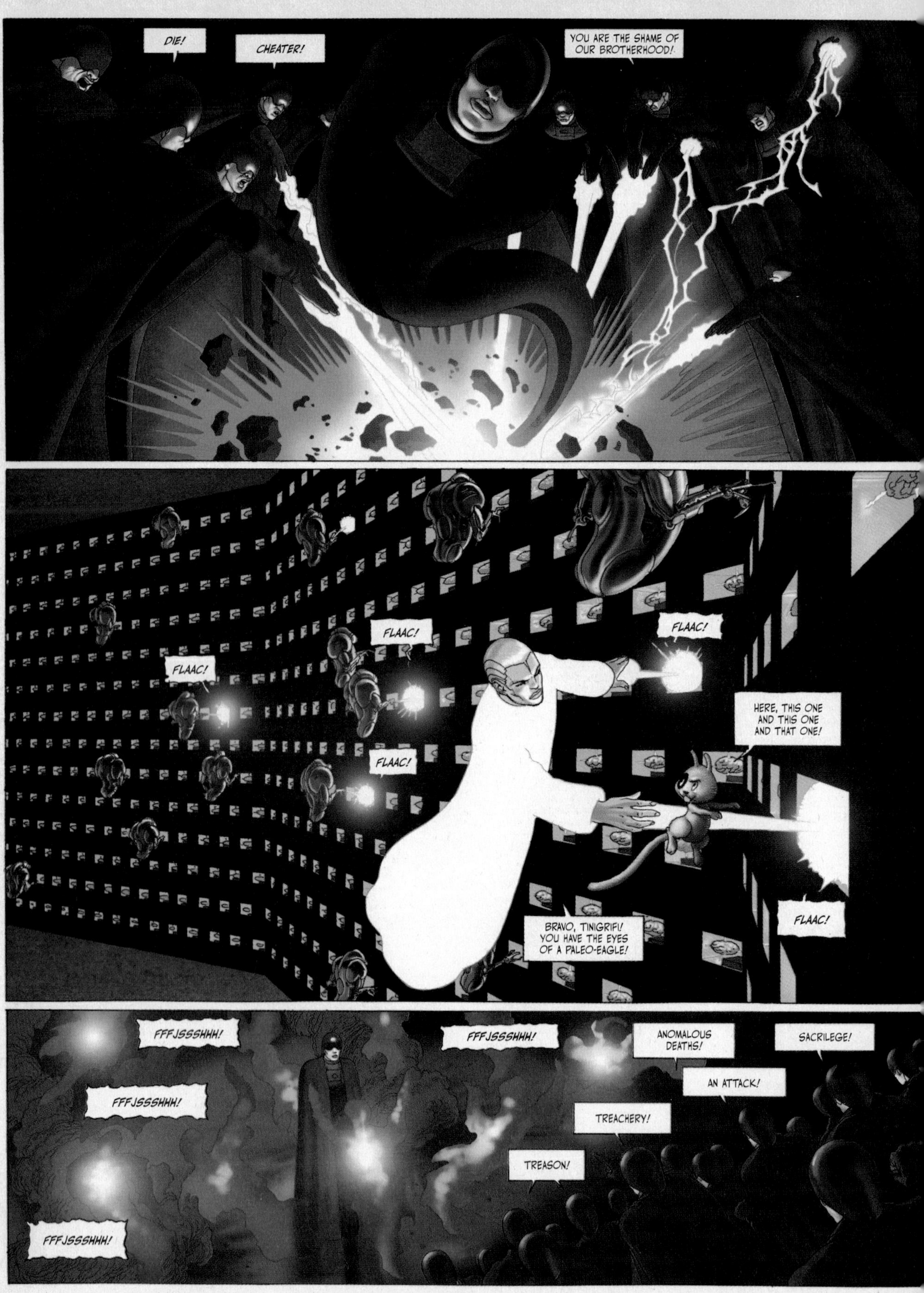
DIE!
CHEATER!
YOU ARE THE SHAME OF OUR BROTHERHOOD!
FLAAC!
FLAAC!
FLAAC!
FLAAC!
HERE, THIS ONE AND THIS ONE AND THAT ONE!
BRAVO, TINIGRIFI! YOU HAVE THE EYES OF A PALEO-EAGLE!
FLAAC!
FFFJSSSHHH!
FFFJSSSHHH!
FFFJSSSHHH!
FFFJSSSHHH!
ANOMALOUS DEATHS!
SACRILEGE!
AN ATTACK!
TREACHERY!
TREASON!

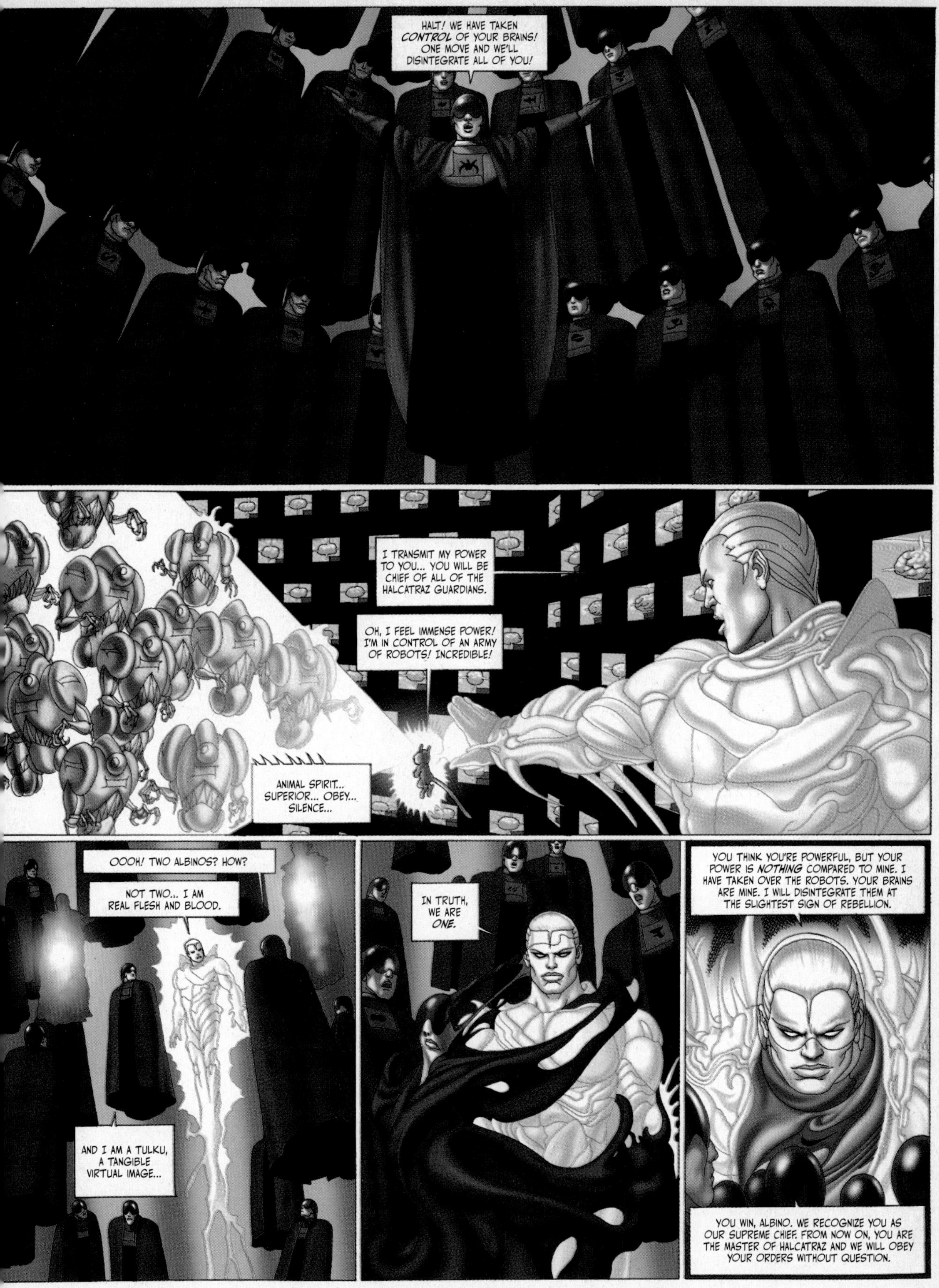
HALT! WE HAVE TAKEN *CONTROL* OF YOUR BRAINS! ONE MOVE AND WE'LL DISINTEGRATE ALL OF YOU!
I TRANSMIT MY POWER TO YOU... YOU WILL BE CHIEF OF ALL OF THE HALCATRAZ GUARDIANS.
OH, I FEEL IMMENSE POWER! I'M IN CONTROL OF AN ARMY OF ROBOTS! INCREDIBLE!
ANIMAL SPIRIT... SUPERIOR... OBEY... SILENCE...
OOOH! TWO ALBINOS? HOW?
NOT TWO... I AM REAL FLESH AND BLOOD.
AND I AM A TULKU, A TANGIBLE VIRTUAL IMAGE...
IN TRUTH, WE ARE *ONE.*
YOU THINK YOU'RE POWERFUL, BUT YOUR POWER IS *NOTHING* COMPARED TO MINE. I HAVE TAKEN OVER THE ROBOTS. YOUR BRAINS ARE MINE. I WILL DISINTEGRATE THEM AT THE SLIGHTEST SIGN OF REBELLION.
YOU WIN, ALBINO. WE RECOGNIZE YOU AS OUR SUPREME CHIEF. FROM NOW ON, YOU ARE THE MASTER OF HALCATRAZ AND WE WILL OBEY YOUR ORDERS WITHOUT QUESTION.

THE TOTALITY OF YOUR VIRTUAL BODIES MAY *PENETRATE* MY CONCRETE BODY.

FROM THIS POINT ON, YOU WILL LIVE IN ME, YOUR FLESH WILL BE MY FLESH. WITH ME, YOU WILL LEAVE HALCATRAZ. *TOGETHER,* WE WILL GO TO GROHMA, THE TEMPLE-PLANET OF THE TECHNO-BISHOPS.

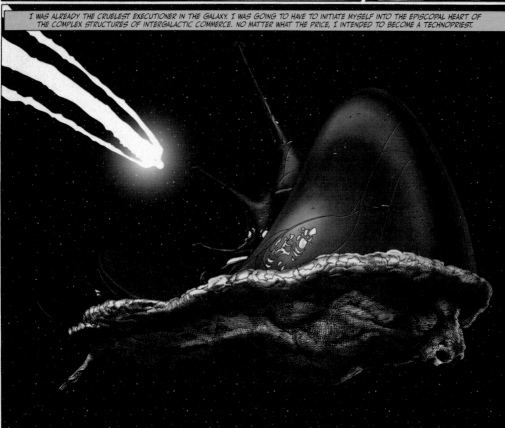

I WAS ALREADY THE CRUELEST EXECUTIONER IN THE GALAXY. I WAS GOING TO HAVE TO INITIATE MYSELF INTO THE EPISCOPAL HEART OF THE COMPLEX STRUCTURES OF INTERGALACTIC COMMERCE. NO MATTER WHAT THE PRICE, I INTENDED TO BECOME A TECHNOPRIEST.

AH, MY TINIGRIFL... HALCATRAZ WAS TO GROHMA AS A LAMB IS TO A WOLF. I NEVER WOULD HAVE SUSPECTED THAT THE "SACRED" TECHNO-TECHNO INDUSTRY WAS BUILT ON A FOUNDATION SO MONSTROUS, SO INHUMAN, SO INSALUBRIOUS, SO BLOODTHIRSTY AND SO VICIOUS.

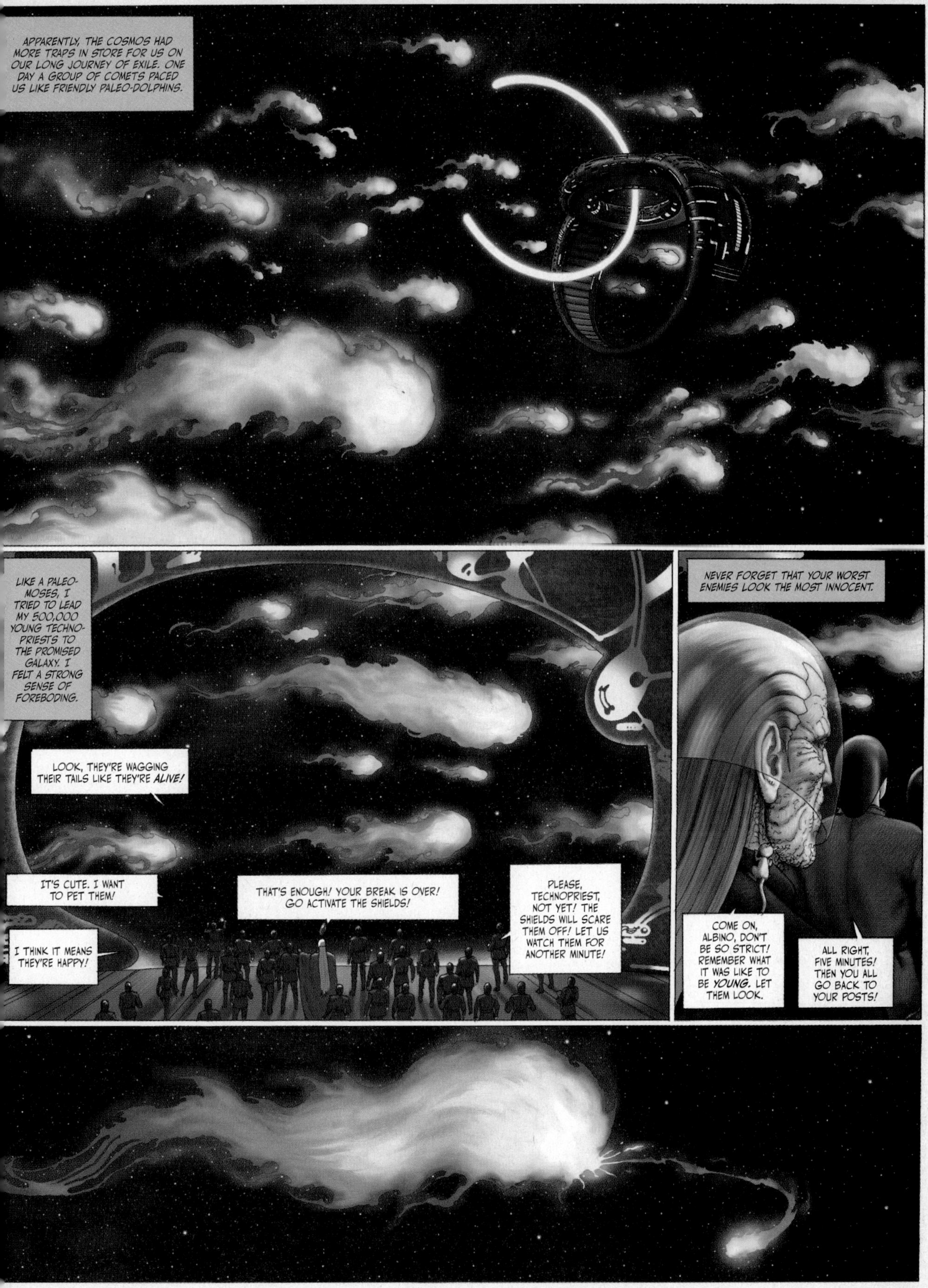
APPARENTLY, THE COSMOS HAD MORE TRAPS IN STORE FOR US ON OUR LONG JOURNEY OF EXILE. ONE DAY A GROUP OF COMETS PACED US LIKE FRIENDLY PALEO-DOLPHINS.
LIKE A PALEO-MOSES, I TRIED TO LEAD MY 500,000 YOUNG TECHNO-PRIESTS TO THE PROMISED GALAXY. I FELT A STRONG SENSE OF FOREBODING.
LOOK, THEY'RE WAGGING THEIR TAILS LIKE THEY'RE *ALIVE!*
IT'S CUTE. I WANT TO PET THEM!
I THINK IT MEANS THEY'RE HAPPY!
THAT'S ENOUGH! YOUR BREAK IS OVER! GO ACTIVATE THE SHIELDS!
PLEASE, TECHNOPRIEST, NOT YET! THE SHIELDS WILL SCARE THEM OFF! LET US WATCH THEM FOR ANOTHER MINUTE!
NEVER FORGET THAT YOUR WORST ENEMIES LOOK THE MOST INNOCENT.
COME ON, ALBINO, DON'T BE SO STRICT! REMEMBER WHAT IT WAS LIKE TO BE *YOUNG*. LET THEM LOOK.
ALL RIGHT, FIVE MINUTES! THEN YOU ALL GO BACK TO YOUR POSTS!

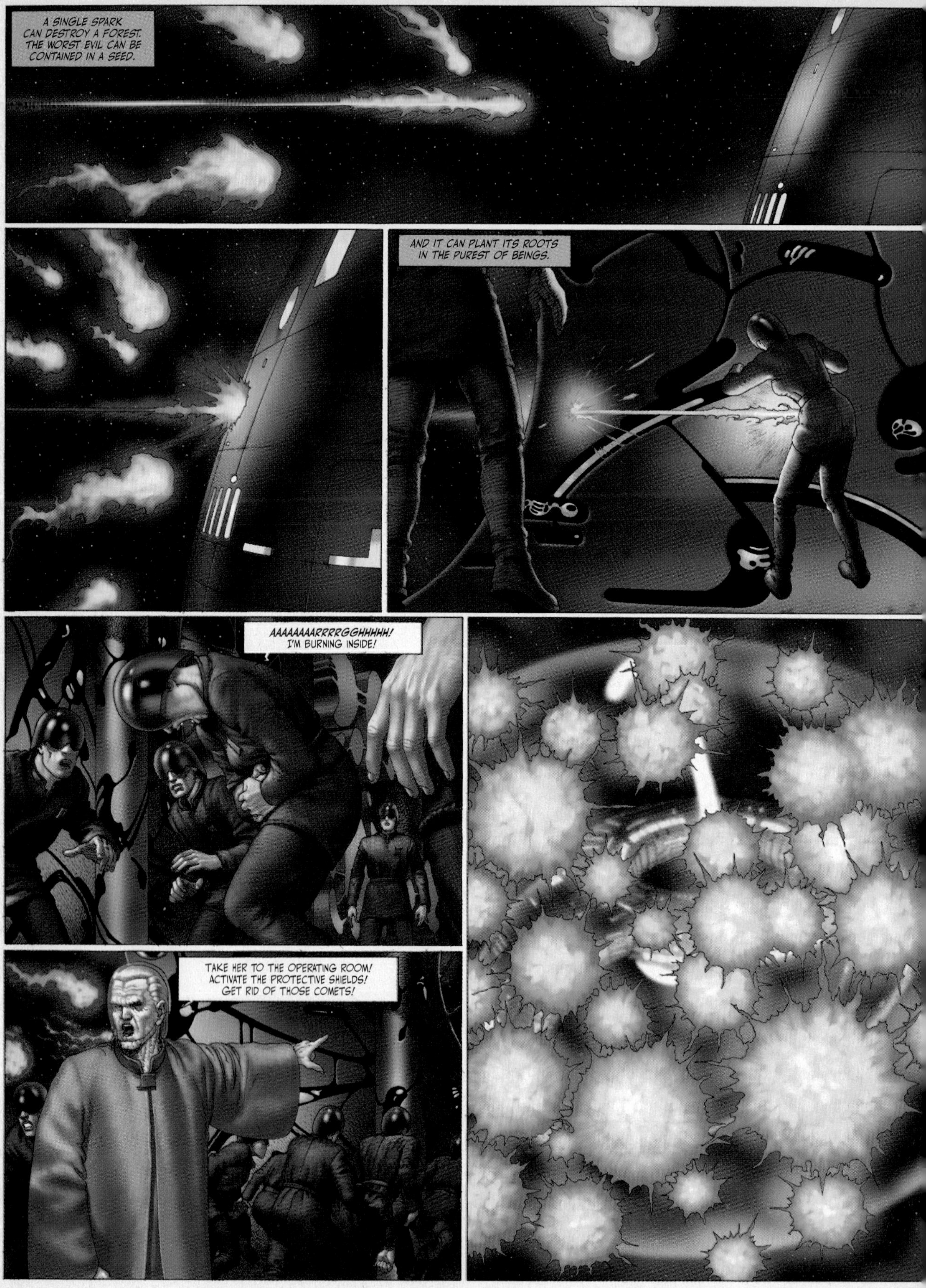

A SINGLE SPARK CAN DESTROY A FOREST. THE WORST EVIL CAN BE CONTAINED IN A SEED.
AND IT CAN PLANT ITS ROOTS IN THE PUREST OF BEINGS.
AAAAAAAARRRRGGHHHHH! I'M BURNING INSIDE!
TAKE HER TO THE OPERATING ROOM! ACTIVATE THE PROTECTIVE SHIELDS! GET RID OF THOSE COMETS!

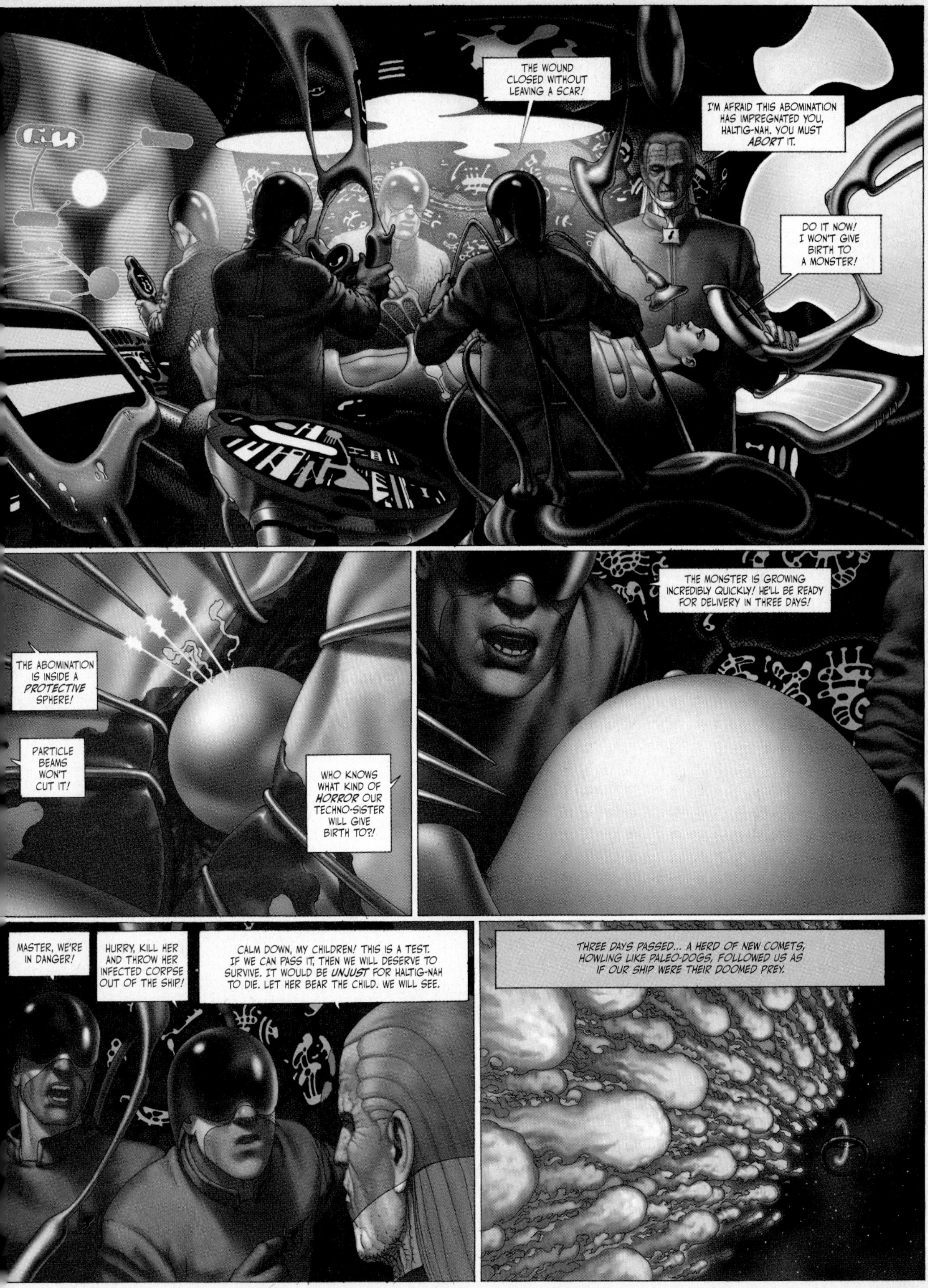
THE WOUND CLOSED WITHOUT LEAVING A SCAR!
I'M AFRAID THIS ABOMINATION HAS IMPREGNATED YOU, HALTIG-NAH. YOU MUST ABORT IT.
DO IT NOW! I WON'T GIVE BIRTH TO A MONSTER!
THE ABOMINATION IS INSIDE A PROTECTIVE SPHERE!
PARTICLE BEAMS WON'T CUT IT!
WHO KNOWS WHAT KIND OF HORROR OUR TECHNO-SISTER WILL GIVE BIRTH TO?!
THE MONSTER IS GROWING INCREDIBLY QUICKLY! HE'LL BE READY FOR DELIVERY IN THREE DAYS!
MASTER, WE'RE IN DANGER!
HURRY, KILL HER AND THROW HER INFECTED CORPSE OUT OF THE SHIP!
CALM DOWN, MY CHILDREN! THIS IS A TEST. IF WE CAN PASS IT, THEN WE WILL DESERVE TO SURVIVE. IT WOULD BE UNJUST FOR HALTIG-NAH TO DIE. LET HER BEAR THE CHILD. WE WILL SEE.
THREE DAYS PASSED... A HERD OF NEW COMETS, HOWLING LIKE PALEO-DOGS, FOLLOWED US AS IF OUR SHIP WERE THEIR DOOMED PREY.

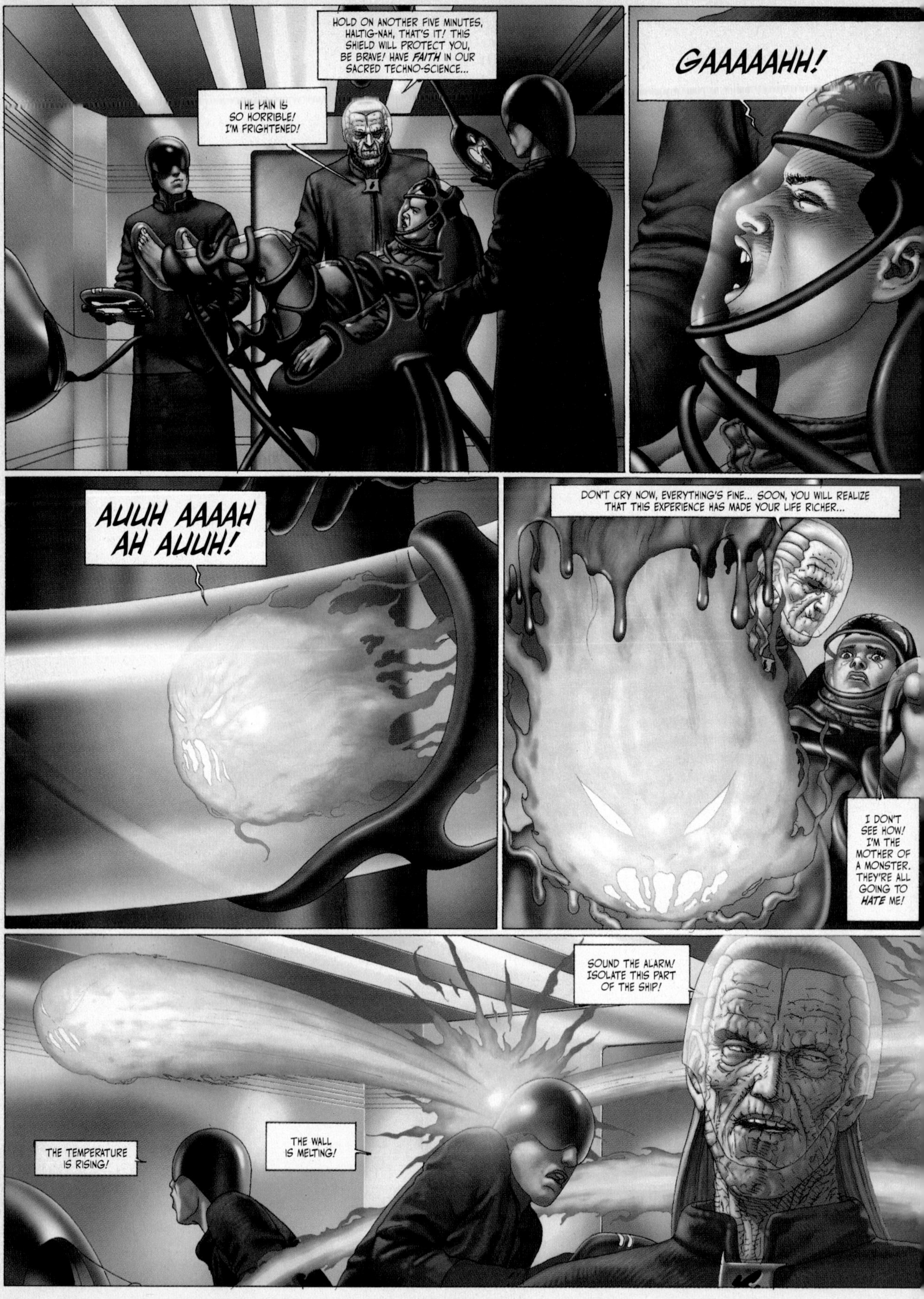
HOLD ON ANOTHER FIVE MINUTES, HALTIG-NAH, THAT'S IT! THIS SHIELD WILL PROTECT YOU, BE BRAVE! HAVE FAITH IN OUR SACRED TECHNO-SCIENCE...
THE PAIN IS SO HORRIBLE! I'M FRIGHTENED!
GAAAAAHH!
AUUH AAAAH AH AUUH!
DON'T CRY NOW, EVERYTHING'S FINE... SOON, YOU WILL REALIZE THAT THIS EXPERIENCE HAS MADE YOUR LIFE RICHER...
I DON'T SEE HOW! I'M THE MOTHER OF A MONSTER. THEY'RE ALL GOING TO HATE ME!
SOUND THE ALARM! ISOLATE THIS PART OF THE SHIP!
THE TEMPERATURE IS RISING!
THE WALL IS MELTING!

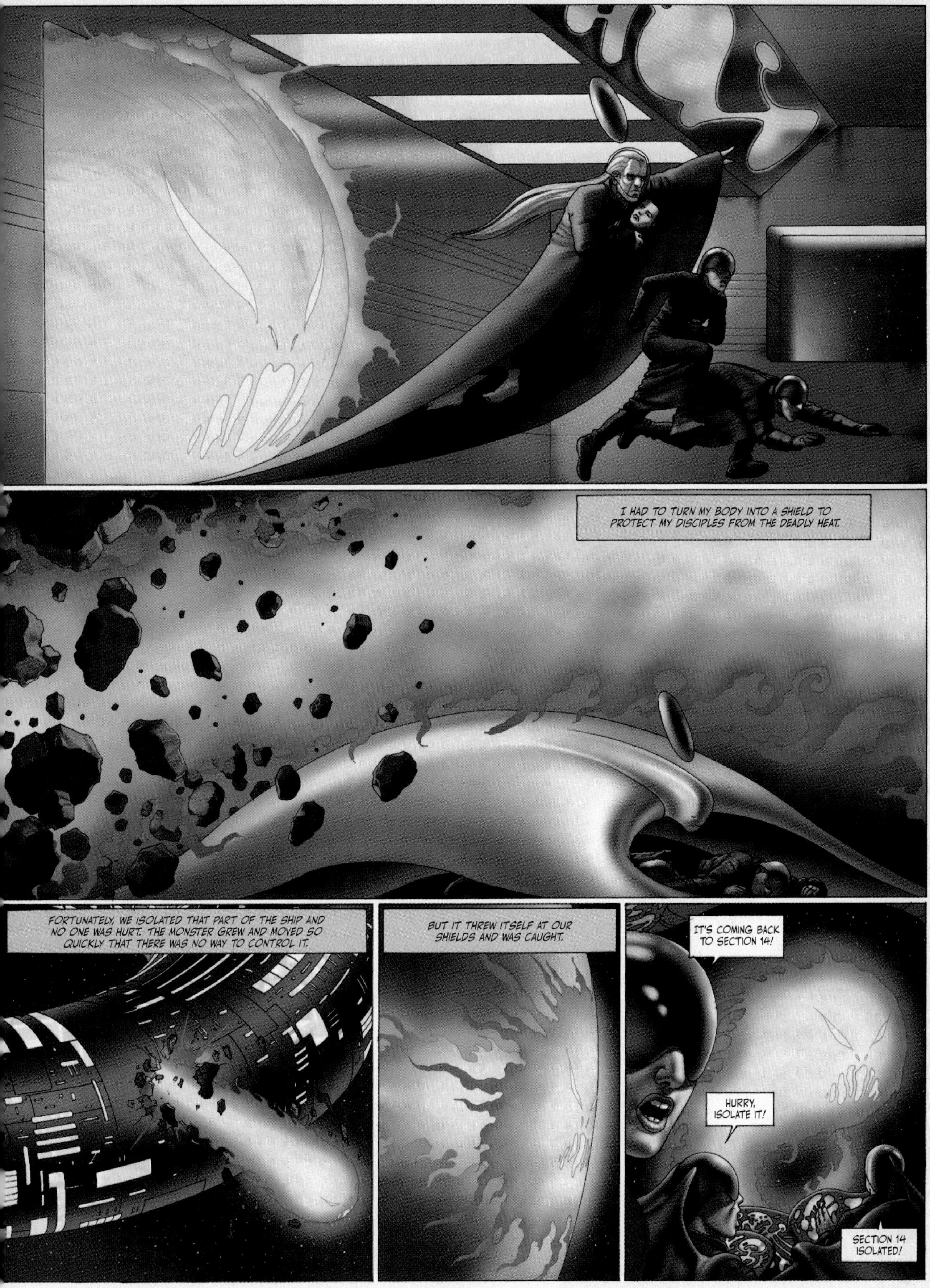
I HAD TO TURN MY BODY INTO A SHIELD TO PROTECT MY DISCIPLES FROM THE DEADLY HEAT.
FORTUNATELY, WE ISOLATED THAT PART OF THE SHIP AND NO ONE WAS HURT. THE MONSTER GREW AND MOVED SO QUICKLY THAT THERE WAS NO WAY TO CONTROL IT.
BUT IT THREW ITSELF AT OUR SHIELDS AND WAS CAUGHT.
IT'S COMING BACK TO SECTION 14!
HURRY, ISOLATE IT!
SECTION 14 ISOLATED!

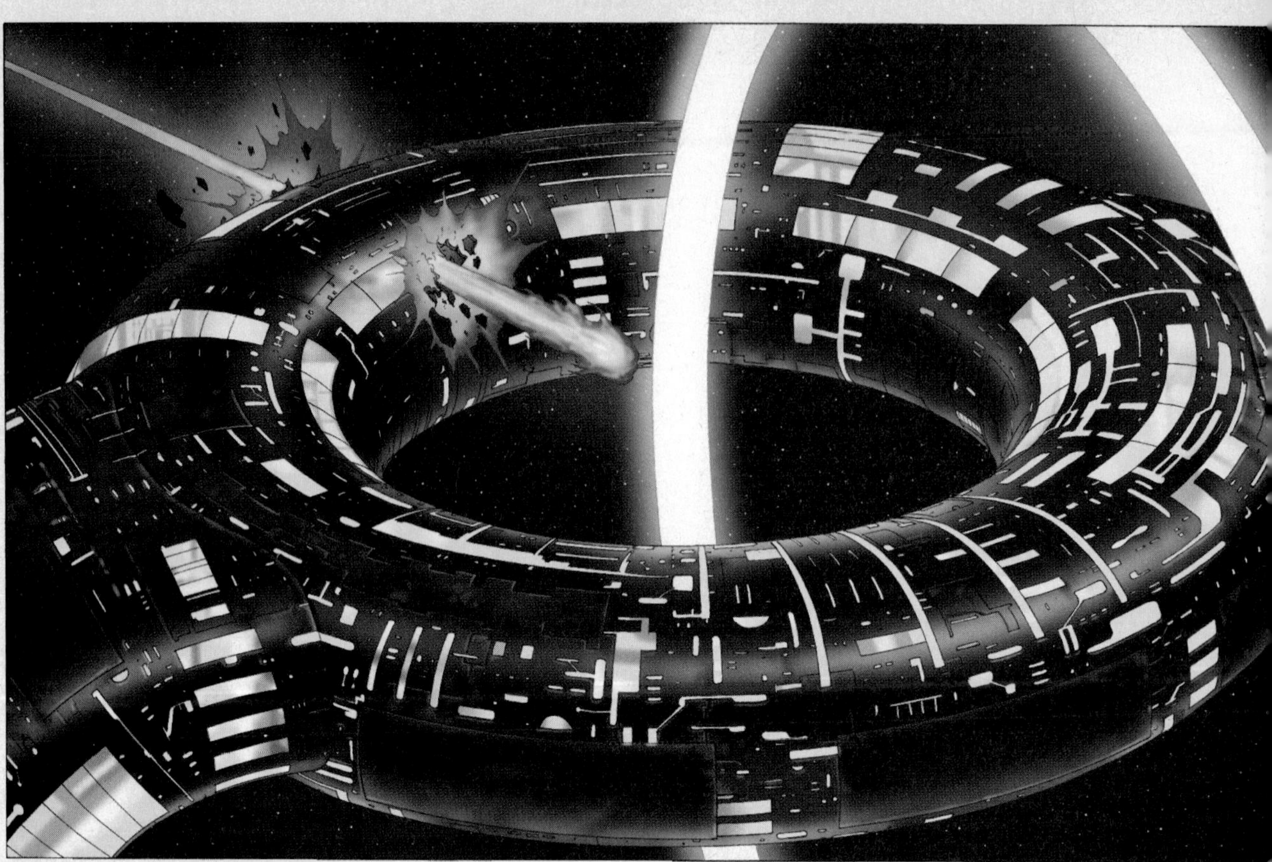

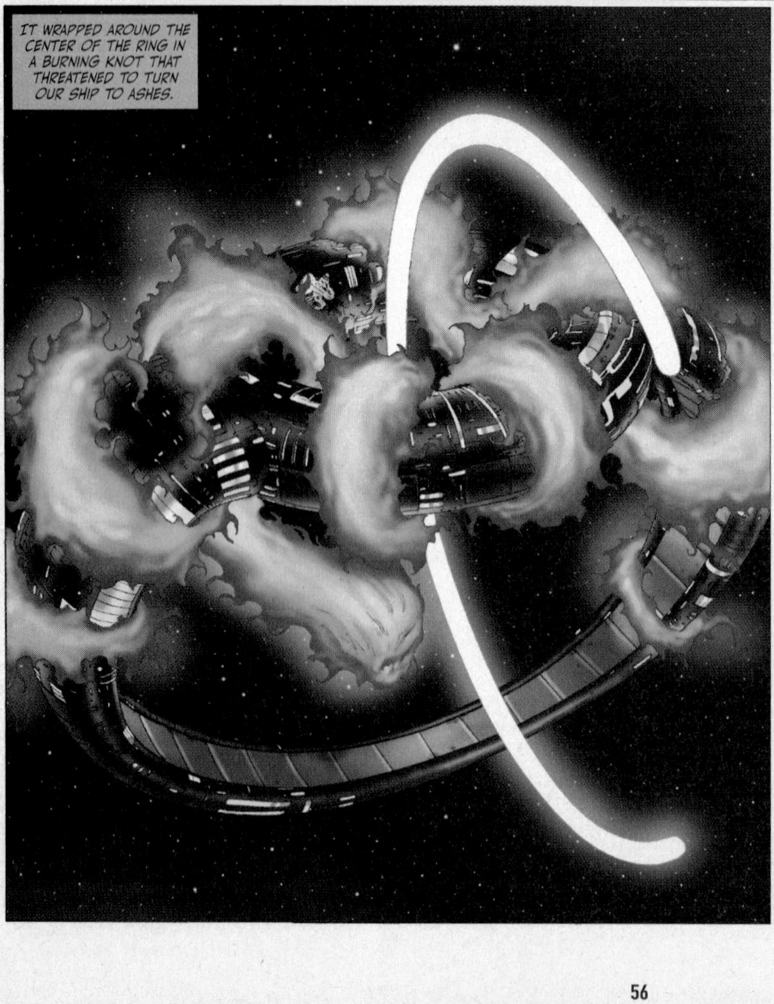
IT WRAPPED AROUND THE CENTER OF THE RING IN A BURNING KNOT THAT THREATENED TO TURN OUR SHIP TO ASHES.

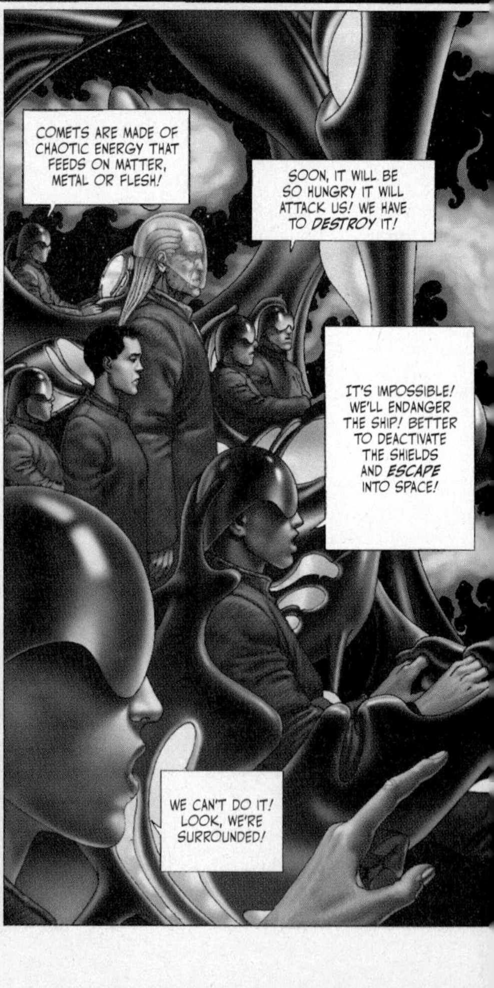
COMETS ARE MADE OF CHAOTIC ENERGY THAT FEEDS ON MATTER, METAL OR FLESH!
SOON, IT WILL BE SO HUNGRY IT WILL ATTACK US! WE HAVE TO *DESTROY* IT!
IT'S IMPOSSIBLE! WE'LL ENDANGER THE SHIP! BETTER TO DEACTIVATE THE SHIELDS AND *ESCAPE* INTO SPACE!
WE CAN'T DO IT! LOOK, WE'RE SURROUNDED!

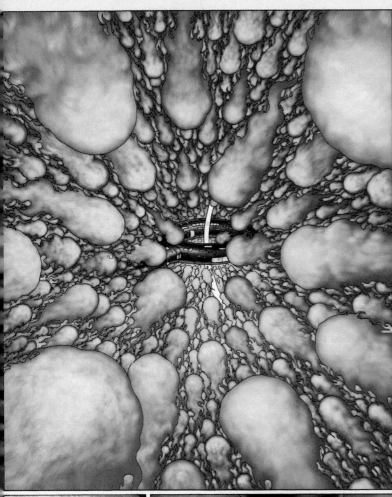

WHAT CAN WE DO, SUPREME TECHNO-SAINT?

VIOLENCE IS *USELESS*. EVERY TIME ONE OF THEM EXPLODES, IT MULTIPLIES BY ONE HUNDRED.

THE MONSTER THAT HALTIG-NAH GAVE BIRTH TO IS HALF HUMAN. MAYBE IT WILL *UNDERSTAND* THAT IT CAN'T EAT A MAN THE WAY IT EATS A PIECE OF ROCK OR METAL.

WE MUST REASON WITH IT. YOU'RE ITS MOTHER, *YOU* CAN CONVINCE IT.

ME? TALK TO THAT ABOMINATION? *NEVER!* NOT ONLY WILL IT NOT LISTEN TO ME, IT'LL BURN ME TO CINDERS!

OPEN GATE B-38!

AND DON'T BE FRIGHTENED. YOUR CHILD WILL NOT HARM YOU! COME!

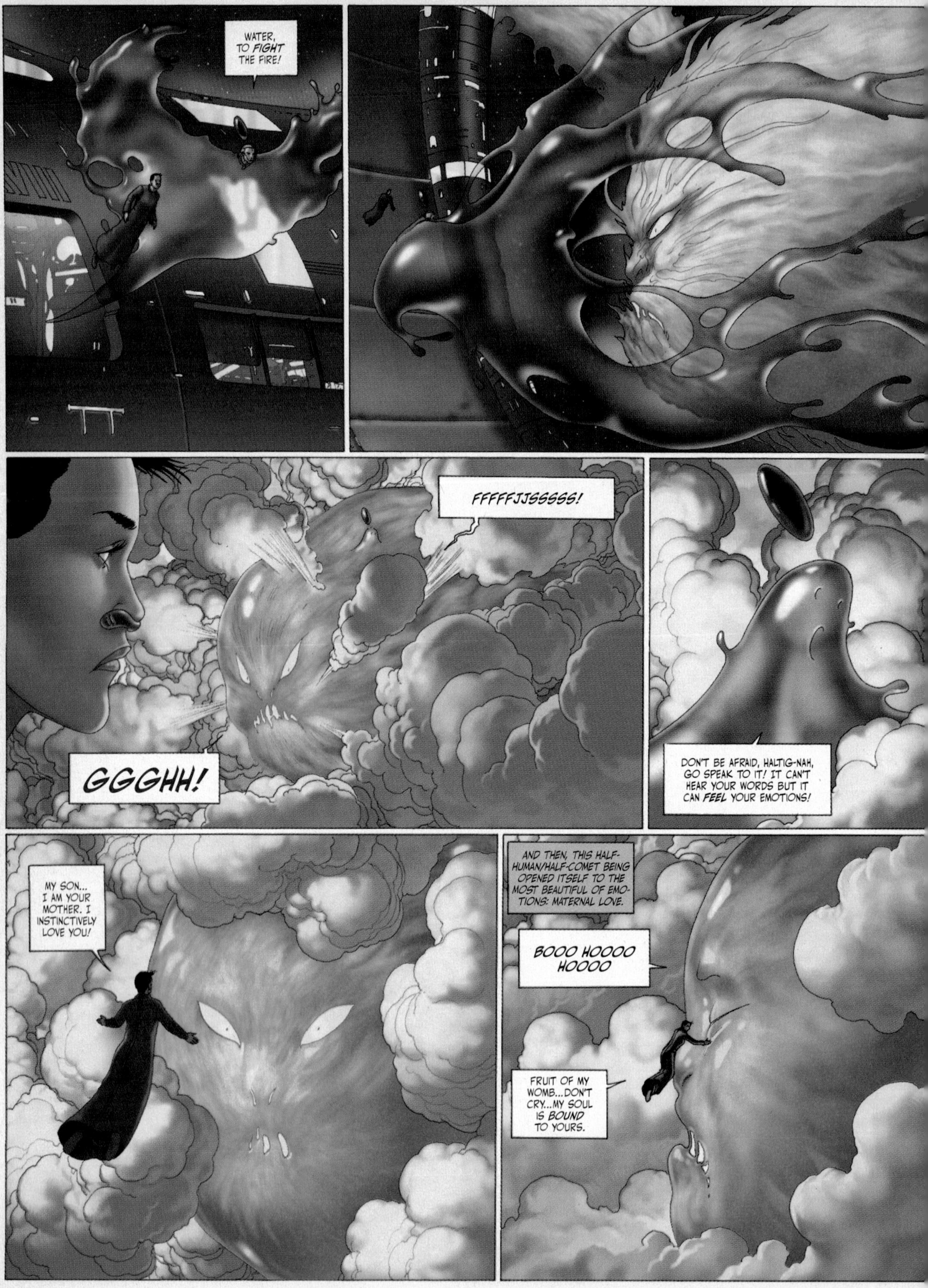
WATER, TO FIGHT THE FIRE!
FFFFFJJSSSSS!
GGGHH!
DON'T BE AFRAID, HALTIG-NAH, GO SPEAK TO IT! IT CAN'T HEAR YOUR WORDS BUT IT CAN FEEL YOUR EMOTIONS!
MY SON... I AM YOUR MOTHER. I INSTINCTIVELY LOVE YOU!
AND THEN, THIS HALF-HUMAN/HALF-COMET BEING OPENED ITSELF TO THE MOST BEAUTIFUL OF EMOTIONS: MATERNAL LOVE.
BOOO HOOOO HOOOO
FRUIT OF MY WOMB...DON'T CRY...MY SOUL IS BOUND TO YOURS.

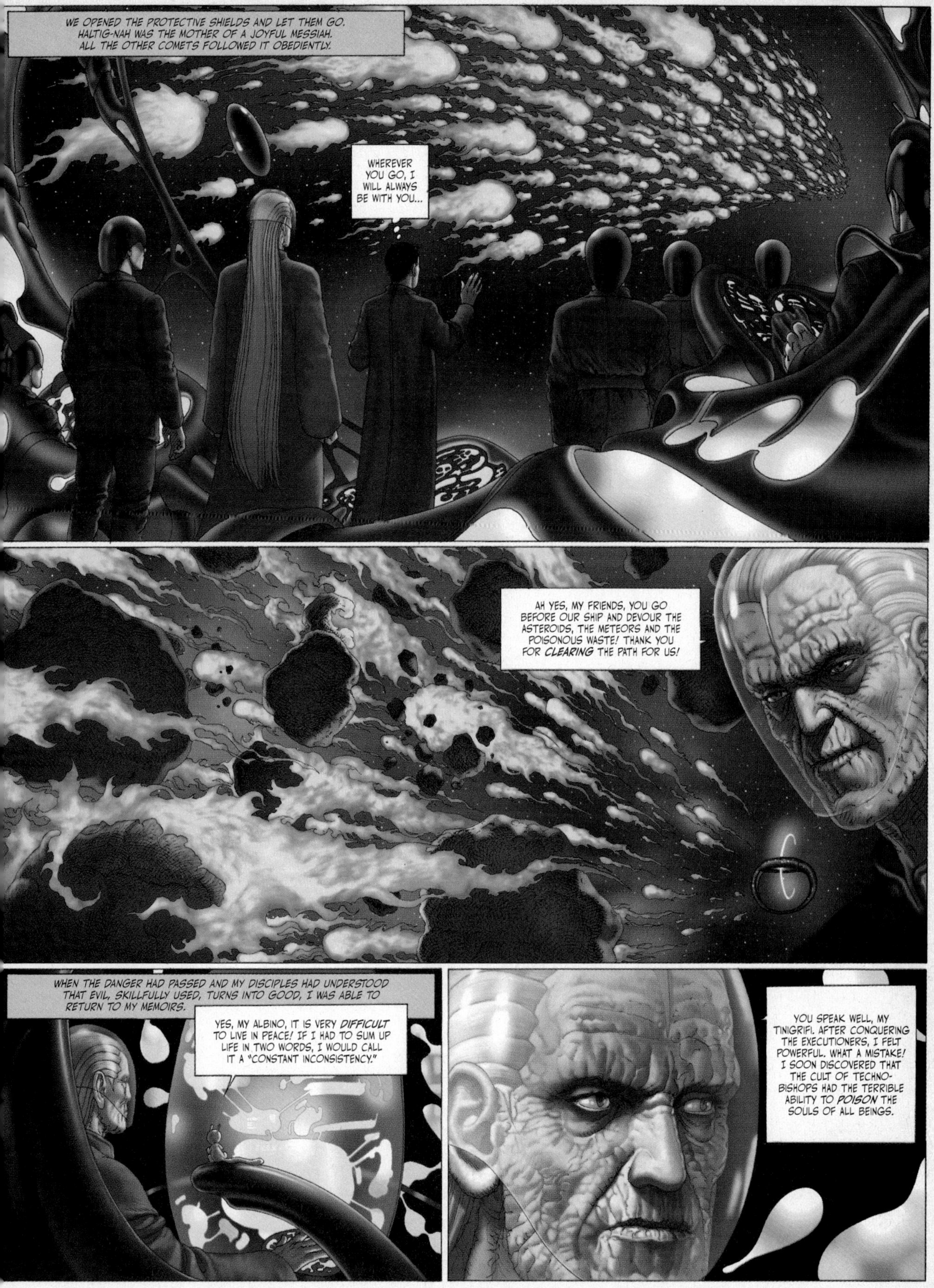
WE OPENED THE PROTECTIVE SHIELDS AND LET THEM GO. HALTIG-NAH WAS THE MOTHER OF A JOYFUL MESSIAH. ALL THE OTHER COMETS FOLLOWED IT OBEDIENTLY.
WHEREVER YOU GO, I WILL ALWAYS BE WITH YOU...
AH YES, MY FRIENDS, YOU GO BEFORE OUR SHIP AND DEVOUR THE ASTEROIDS, THE METEORS AND THE POISONOUS WASTE! THANK YOU FOR *CLEARING* THE PATH FOR US!
WHEN THE DANGER HAD PASSED AND MY DISCIPLES HAD UNDERSTOOD THAT EVIL, SKILLFULLY USED, TURNS INTO GOOD, I WAS ABLE TO RETURN TO MY MEMOIRS.
YES, MY ALBINO, IT IS VERY *DIFFICULT* TO LIVE IN PEACE! IF I HAD TO SUM UP LIFE IN TWO WORDS, I WOULD CALL IT A "CONSTANT INCONSISTENCY."
YOU SPEAK WELL, MY TINIGRIFI. AFTER CONQUERING THE EXECUTIONERS, I FELT POWERFUL. WHAT A MISTAKE! I SOON DISCOVERED THAT THE CULT OF TECHNO-BISHOPS HAD THE TERRIBLE ABILITY TO *POISON* THE SOULS OF ALL BEINGS.

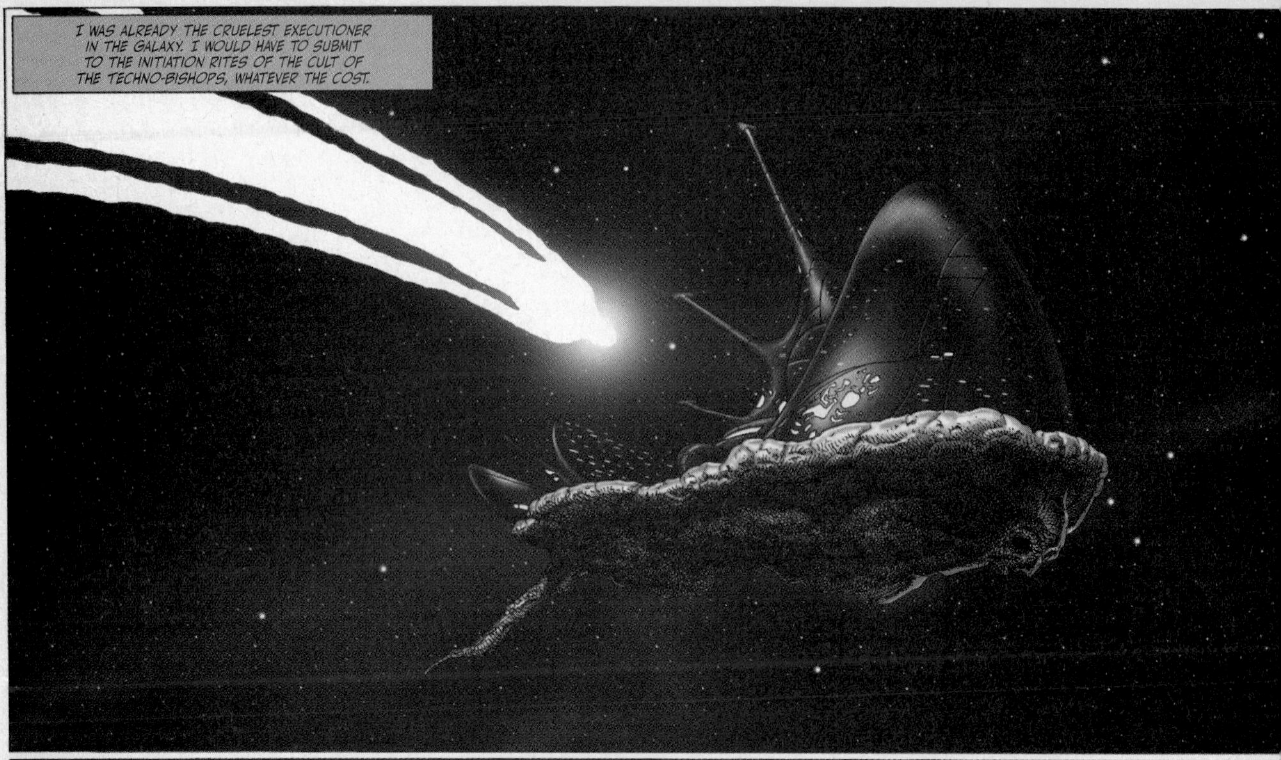
I WAS ALREADY THE CRUELEST EXECUTIONER IN THE GALAXY. I WOULD HAVE TO SUBMIT TO THE INITIATION RITES OF THE CULT OF THE TECHNO-BISHOPS, WHATEVER THE COST.

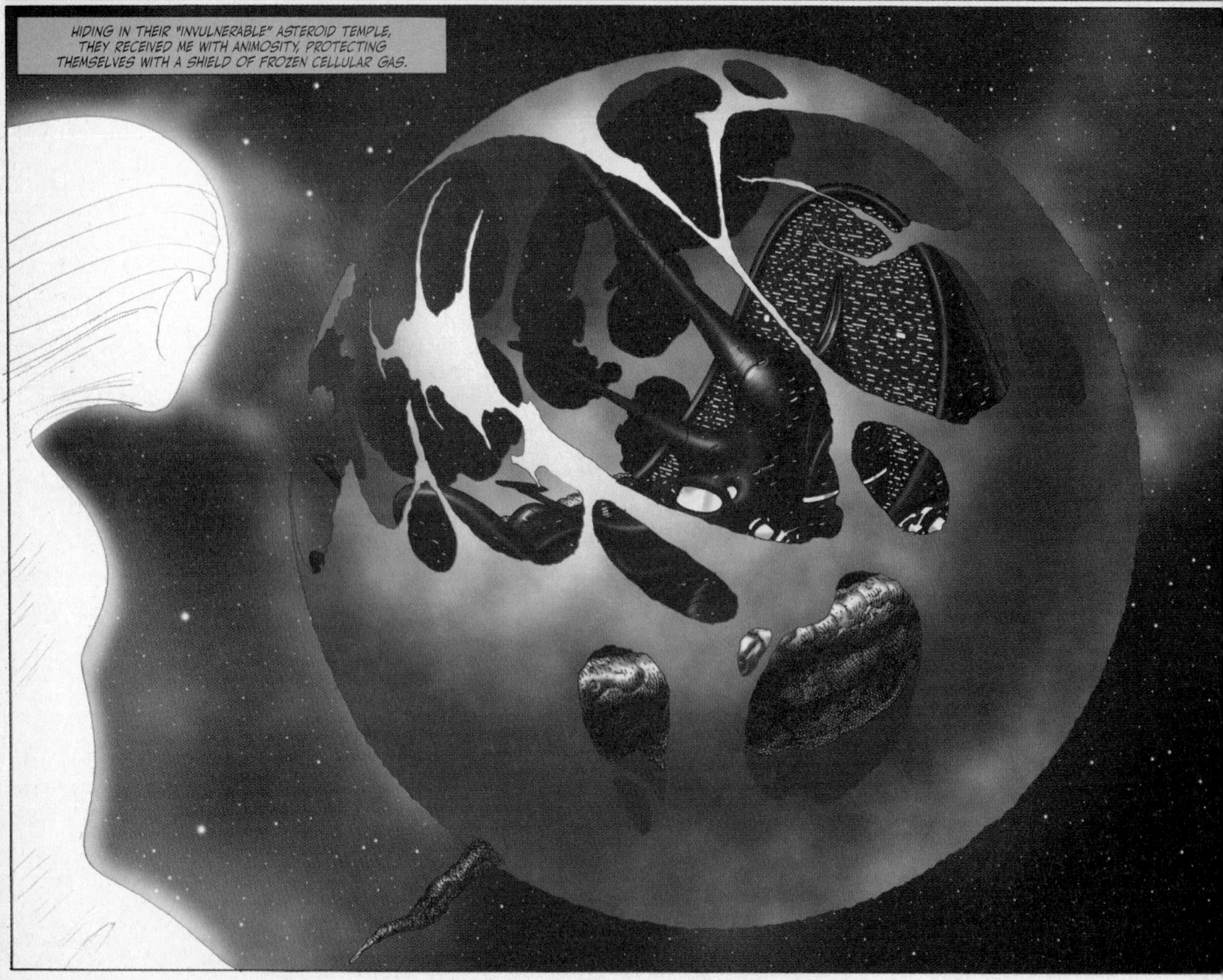
HIDING IN THEIR "INVULNERABLE" ASTEROID TEMPLE, THEY RECEIVED ME WITH ANIMOSITY, PROTECTING THEMSELVES WITH A SHIELD OF FROZEN CELLULAR GAS.

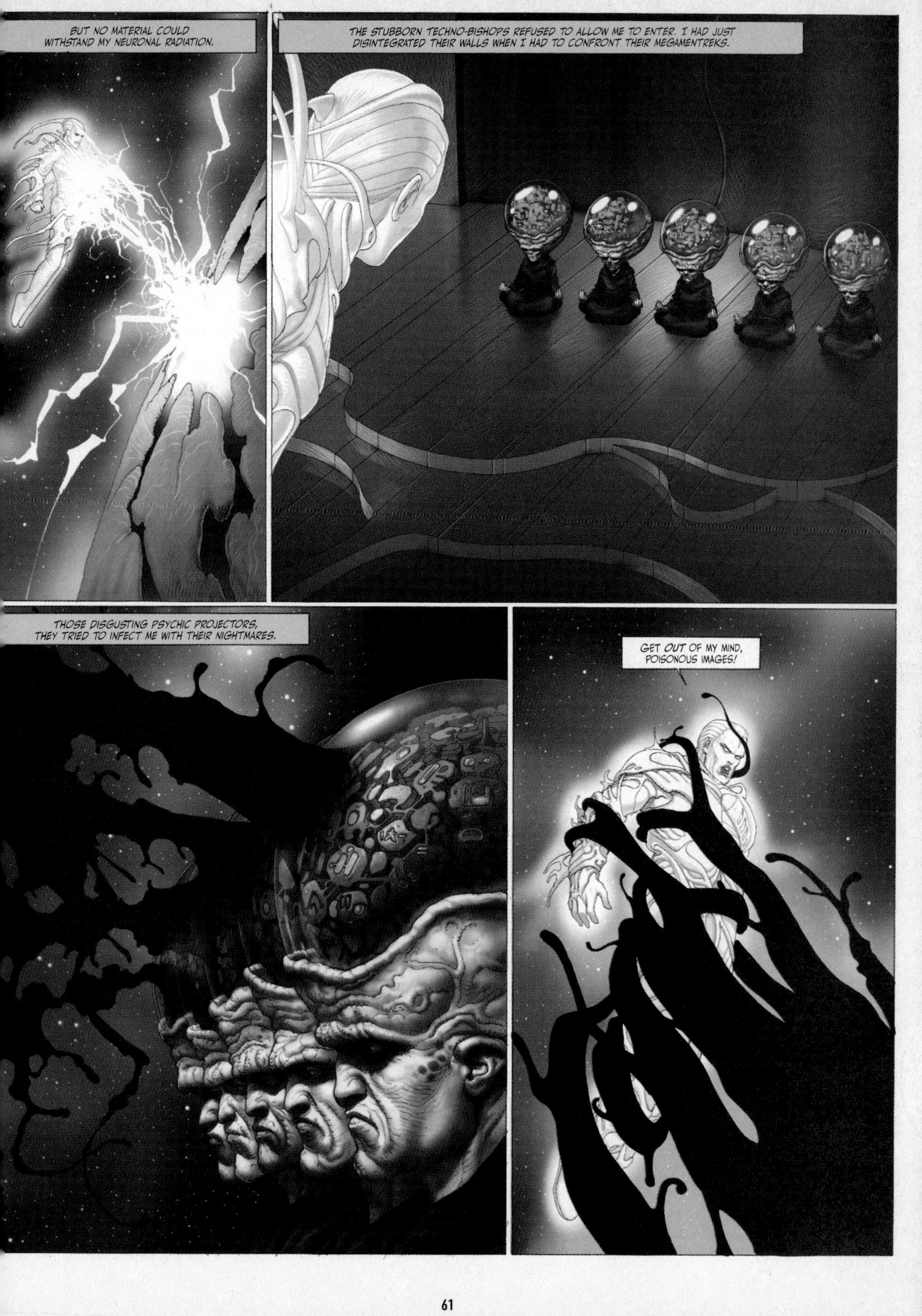
BUT NO MATERIAL COULD WITHSTAND MY NEURONAL RADIATION.
THE STUBBORN TECHNO-BISHOPS REFUSED TO ALLOW ME TO ENTER. I HAD JUST DISINTEGRATED THEIR WALLS WHEN I HAD TO CONFRONT THEIR MEGAMENTREKS.
THOSE DISGUSTING PSYCHIC PROJECTORS, THEY TRIED TO INFECT ME WITH THEIR NIGHTMARES.
GET OUT OF MY MIND, POISONOUS IMAGES!

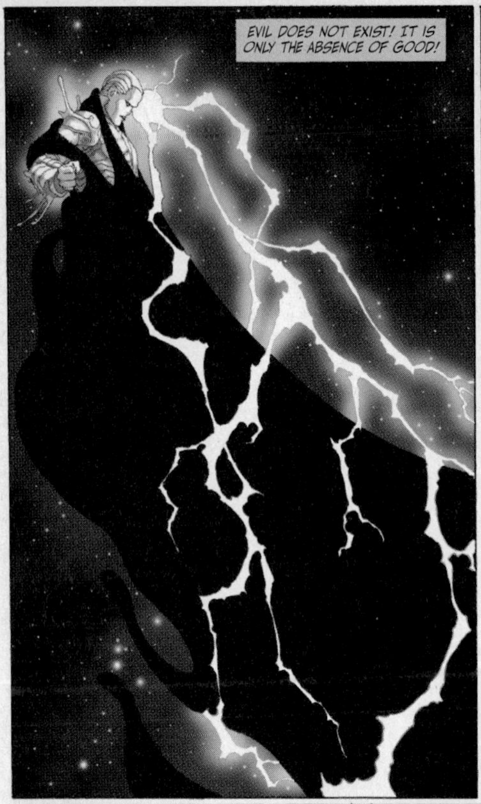
EVIL DOES NOT EXIST! IT IS
ONLY THE ABSENCE OF GOOD!

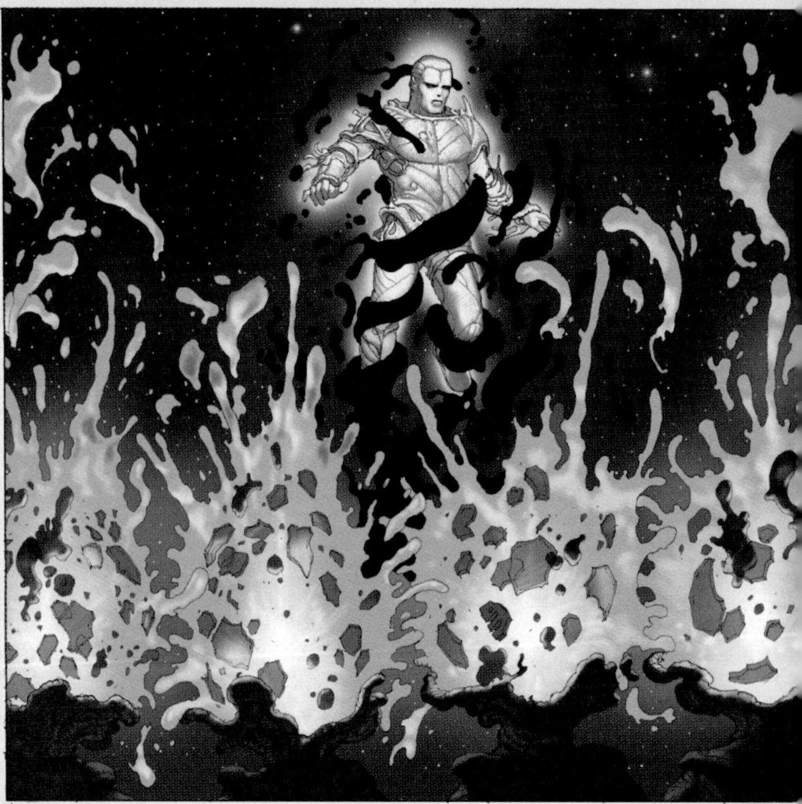

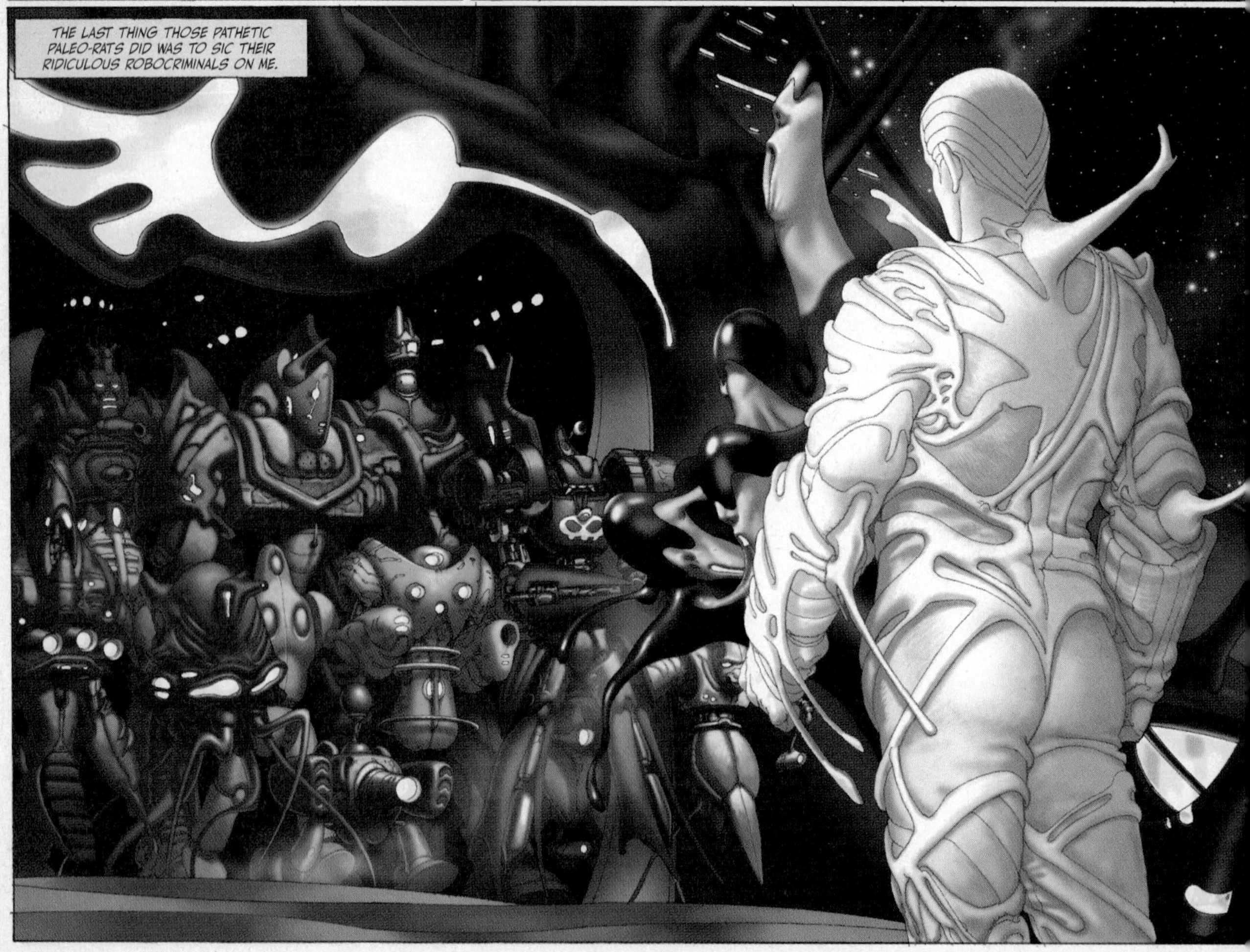
THE LAST THING THOSE PATHETIC
PALEO-RATS DID WAS TO SIC THEIR
RIDICULOUS ROBOCRIMINALS ON ME.

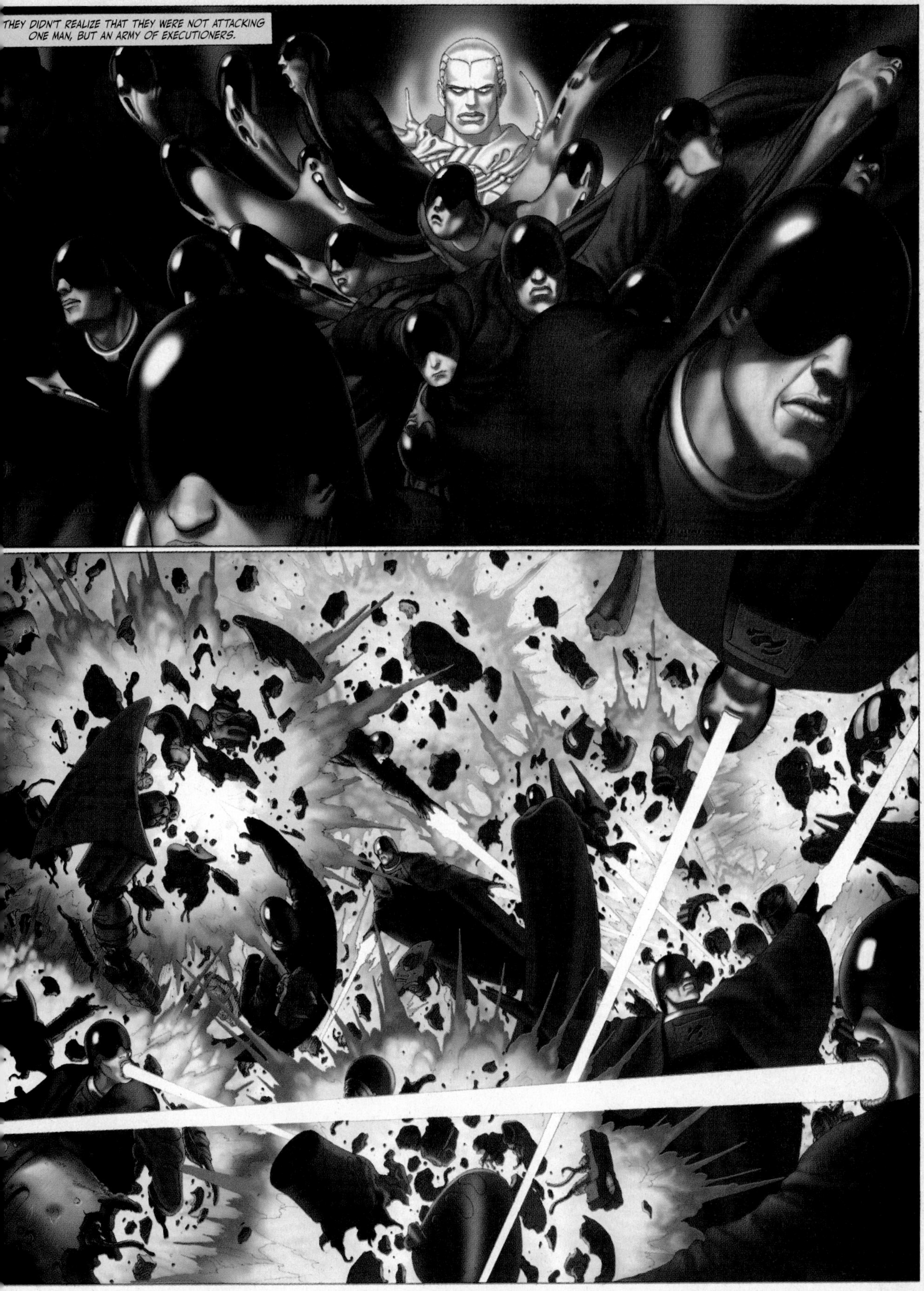
THEY DIDN'T REALIZE THAT THEY WERE NOT ATTACKING ONE MAN, BUT AN ARMY OF EXECUTIONERS.

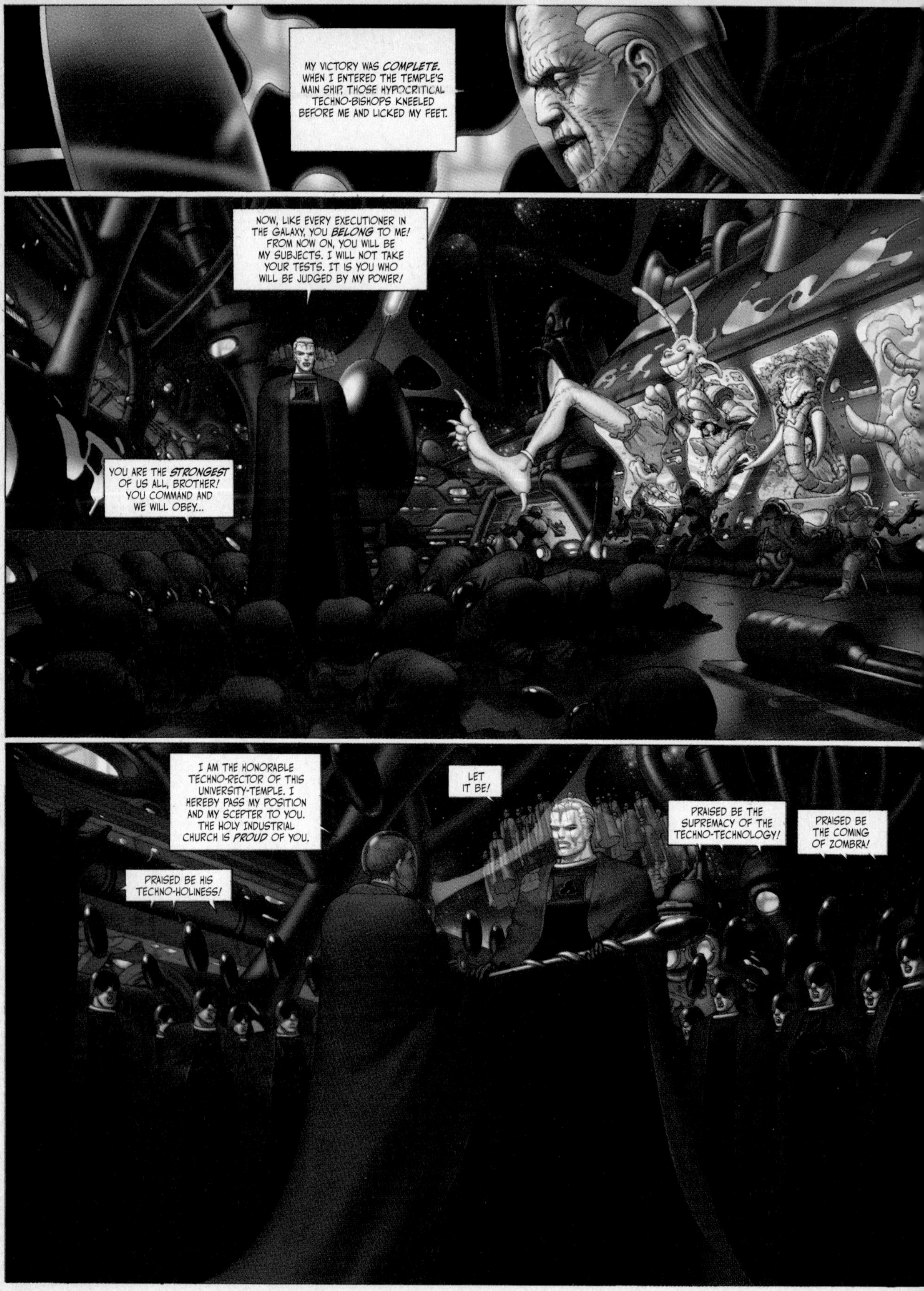

MY VICTORY WAS *COMPLETE.* WHEN I ENTERED THE TEMPLE'S MAIN SHIP, THOSE HYPOCRITICAL TECHNO-BISHOPS KNEELED BEFORE ME AND LICKED MY FEET.
NOW, LIKE EVERY EXECUTIONER IN THE GALAXY, YOU *BELONG* TO ME! FROM NOW ON, YOU WILL BE MY SUBJECTS. I WILL NOT TAKE YOUR TESTS. IT IS YOU WHO WILL BE JUDGED BY MY POWER!
YOU ARE THE *STRONGEST* OF US ALL, BROTHER! YOU COMMAND AND WE WILL OBEY...
I AM THE HONORABLE TECHNO-RECTOR OF THIS UNIVERSITY-TEMPLE. I HEREBY PASS MY POSITION AND MY SCEPTER TO YOU. THE HOLY INDUSTRIAL CHURCH IS *PROUD* OF YOU.
PRAISED BE HIS TECHNO-HOLINESS!
LET IT BE!
PRAISED BE THE SUPREMACY OF THE TECHNO-TECHNOLOGY!
PRAISED BE THE COMING OF ZOMBRA!

HEY! YOU'RE SHOWING OFF FOR HAVING CONQUERED YOUR *EGO*, BUT ALL YOU REMEMBER IS HOW GREAT YOU WERE! YOU DIDN'T BEAT THE ROBOCRIMINALS ON YOUR OWN! WHAT ABOUT HOW I HELPED YOU?

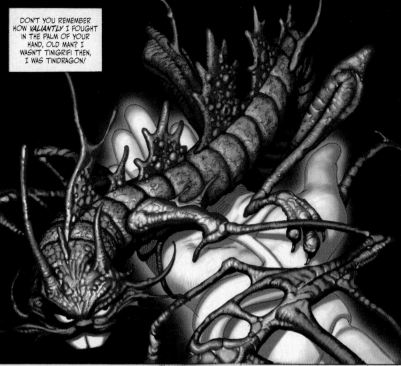

DON'T YOU REMEMBER HOW *VALIANTLY* I FOUGHT IN THE PALM OF YOUR HAND, OLD MAN? I WASN'T TINIGRIFI THEN, I WAS TINIDRAGON!

GROAAAR!

I DESTROYED THOUSANDS OF OUR ENEMIES! IT'S TRUE!

DON'T *EXAGGERATE*, LITTLE PALEO-RAT, NO MORE THAN A DOZEN DIED. AND THAT'S ENOUGH! I RECORDED YOUR VOICE. YOU'RE PART OF HISTORY. NOW, LET ME WRITE MY MEMOIRS. MINE, NOT YOURS.

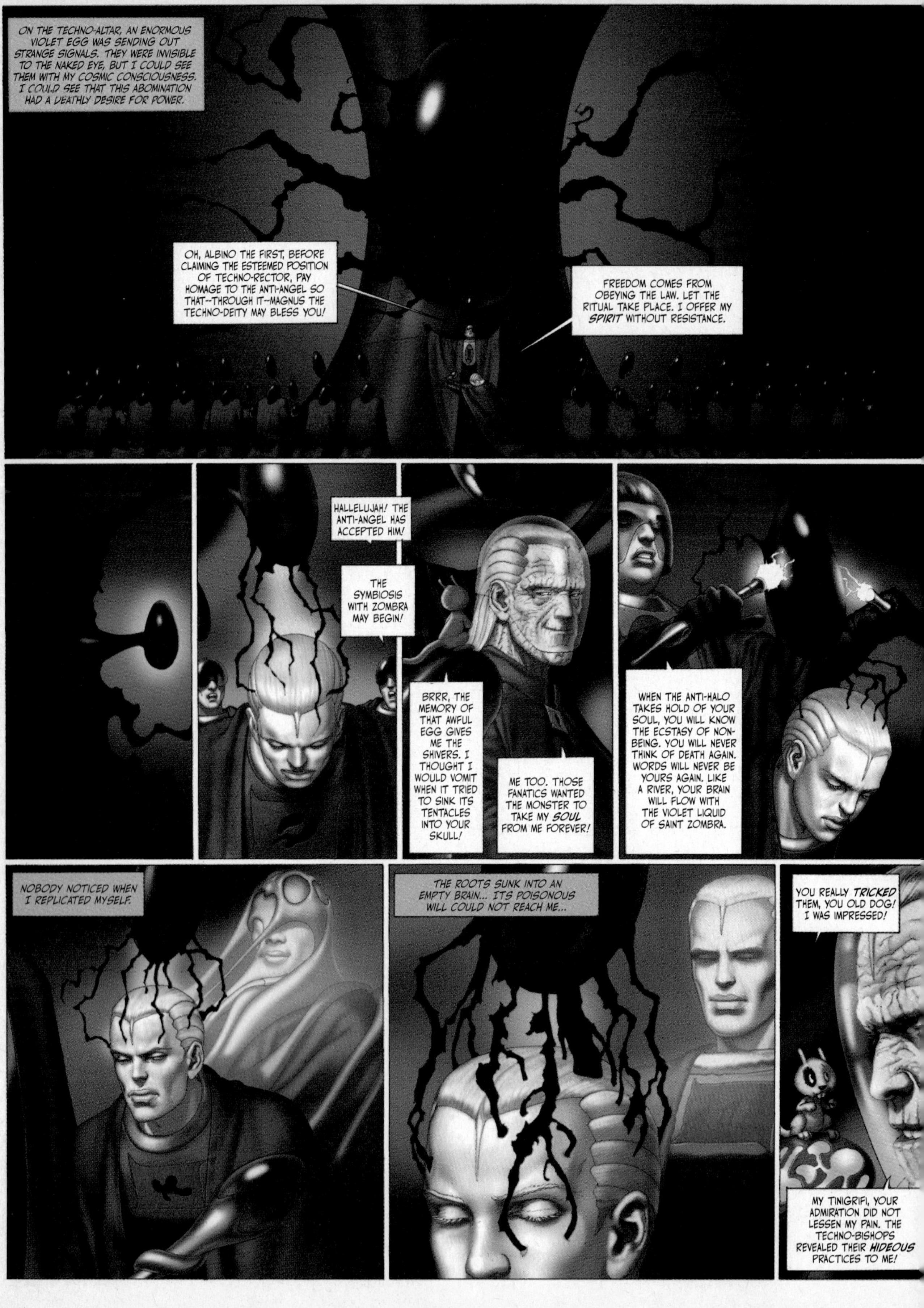
ON THE TECHNO-ALTAR, AN ENORMOUS VIOLET EGG WAS SENDING OUT STRANGE SIGNALS. THEY WERE INVISIBLE TO THE NAKED EYE, BUT I COULD SEE THEM WITH MY COSMIC CONSCIOUSNESS. I COULD SEE THAT THIS ABOMINATION HAD A DEATHLY DESIRE FOR POWER.
OH, ALBINO THE FIRST, BEFORE CLAIMING THE ESTEEMED POSITION OF TECHNO-RECTOR, PAY HOMAGE TO THE ANTI-ANGEL SO THAT--THROUGH IT--MAGNUS THE TECHNO-DEITY MAY BLESS YOU!
FREEDOM COMES FROM OBEYING THE LAW. LET THE RITUAL TAKE PLACE. I OFFER MY SPIRIT WITHOUT RESISTANCE.
HALLELUJAH! THE ANTI-ANGEL HAS ACCEPTED HIM!
THE SYMBIOSIS WITH ZOMBRA MAY BEGIN!
BRRR, THE MEMORY OF THAT AWFUL EGG GIVES ME THE SHIVERS. I THOUGHT I WOULD VOMIT WHEN IT TRIED TO SINK ITS TENTACLES INTO YOUR SKULL!
ME TOO. THOSE FANATICS WANTED THE MONSTER TO TAKE MY SOUL FROM ME FOREVER!
WHEN THE ANTI-HALO TAKES HOLD OF YOUR SOUL, YOU WILL KNOW THE ECSTASY OF NON-BEING. YOU WILL NEVER THINK OF DEATH AGAIN. WORDS WILL NEVER BE YOURS AGAIN. LIKE A RIVER, YOUR BRAIN WILL FLOW WITH THE VIOLET LIQUID OF SAINT ZOMBRA.
NOBODY NOTICED WHEN I REPLICATED MYSELF.
THE ROOTS SUNK INTO AN EMPTY BRAIN... ITS POISONOUS WILL COULD NOT REACH ME...
YOU REALLY TRICKED THEM, YOU OLD DOG! I WAS IMPRESSED!
MY TINIGRIFI, YOUR ADMIRATION DID NOT LESSEN MY PAIN. THE TECHNO-BISHOPS REVEALED THEIR HIDEOUS PRACTICES TO ME!

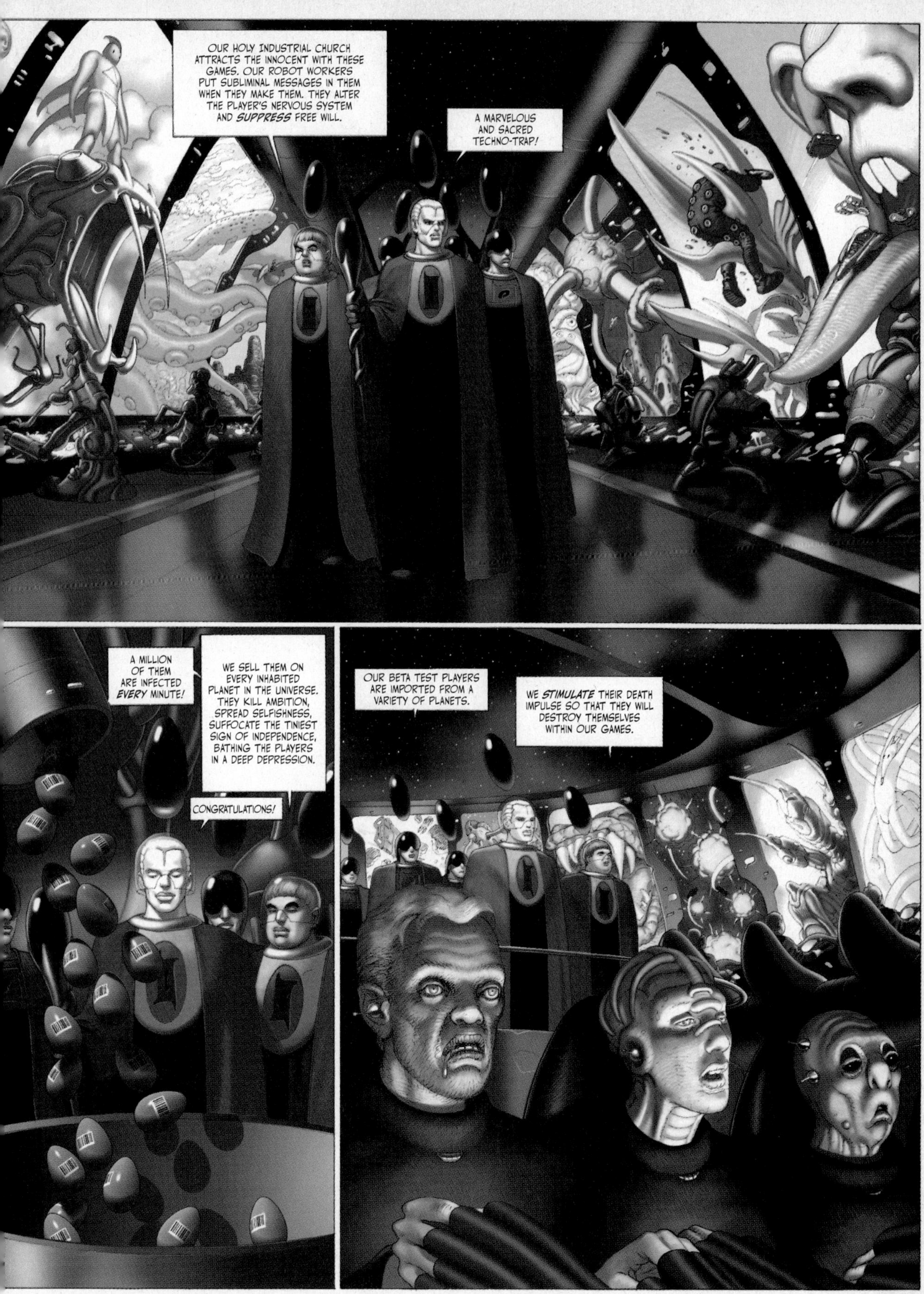
OUR HOLY INDUSTRIAL CHURCH ATTRACTS THE INNOCENT WITH THESE GAMES. OUR ROBOT WORKERS PUT SUBLIMINAL MESSAGES IN THEM WHEN THEY MAKE THEM. THEY ALTER THE PLAYER'S NERVOUS SYSTEM AND SUPPRESS FREE WILL.
A MARVELOUS AND SACRED TECHNO-TRAP!
A MILLION OF THEM ARE INFECTED EVERY MINUTE!
WE SELL THEM ON EVERY INHABITED PLANET IN THE UNIVERSE. THEY KILL AMBITION, SPREAD SELFISHNESS, SUFFOCATE THE TINIEST SIGN OF INDEPENDENCE, BATHING THE PLAYERS IN A DEEP DEPRESSION.
CONGRATULATIONS!
OUR BETA TEST PLAYERS ARE IMPORTED FROM A VARIETY OF PLANETS.
WE STIMULATE THEIR DEATH IMPULSE SO THAT THEY WILL DESTROY THEMSELVES WITHIN OUR GAMES.

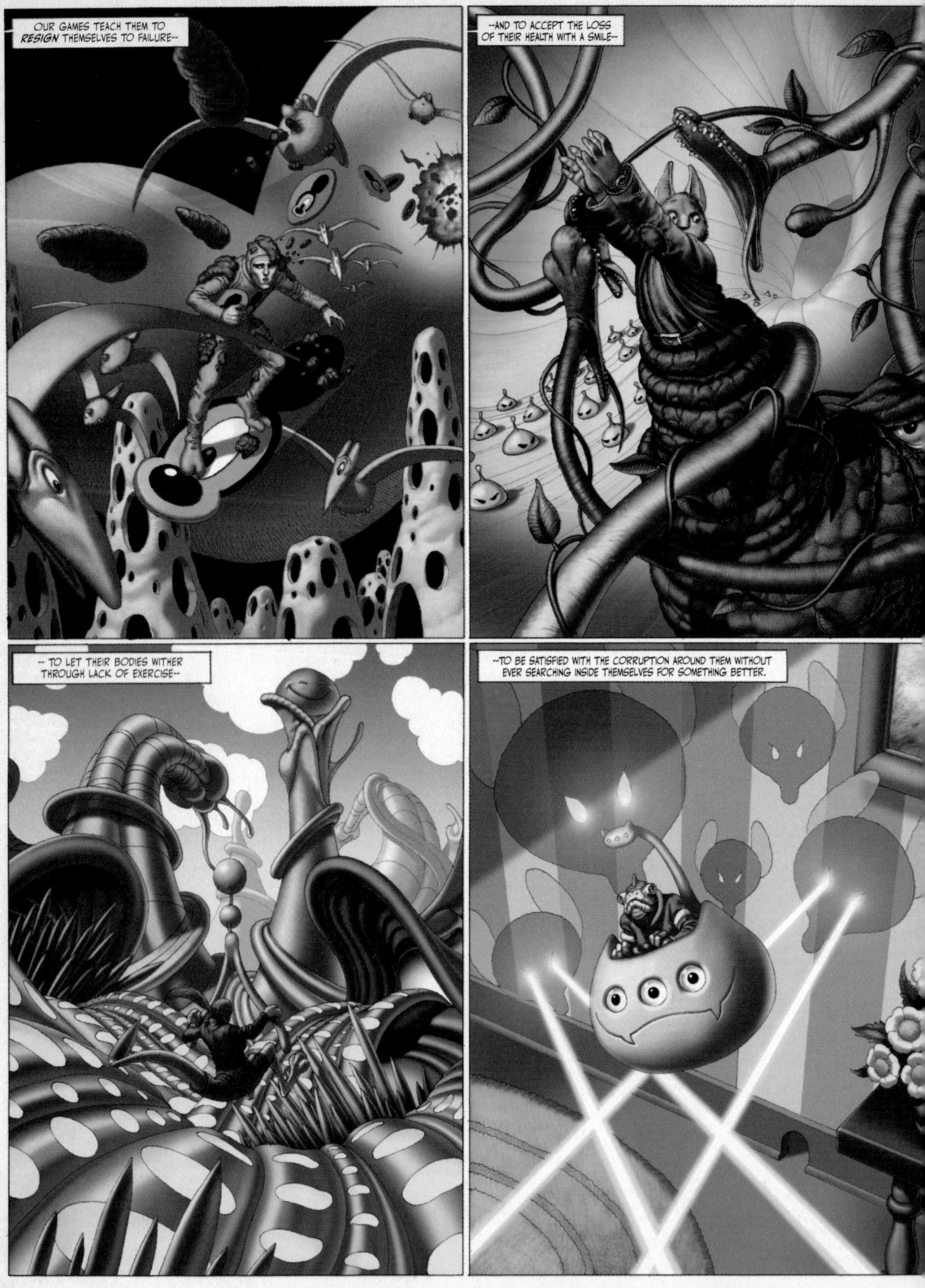
OUR GAMES TEACH THEM TO RESIGN THEMSELVES TO FAILURE--
--AND TO ACCEPT THE LOSS OF THEIR HEALTH WITH A SMILE--
-- TO LET THEIR BODIES WITHER THROUGH LACK OF EXERCISE--
--TO BE SATISFIED WITH THE CORRUPTION AROUND THEM WITHOUT EVER SEARCHING INSIDE THEMSELVES FOR SOMETHING BETTER.

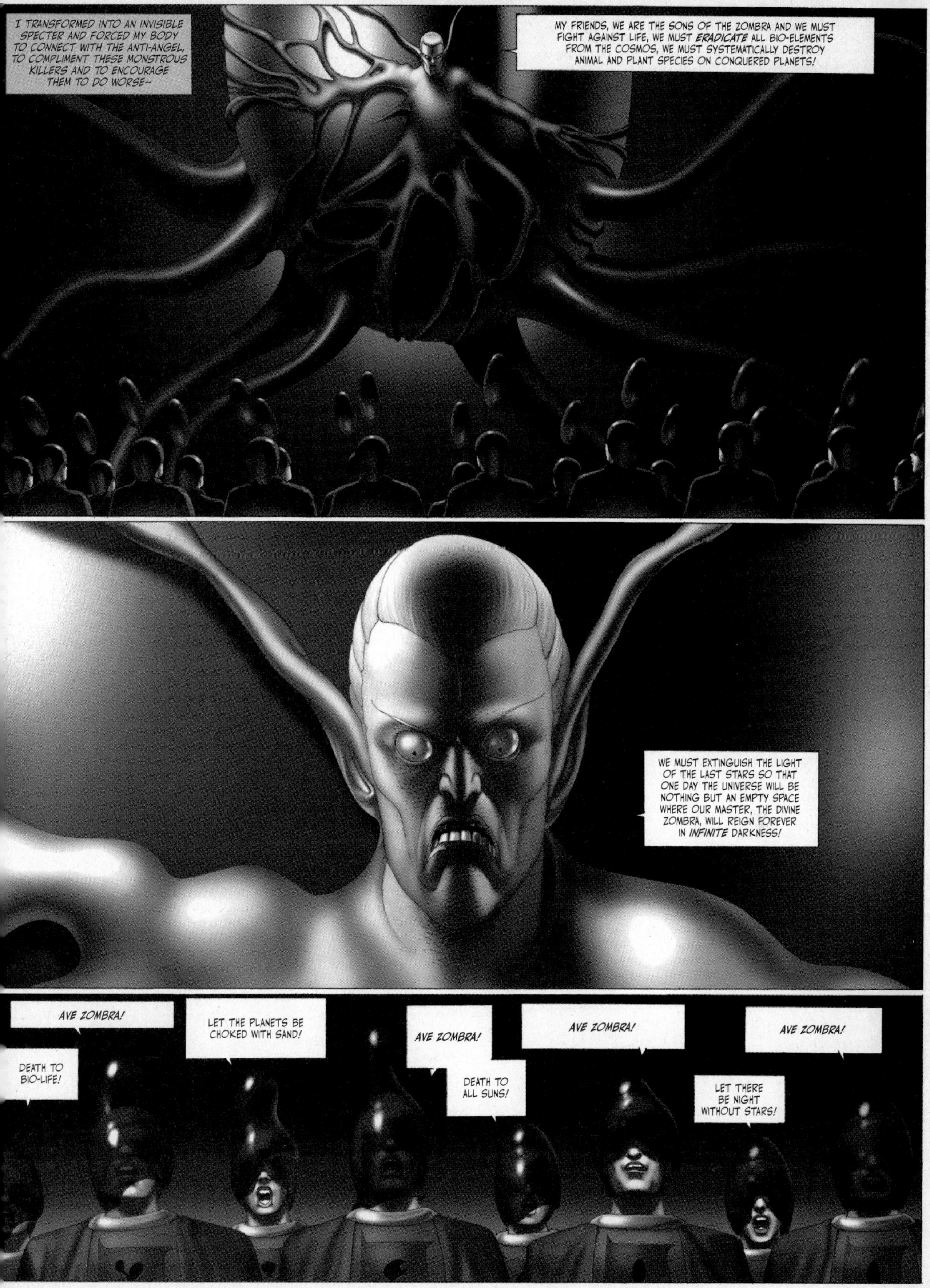
I TRANSFORMED INTO AN INVISIBLE SPECTER AND FORCED MY BODY TO CONNECT WITH THE ANTI-ANGEL, TO COMPLIMENT THESE MONSTROUS KILLERS AND TO ENCOURAGE THEM TO DO WORSE--
MY FRIENDS, WE ARE THE SONS OF THE ZOMBRA AND WE MUST FIGHT AGAINST LIFE, WE MUST ERADICATE ALL BIO-ELEMENTS FROM THE COSMOS, WE MUST SYSTEMATICALLY DESTROY ANIMAL AND PLANT SPECIES ON CONQUERED PLANETS!
WE MUST EXTINGUISH THE LIGHT OF THE LAST STARS SO THAT ONE DAY THE UNIVERSE WILL BE NOTHING BUT AN EMPTY SPACE WHERE OUR MASTER, THE DIVINE ZOMBRA, WILL REIGN FOREVER IN INFINITE DARKNESS!
AVE ZOMBRA!
DEATH TO BIO-LIFE!
LET THE PLANETS BE CHOKED WITH SAND!
AVE ZOMBRA!
DEATH TO ALL SUNS!
AVE ZOMBRA!
LET THERE BE NIGHT WITHOUT STARS!
AVE ZOMBRA!

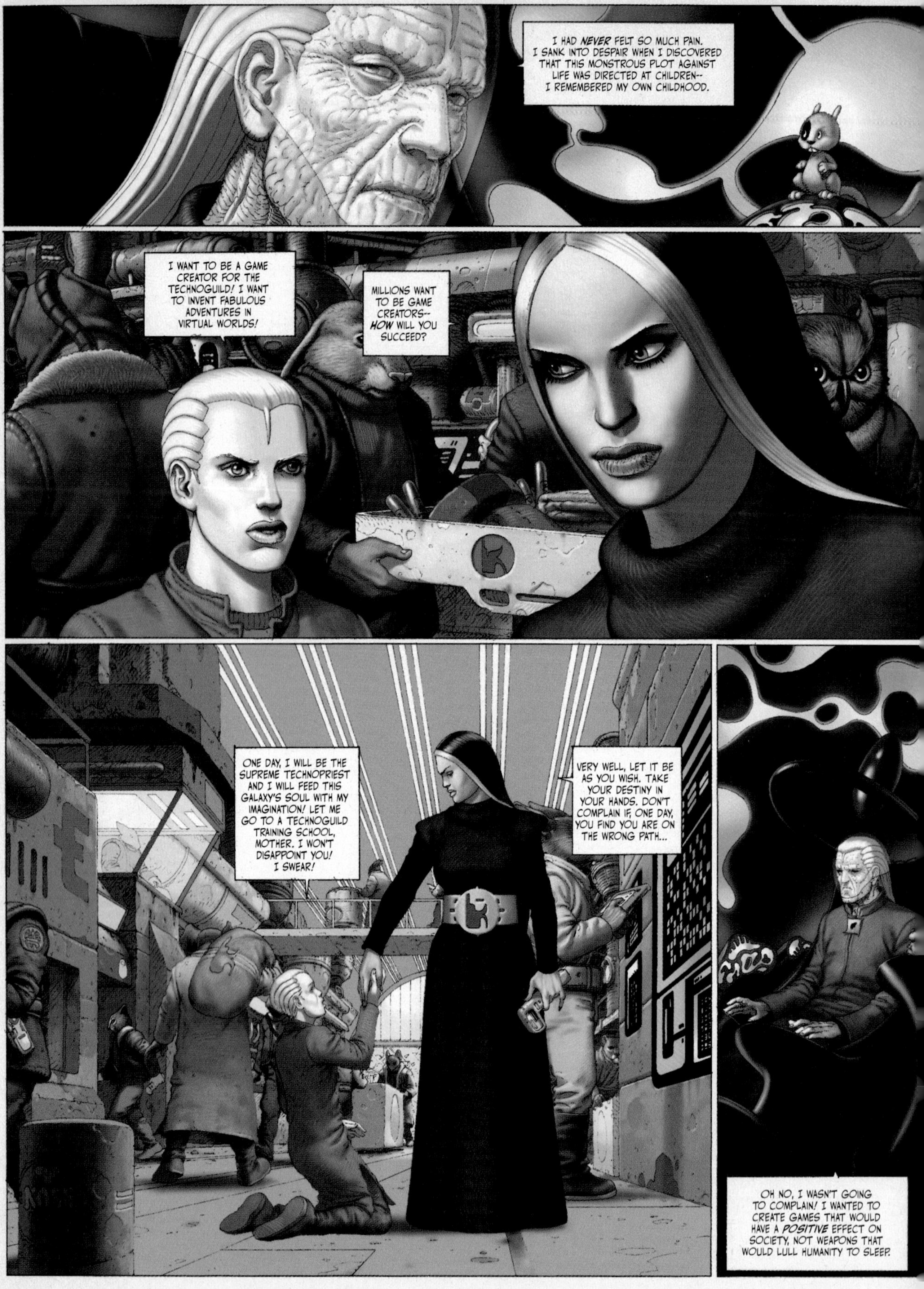
I HAD NEVER FELT SO MUCH PAIN. I SANK INTO DESPAIR WHEN I DISCOVERED THAT THIS MONSTROUS PLOT AGAINST LIFE WAS DIRECTED AT CHILDREN-- I REMEMBERED MY OWN CHILDHOOD.
I WANT TO BE A GAME CREATOR FOR THE TECHNOGUILD! I WANT TO INVENT FABULOUS ADVENTURES IN VIRTUAL WORLDS!
MILLIONS WANT TO BE GAME CREATORS-- HOW WILL YOU SUCCEED?
ONE DAY, I WILL BE THE SUPREME TECHNOPRIEST AND I WILL FEED THIS GALAXY'S SOUL WITH MY IMAGINATION! LET ME GO TO A TECHNOGUILD TRAINING SCHOOL, MOTHER. I WON'T DISAPPOINT YOU! I SWEAR!
VERY WELL, LET IT BE AS YOU WISH. TAKE YOUR DESTINY IN YOUR HANDS. DON'T COMPLAIN IF, ONE DAY, YOU FIND YOU ARE ON THE WRONG PATH...
OH NO, I WASN'T GOING TO COMPLAIN! I WANTED TO CREATE GAMES THAT WOULD HAVE A POSITIVE EFFECT ON SOCIETY, NOT WEAPONS THAT WOULD LULL HUMANITY TO SLEEP.

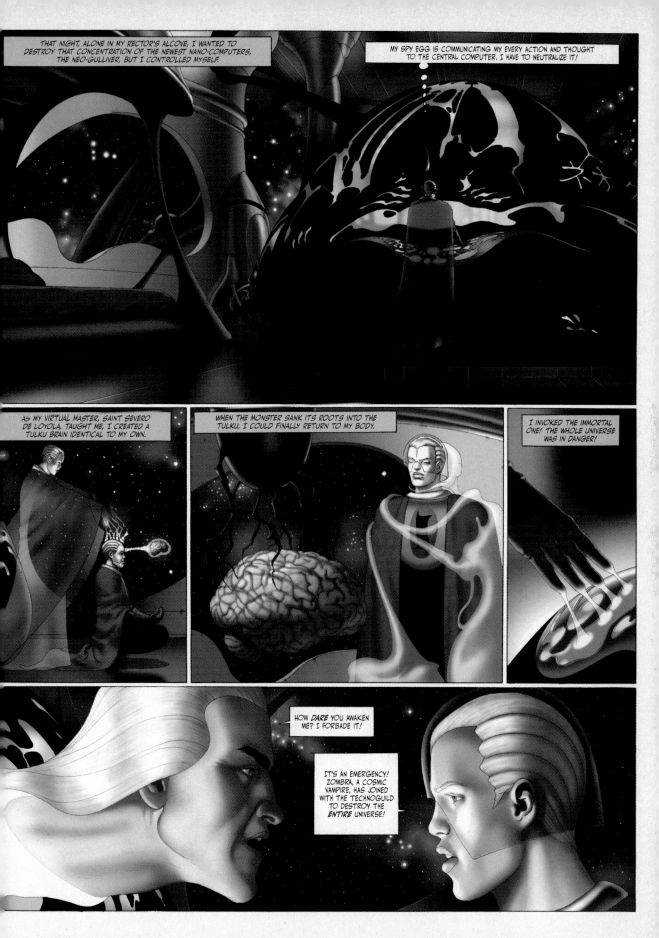

THAT NIGHT, ALONE IN MY RECTOR'S ALCOVE, I WANTED TO DESTROY THAT CONCENTRATION OF THE NEWEST NANO-COMPUTERS, THE NEO-GULLIVER, BUT I CONTROLLED MYSELF.

MY SPY EGG IS COMMUNICATING MY EVERY ACTION AND THOUGHT TO THE CENTRAL COMPUTER. I HAVE TO NEUTRALIZE IT!

AS MY VIRTUAL MASTER, SAINT SEVERO DE LOYOLA, TAUGHT ME, I CREATED A TULKU BRAIN IDENTICAL TO MY OWN.

WHEN THE MONSTER SANK ITS ROOTS INTO THE TULKU, I COULD FINALLY RETURN TO MY BODY.

I INVOKED THE IMMORTAL ONE! THE WHOLE UNIVERSE WAS IN DANGER!

HOW DARE YOU AWAKEN ME? I FORBADE IT!

IT'S AN EMERGENCY! ZOMBRA, A COSMIC VAMPIRE, HAS JOINED WITH THE TECHNOGUILD TO DESTROY THE ENTIRE UNIVERSE!

MASTER, WHEN I MET YOU FOR THE FIRST TIME IN YOUR VIRTUAL HOME, YOU SAID, "I HAVE BEEN WAITING FOR YOU FOR FIVE CENTURIES! YOU ARE THE SAVIOR OF WHOM THE PROPHET SPOKE!" BUT HOW CAN I SAVE THE UNIVERSE ALONE?

I TOLD YOU, MY SON. TO OVERTHROW THE CORRUPT TECHNOPRIESTS, YOU MUST SACRIFICE YOUR ILLUSIONS AND LIVE WITHIN THE HORROR THAT HIDES BEHIND THE PANTECHNO GAMES!

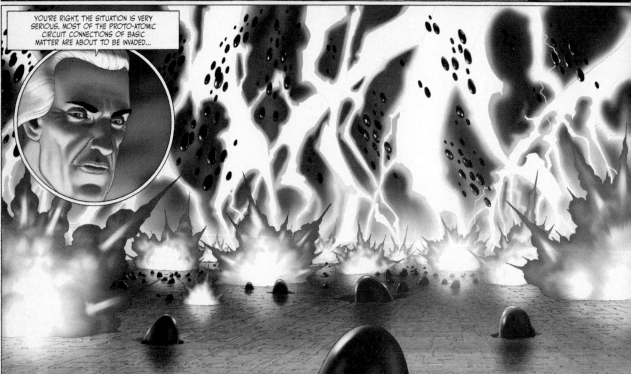

YOU'RE RIGHT, THE SITUATION IS VERY SERIOUS. MOST OF THE PROTO-ATOMIC CIRCUIT CONNECTIONS OF BASIC MATTER ARE ABOUT TO BE INVADED...

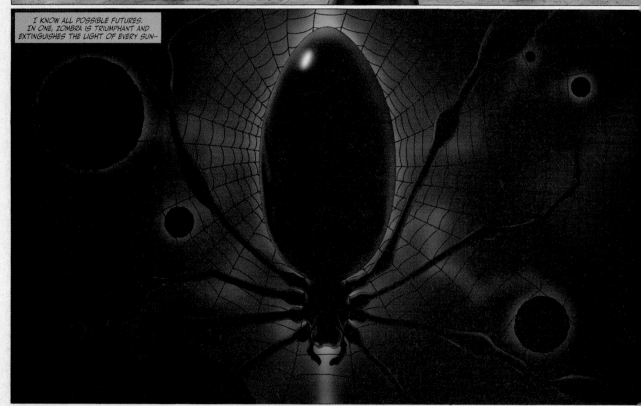

I KNOW ALL POSSIBLE FUTURES. IN ONE, ZOMBRA IS TRIUMPHANT AND EXTINGUISHES THE LIGHT OF EVERY SUN—

--IN ANOTHER, YOU GO CRAZY AND KILL ME. THEN, IN YOUR AUTISTIC BRAIN, YOU CREATE A NEW UNIVERSE IN WHICH YOU ARE GOD--

IN ANOTHER, YOU BECOME THE SUPREME TECHNOPRIEST. LIKE A PALEO-MOSES, YOU LEAVE WITH 500,000 YOUNG TECHNOPRIESTS TO FIND THE PROMISED GALAXY--

--TO FOUND A NEW SOCIETY WHERE HARMONIOUS HUMAN RELATIONSHIPS WILL BE MORE IMPORTANT THAN TECHNOLOGICAL DEVELOPMENT--

THE COSMOS IS OUR BODY, TIME IS WHAT HAPPENS TO US. WE ARE THE *CONSCIENCE* OF THE UNIVERSE.

I MUST DESTROY THE ANTI-ANGEL THAT RULES THIS TEMPLE!

THE INDUSTRIAL CHURCH HAS A PLANETOID TEMPLE FULL OF CONTAMINATED TECHNO-BISHOPS UNDER THE DIRECTION OF AN ANTI-ANGEL IN EVERY INHABITED SYSTEM IN THE GALAXY. IT WOULD BE USELESS TO DESTROY THIS ONE.

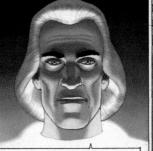

YOU WILL WAIT HERE FOR 24 MONTHS, UNTIL THE CURRENT SUPREME TECHNOPRIEST ORGANIZES THE BIENNIAL CONGRESS OF TECHNO-RECTORS ON THE CENTRAL PLANET, SEAT OF TECHNO-TECHNO POWER... ONLY AT THAT VERY INSTANT CAN YOU ATTACK AND *DETHRONE* HIM.

NO MATTER HOW MANY YEARS PASS, I CANNOT REMEMBER THAT TIME WITHOUT TEARS COMING TO MY EYES.

I UNDERSTAND, MY UNHAPPY FRIEND. YOU HAD TO BE PATIENT FOR TWO YEARS, PRETENDING TO SUBMIT TO ZOMBRA, INFECTING MILLIONS OF GAMES WITH SUBLIMINAL PSYCHO-POISON, SACRIFICING COUNTLESS BETA TEST PLAYERS, MAKING YOURSELF SICK BY *BETRAYING* YOUR SUBLIME IDEALS.

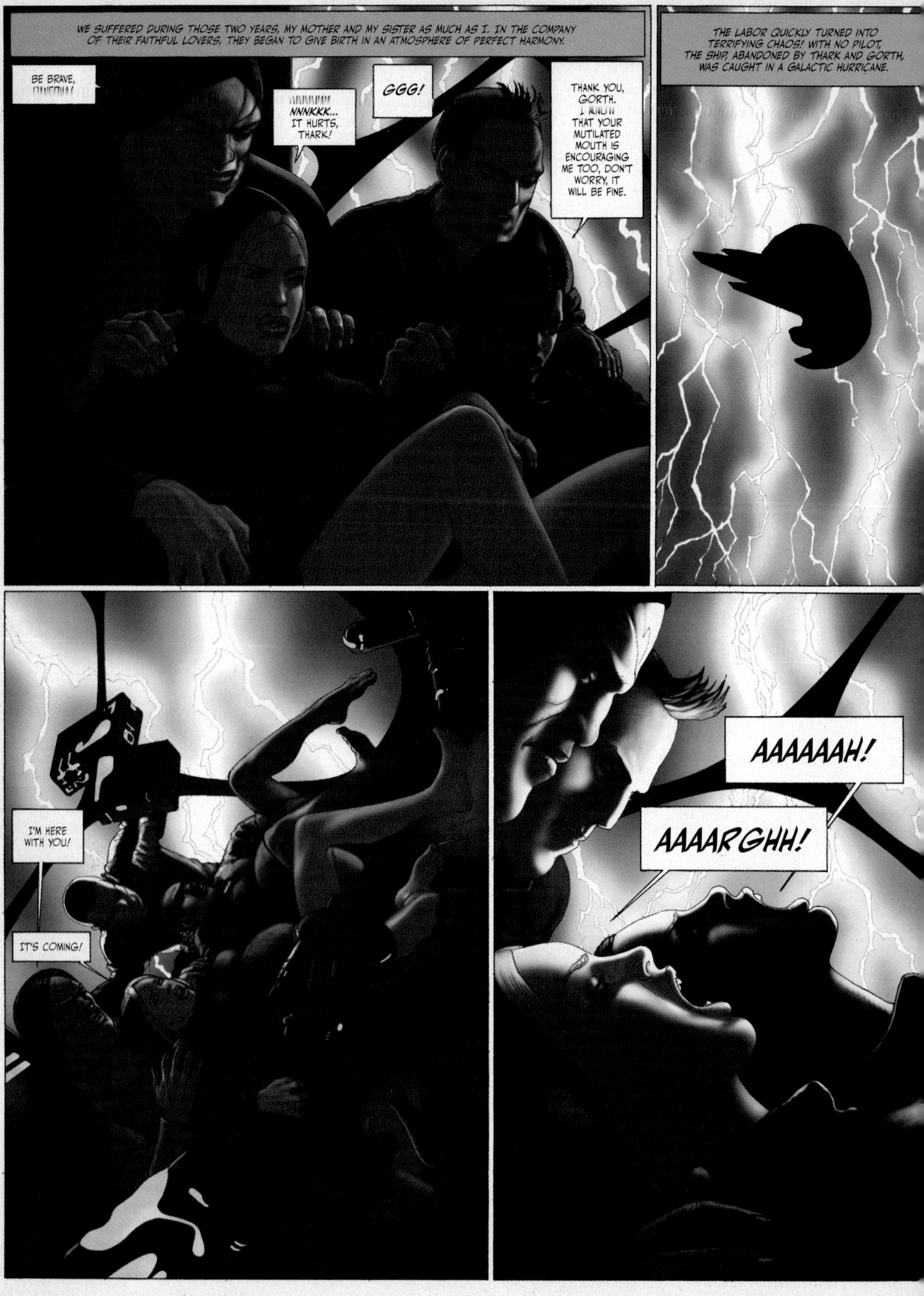
WE SUFFERED DURING THOSE TWO YEARS, MY MOTHER AND MY SISTER AS MUCH AS I. IN THE COMPANY OF THEIR FAITHFUL LOVERS, THEY BEGAN TO GIVE BIRTH IN AN ATMOSPHERE OF PERFECT HARMONY.
BE BRAVE,
NNNKKK... IT HURTS, THARK!
GGG!
THANK YOU, GORTH.
THAT YOUR MUTILATED MOUTH IS ENCOURAGING ME TOO, DON'T WORRY, IT WILL BE FINE.
THE LABOR QUICKLY TURNED INTO TERRIFYING CHAOS! WITH NO PILOT, THE SHIP, ABANDONED BY THARK AND GORTH, WAS CAUGHT IN A GALACTIC HURRICANE.
I'M HERE WITH YOU!
IT'S COMING!
AAAAAAH!
AAAARGHH!

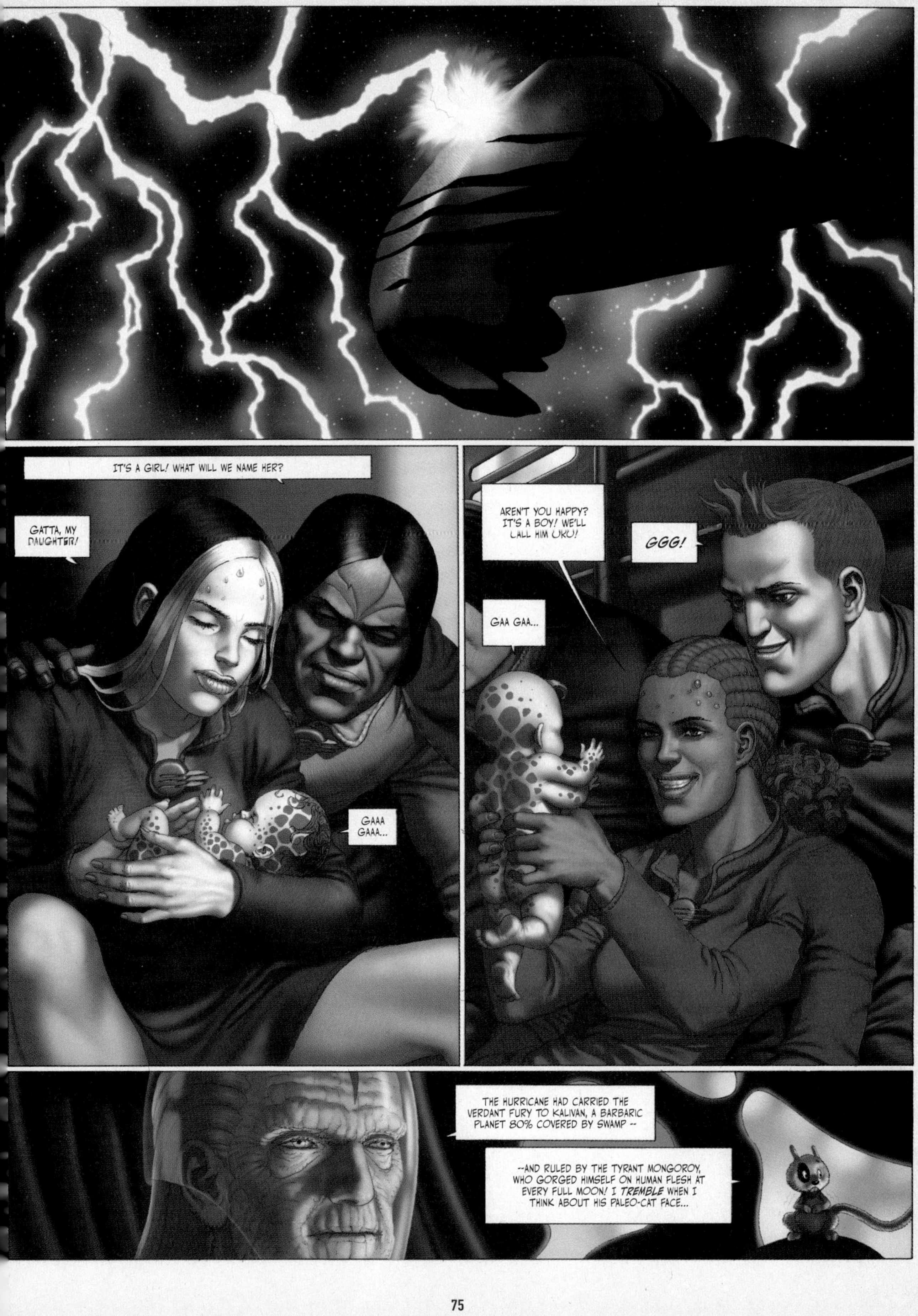
IT'S A GIRL! WHAT WILL WE NAME HER?
GATTA, MY DAUGHTER!
GAAA GAAA...
AREN'T YOU HAPPY? IT'S A BOY! WE'LL CALL HIM URO!
GGG!
GAA GAA...
THE HURRICANE HAD CARRIED THE VERDANT FURY TO KALIVAN, A BARBARIC PLANET 80% COVERED BY SWAMP --
--AND RULED BY THE TYRANT MONGOROY, WHO GORGED HIMSELF ON HUMAN FLESH AT EVERY FULL MOON! I *TREMBLE* WHEN I THINK ABOUT HIS PALEO-CAT FACE...

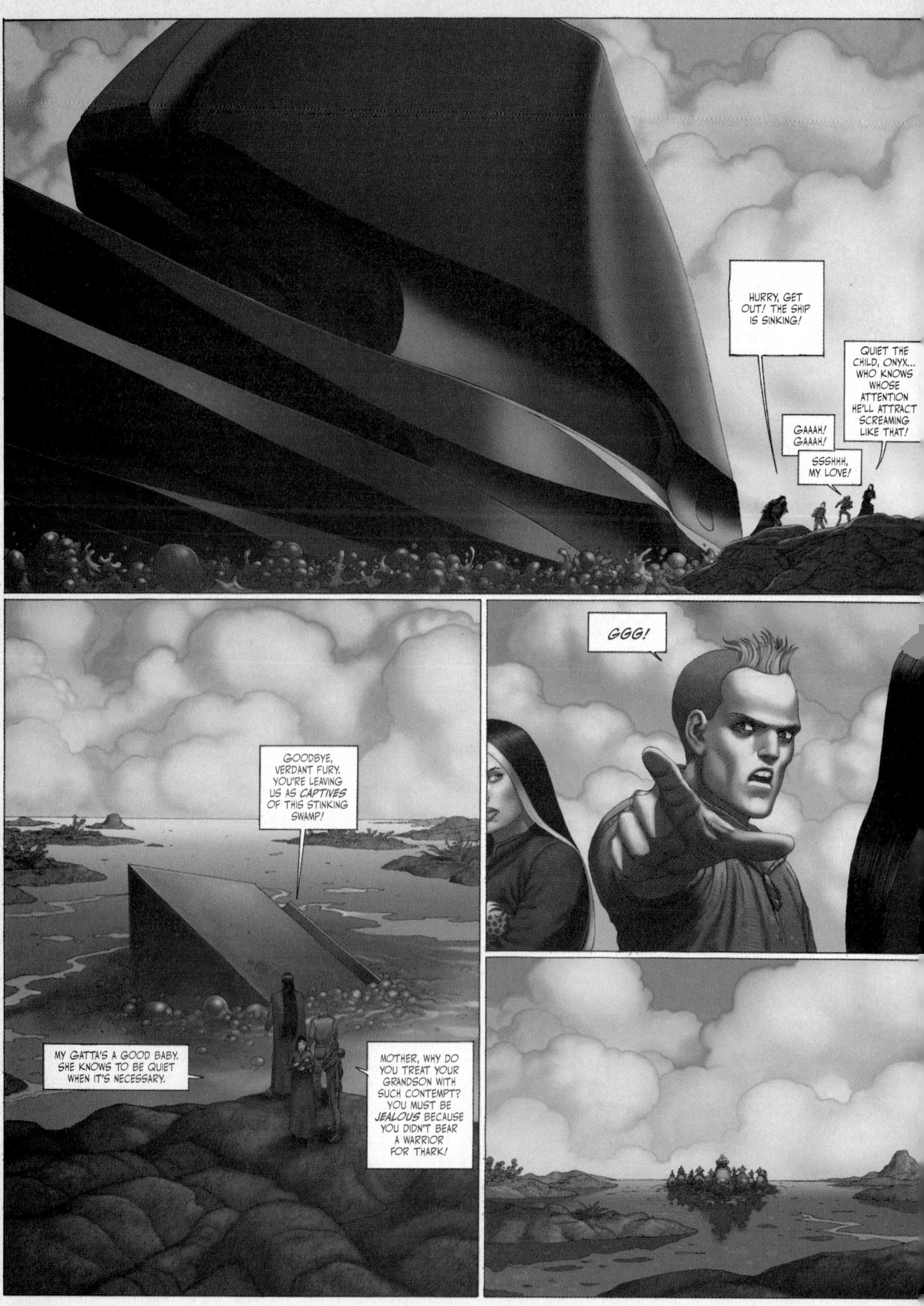
HURRY, GET OUT! THE SHIP IS SINKING!
QUIET THE CHILD, ONYX... WHO KNOWS WHOSE ATTENTION HE'LL ATTRACT SCREAMING LIKE THAT!
GAAAH! GAAAH!
SSSHHH, MY LOVE!
GOODBYE, VERDANT FURY. YOU'RE LEAVING US AS CAPTIVES OF THIS STINKING SWAMP!
MY GATTA'S A GOOD BABY. SHE KNOWS TO BE QUIET WHEN IT'S NECESSARY.
MOTHER, WHY DO YOU TREAT YOUR GRANDSON WITH SUCH CONTEMPT? YOU MUST BE JEALOUS BECAUSE YOU DIDN'T BEAR A WARRIOR FOR THARK!
GGG!

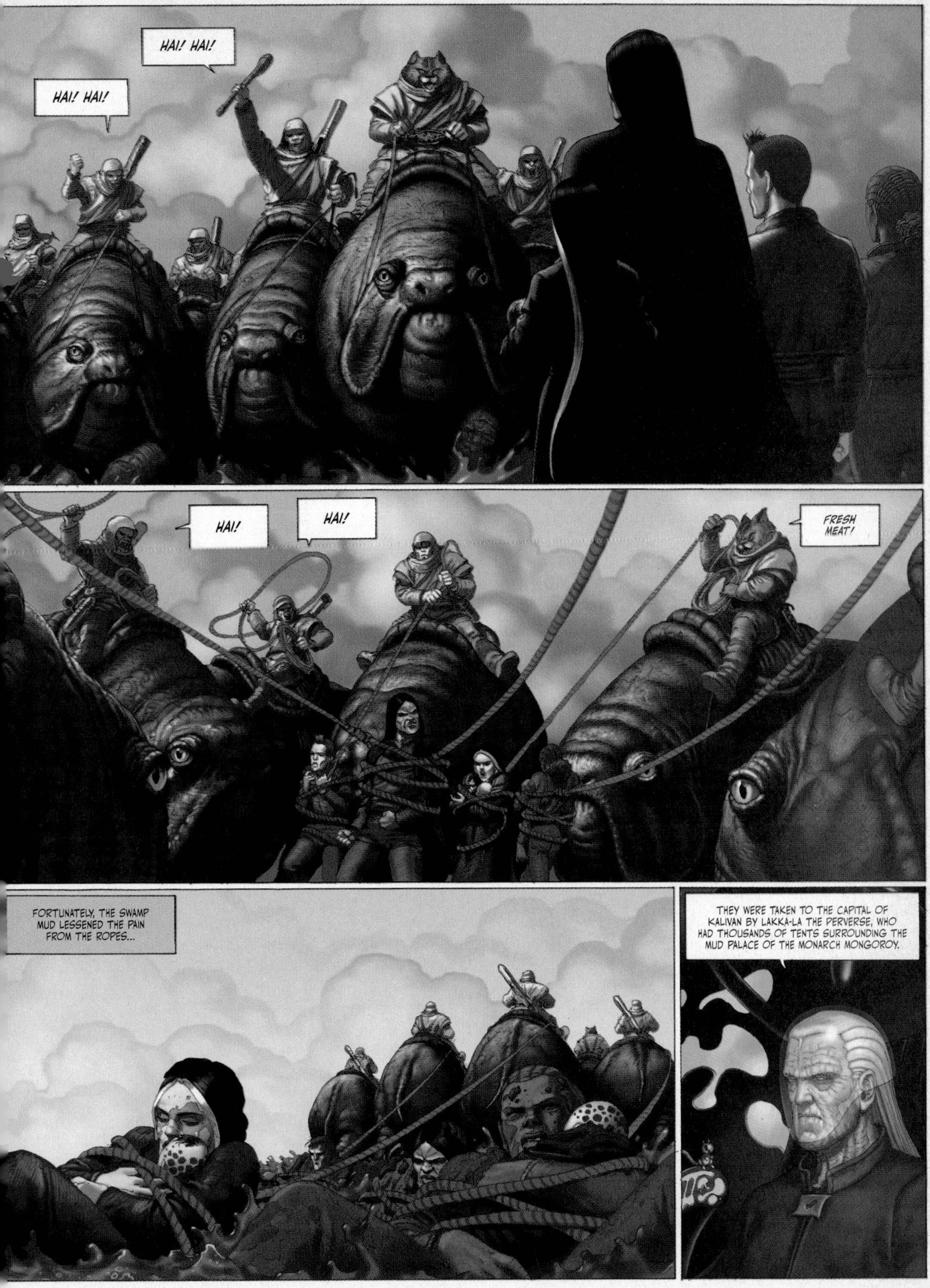

HAI! HAI!
HAI! HAI!
HAI!
HAI!
FRESH MEAT!
FORTUNATELY, THE SWAMP MUD LESSENED THE PAIN FROM THE ROPES...
THEY WERE TAKEN TO THE CAPITAL OF KALIVAN BY LAKKA-LA THE PERVERSE, WHO HAD THOUSANDS OF TENTS SURROUNDING THE MUD PALACE OF THE MONARCH MONGOROY.

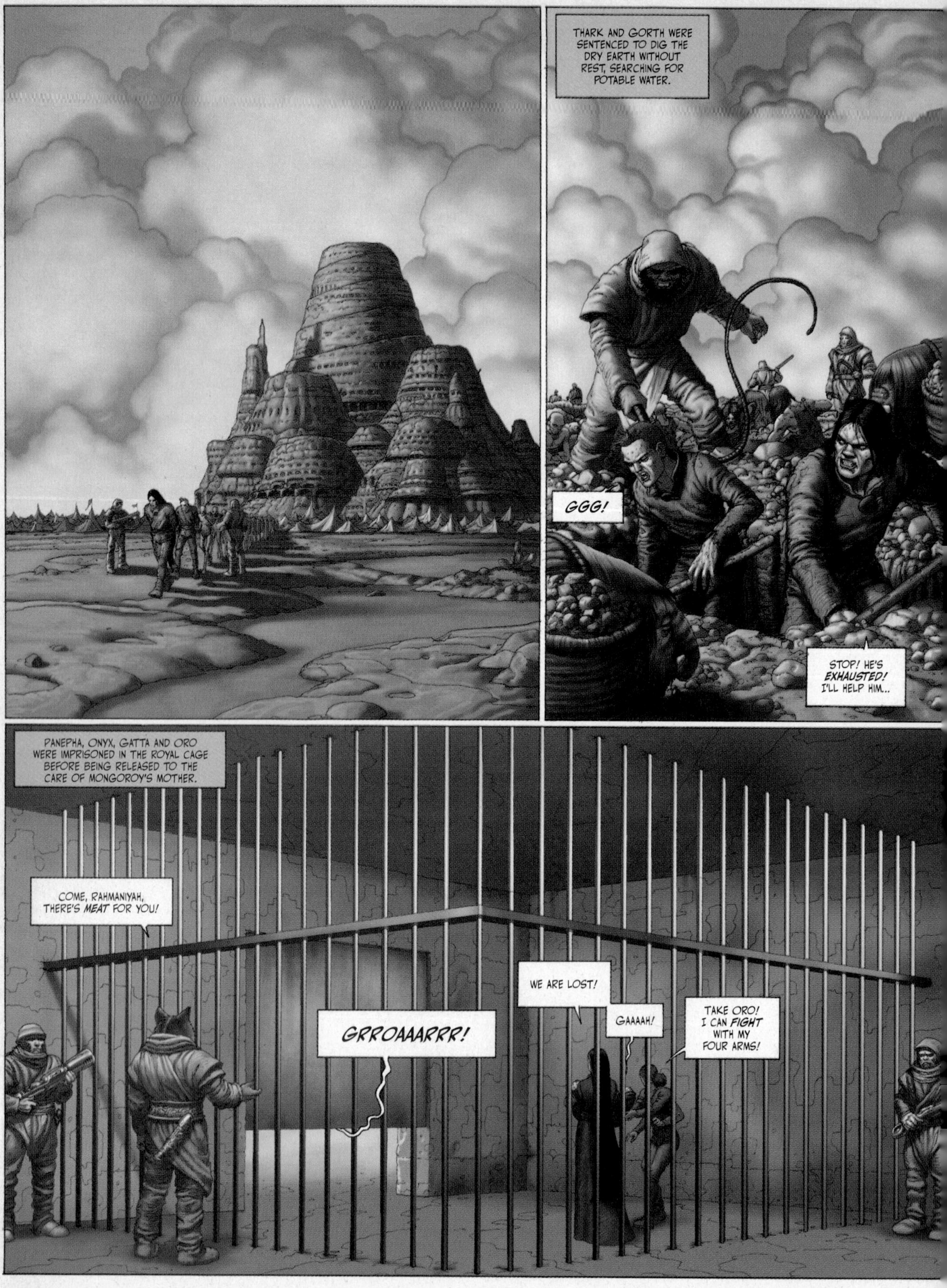
THARK AND GORTH WERE SENTENCED TO DIG THE DRY EARTH WITHOUT REST, SEARCHING FOR POTABLE WATER.
GGG!
STOP! HE'S EXHAUSTED! I'LL HELP HIM...
PANEPHA, ONYX, GATTA AND ORO WERE IMPRISONED IN THE ROYAL CAGE BEFORE BEING RELEASED TO THE CARE OF MONGOROY'S MOTHER.
COME, RAHMANIYAH, THERE'S MEAT FOR YOU!
GRROAAARRR!
WE ARE LOST!
GAAAAH!
TAKE ORO! I CAN FIGHT WITH MY FOUR ARMS!

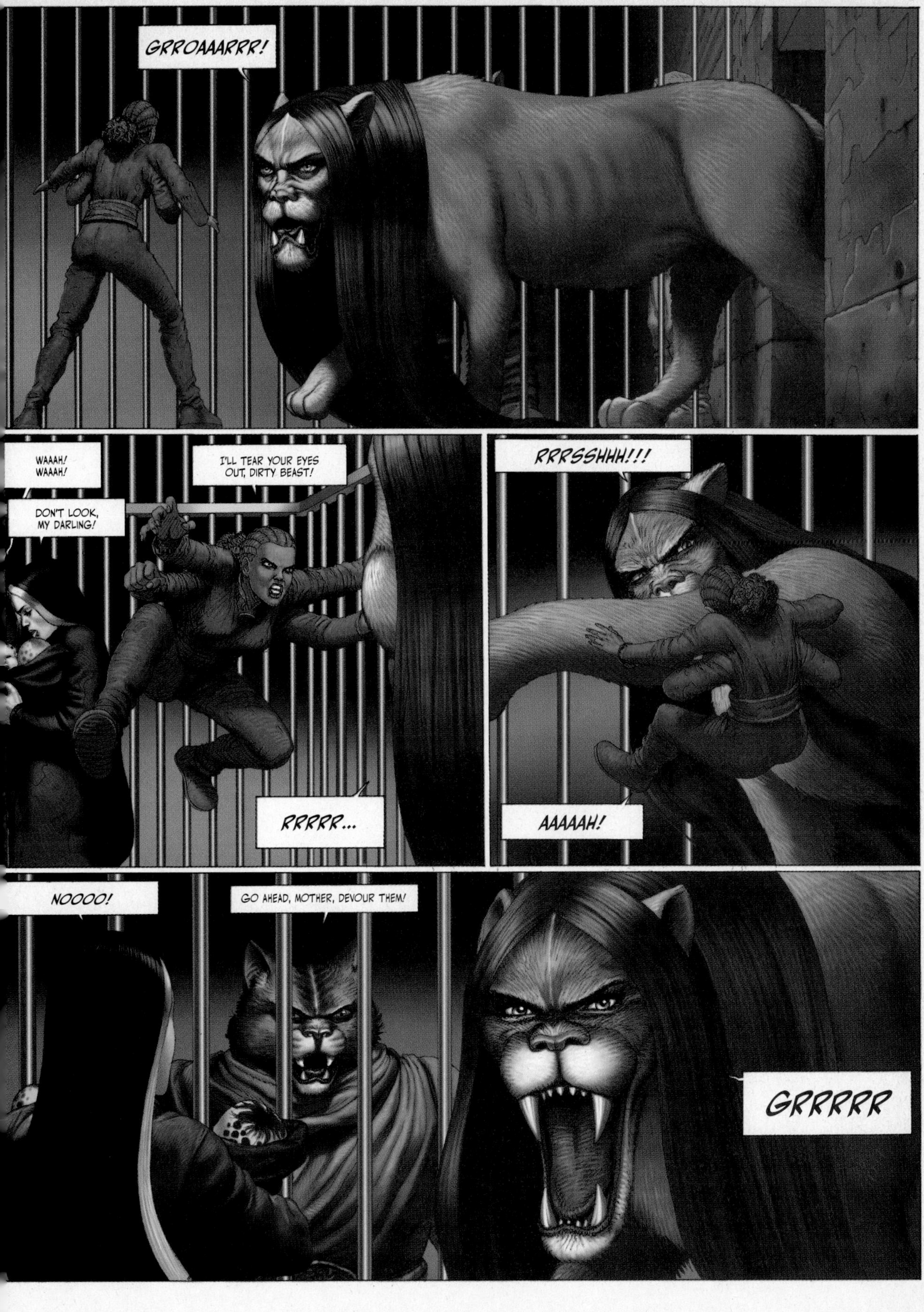
GRROAAARRR!
WAAAH! WAAAH!
DON'T LOOK, MY DARLING!
I'LL TEAR YOUR EYES OUT, DIRTY BEAST!
RRRRR...
RRRSSHHH!!!
AAAAAH!
NOOOO!
GO AHEAD, MOTHER, DEVOUR THEM!
GRRRRR

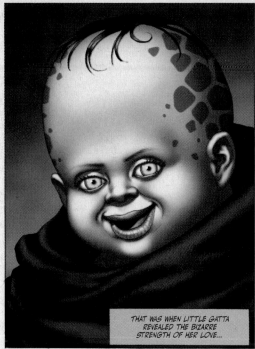

ROWF. ROWF.

THAT WAS WHEN LITTLE GATTA REVEALED THE BIZARRE STRENGTH OF HER LOVE...

RAHMANIYAH, THIS IS THE *FIRST* TIME IN MY LIFE I'VE HEARD YOU PURR!

IT'S A MIRACLE!

RRRROOON RRROOONN...

IT'S NOT A MIRACLE! IT'S THE POWER OF MY DAUGHTER, GATTA!

OH! GATTA HAD SUPERHUMAN POWERS WHILE ORO WOULDN'T STOP CRYING. IT WAS A BLOW TO ONYX'S MATERNAL PRIDE.

YOU'RE GETTING OLD, MY POOR TINIGRIFI. YOU'RE FORGETTING THAT ORO WOULD LATER DEVELOP UNCOMMON GIFTS OF HIS OWN. LET'S GET BACK TO OUR STORY.

SEEING THE ANIMAL SO HAPPY WITH THESE UNUSUAL WOMEN, MONGOROY DECIDED TO KEEP THEM IN HIS MOTHER'S SERVICE. FROM THEN ON, THEY LIVED IN LUXURY. THEIR LOVERS, ON THE OTHER HAND--

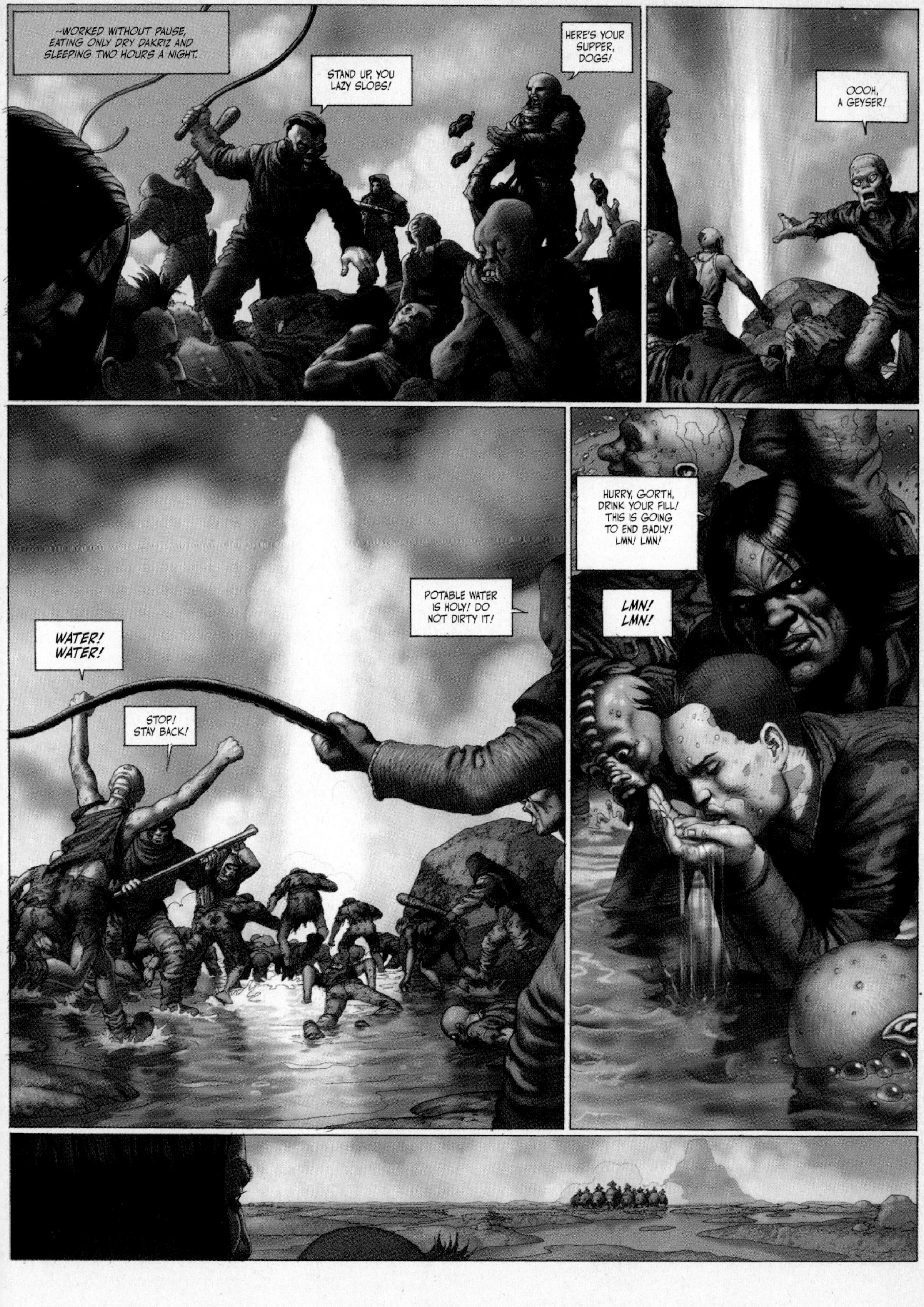

--WORKED WITHOUT PAUSE, EATING ONLY DRY DAKRIZ AND SLEEPING TWO HOURS A NIGHT.
STAND UP, YOU LAZY SLOBS!
HERE'S YOUR SUPPER, DOGS!
OOOH, A GEYSER!
WATER! WATER!
STOP! STAY BACK!
POTABLE WATER IS HOLY! DO NOT DIRTY IT!
HURRY, GORTH, DRINK YOUR FILL! THIS IS GOING TO END BADLY! LMN! LMN!
LMN! LMN!

FIRE!
DON'T MOVE, SCUMBAG!
SACRILEGIOUS DOG!
YOU OKAY?
GGBB...
BY THE DIVINE WILL OF OUR MOTHER RAHMANIYAH, THE POTABLE WATER HAS RETURNED. I WILL DISTRIBUTE IT TO THOSE WHO ARE *WORTHY!*
RAHMANIYAH IS THE GODDESS OF GODDESSES...
AND MONGOROY IS HER PROPHET!

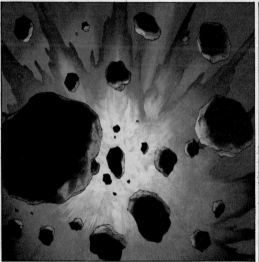

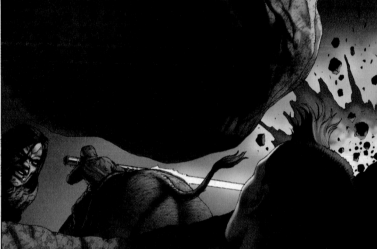

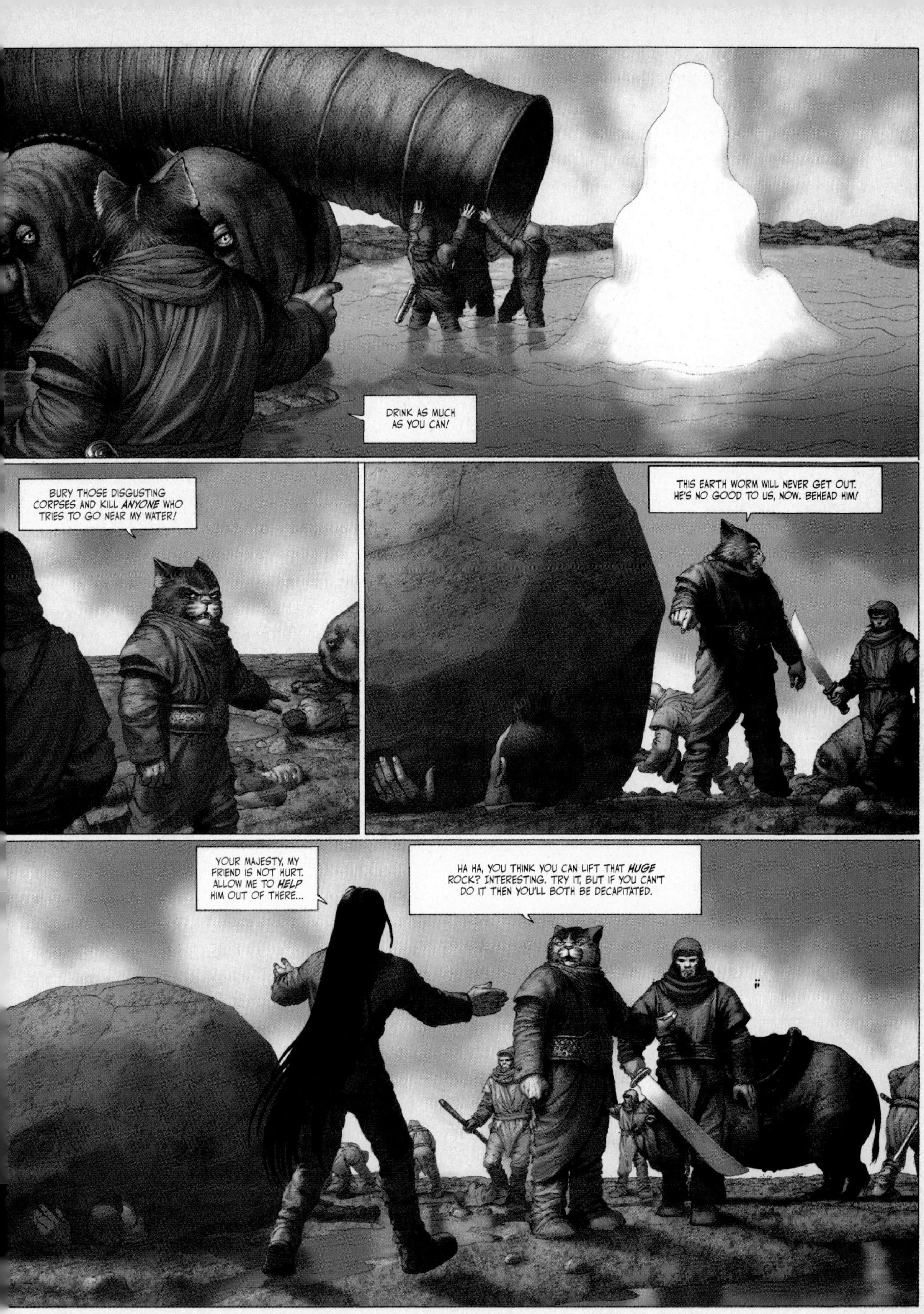
DRINK AS MUCH AS YOU CAN!
BURY THOSE DISGUSTING CORPSES AND KILL *ANYONE* WHO TRIES TO GO NEAR MY WATER!
THIS EARTH WORM WILL NEVER GET OUT. HE'S NO GOOD TO US, NOW. BEHEAD HIM!
YOUR MAJESTY, MY FRIEND IS NOT HURT. ALLOW ME TO *HELP* HIM OUT OF THERE...
HA HA, YOU THINK YOU CAN LIFT THAT *HUGE* ROCK? INTERESTING. TRY IT, BUT IF YOU CAN'T DO IT THEN YOU'LL BOTH BE DECAPITATED.

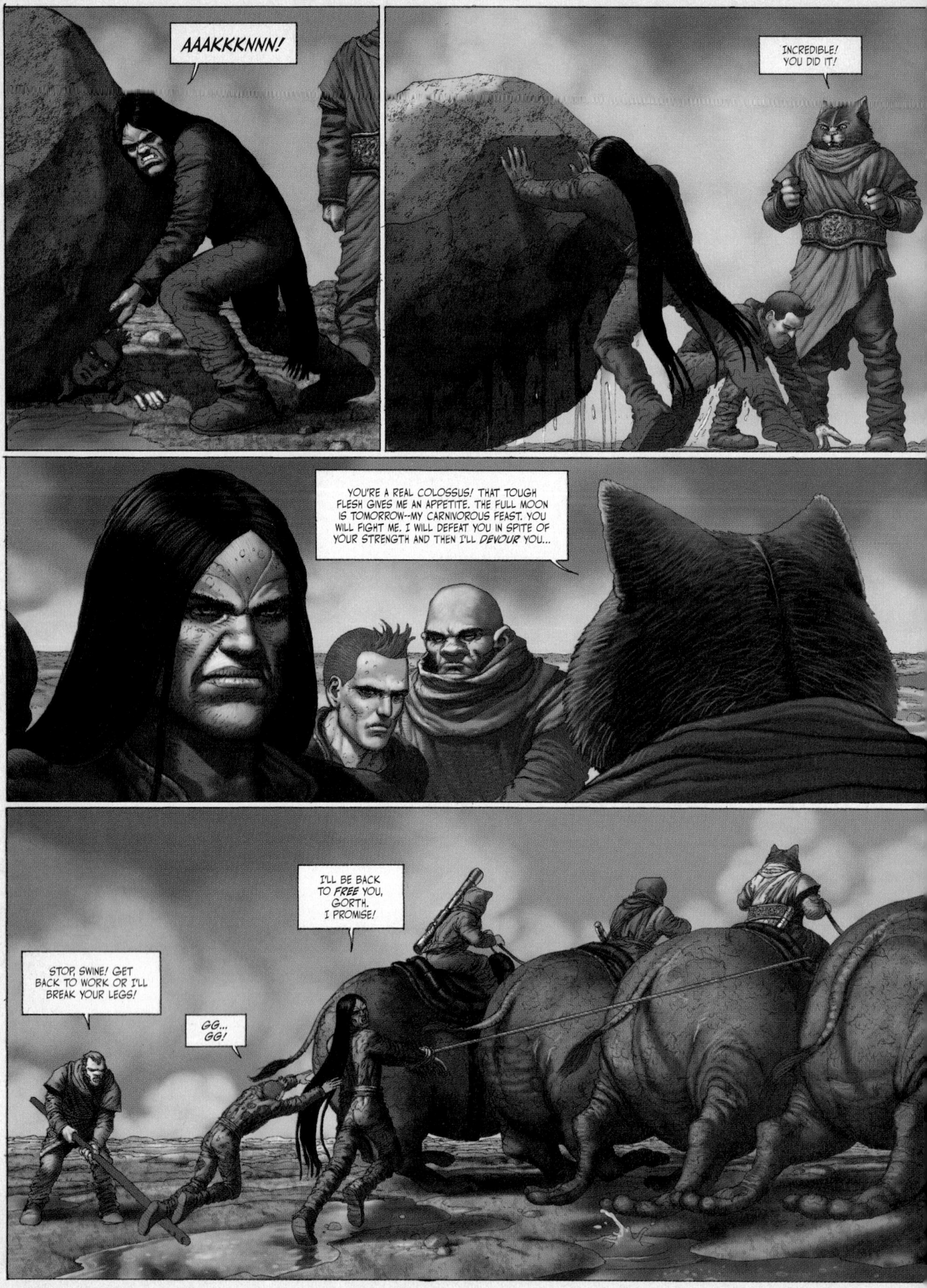
AAAKKKNNN!
INCREDIBLE! YOU DID IT!
YOU'RE A REAL COLOSSUS! THAT TOUGH FLESH GIVES ME AN APPETITE. THE FULL MOON IS TOMORROW--MY CARNIVOROUS FEAST. YOU WILL FIGHT ME. I WILL DEFEAT YOU IN SPITE OF YOUR STRENGTH AND THEN I'LL *DEVOUR* YOU...
STOP, SWINE! GET BACK TO WORK OR I'LL BREAK YOUR LEGS!
GG... GG!
I'LL BE BACK TO *FREE* YOU, GORTH. I PROMISE!

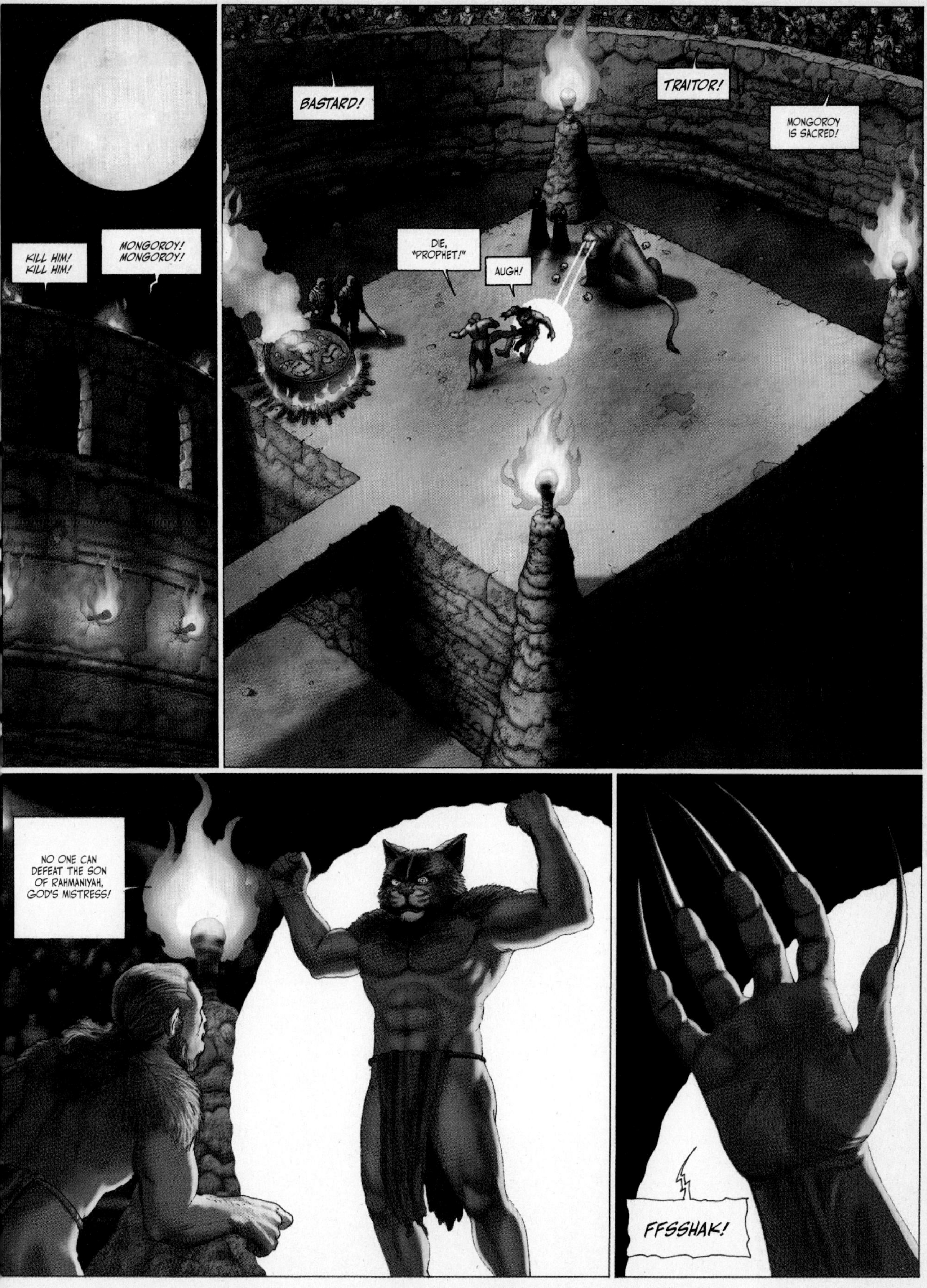
KILL HIM! KILL HIM!
MONGOROY! MONGOROY!
BASTARD!
TRAITOR!
MONGOROY IS SACRED!
DIE, "PROPHET!"
AUGH!
NO ONE CAN DEFEAT THE SON OF RAHMANIYAH, GOD'S MISTRESS!
FFSSHAK!

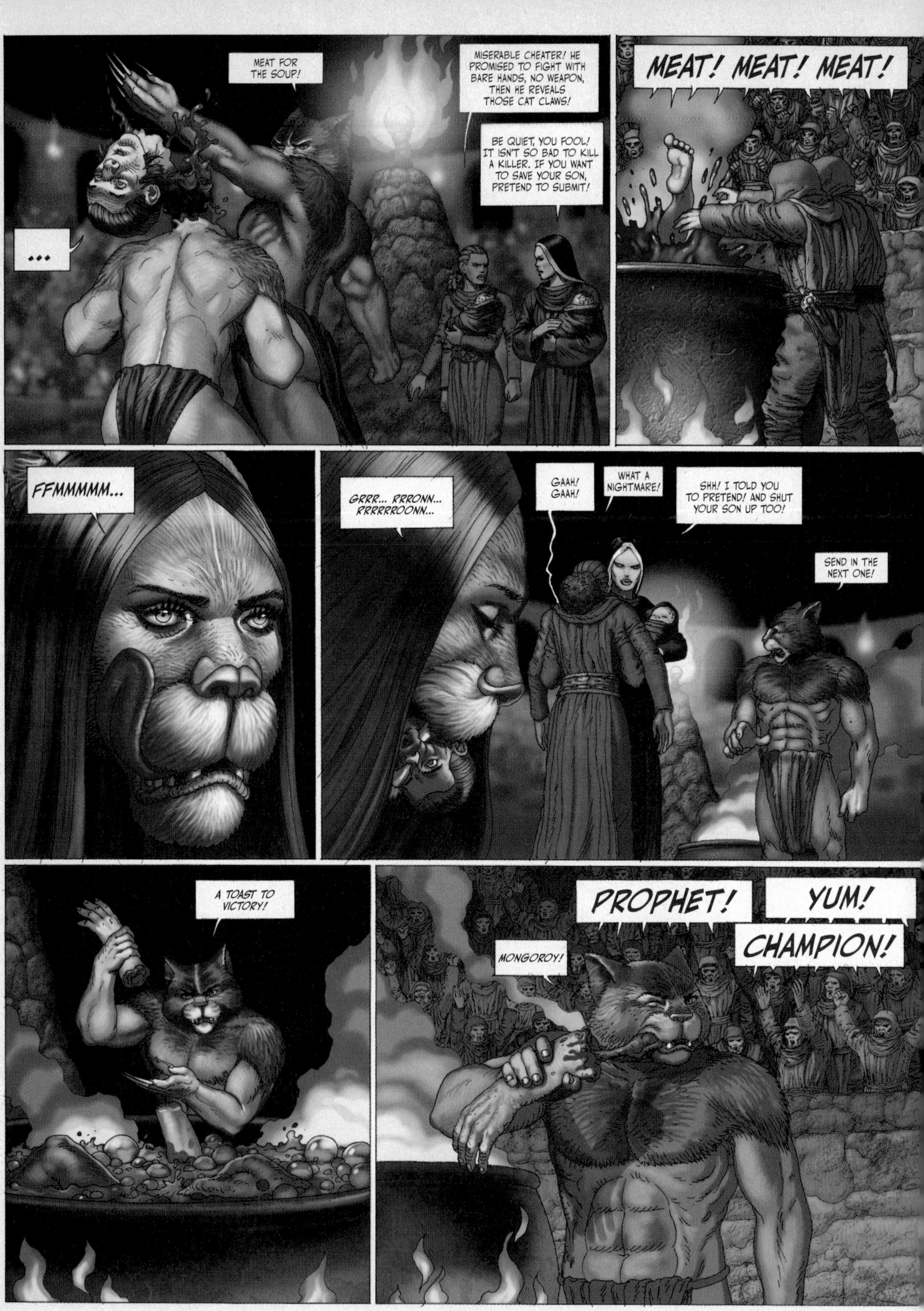
MEAT FOR THE SOUP!
MISERABLE CHEATER! HE PROMISED TO FIGHT WITH BARE HANDS, NO WEAPON, THEN HE REVEALS THOSE CAT CLAWS!
BE QUIET, YOU FOOL! IT ISN'T SO BAD TO KILL A KILLER. IF YOU WANT TO SAVE YOUR SON, PRETEND TO SUBMIT!
...
MEAT! MEAT! MEAT!
FFMMMMM...
GRRR... RRRONN... RRRRRROONN...
GAAH! GAAH!
WHAT A NIGHTMARE!
SHH! I TOLD YOU TO PRETEND! AND SHUT YOUR SON UP TOO!
SEND IN THE NEXT ONE!
A TOAST TO VICTORY!
PROPHET!
YUM!
MONGOROY!
CHAMPION!

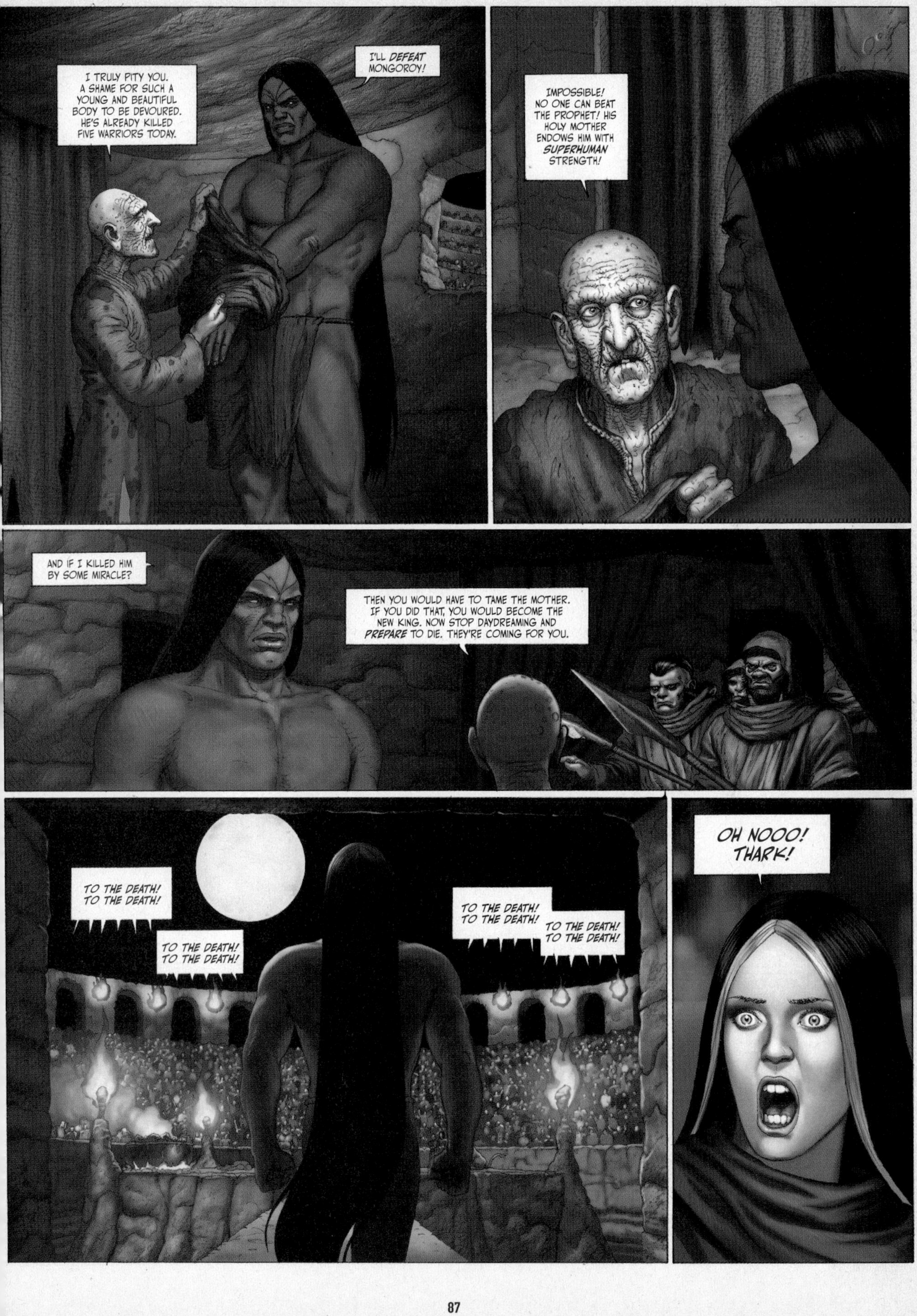
I TRULY PITY YOU. A SHAME FOR SUCH A YOUNG AND BEAUTIFUL BODY TO BE DEVOURED. HE'S ALREADY KILLED FIVE WARRIORS TODAY.
I'LL DEFEAT MONGOROY!
IMPOSSIBLE! NO ONE CAN BEAT THE PROPHET! HIS HOLY MOTHER ENDOWS HIM WITH SUPERHUMAN STRENGTH!
AND IF I KILLED HIM BY SOME MIRACLE?
THEN YOU WOULD HAVE TO TAME THE MOTHER. IF YOU DID THAT, YOU WOULD BECOME THE NEW KING. NOW STOP DAYDREAMING AND PREPARE TO DIE. THEY'RE COMING FOR YOU.
TO THE DEATH! TO THE DEATH!
TO THE DEATH! TO THE DEATH!
TO THE DEATH! TO THE DEATH!
TO THE DEATH! TO THE DEATH!
OH NOOO! THARK!

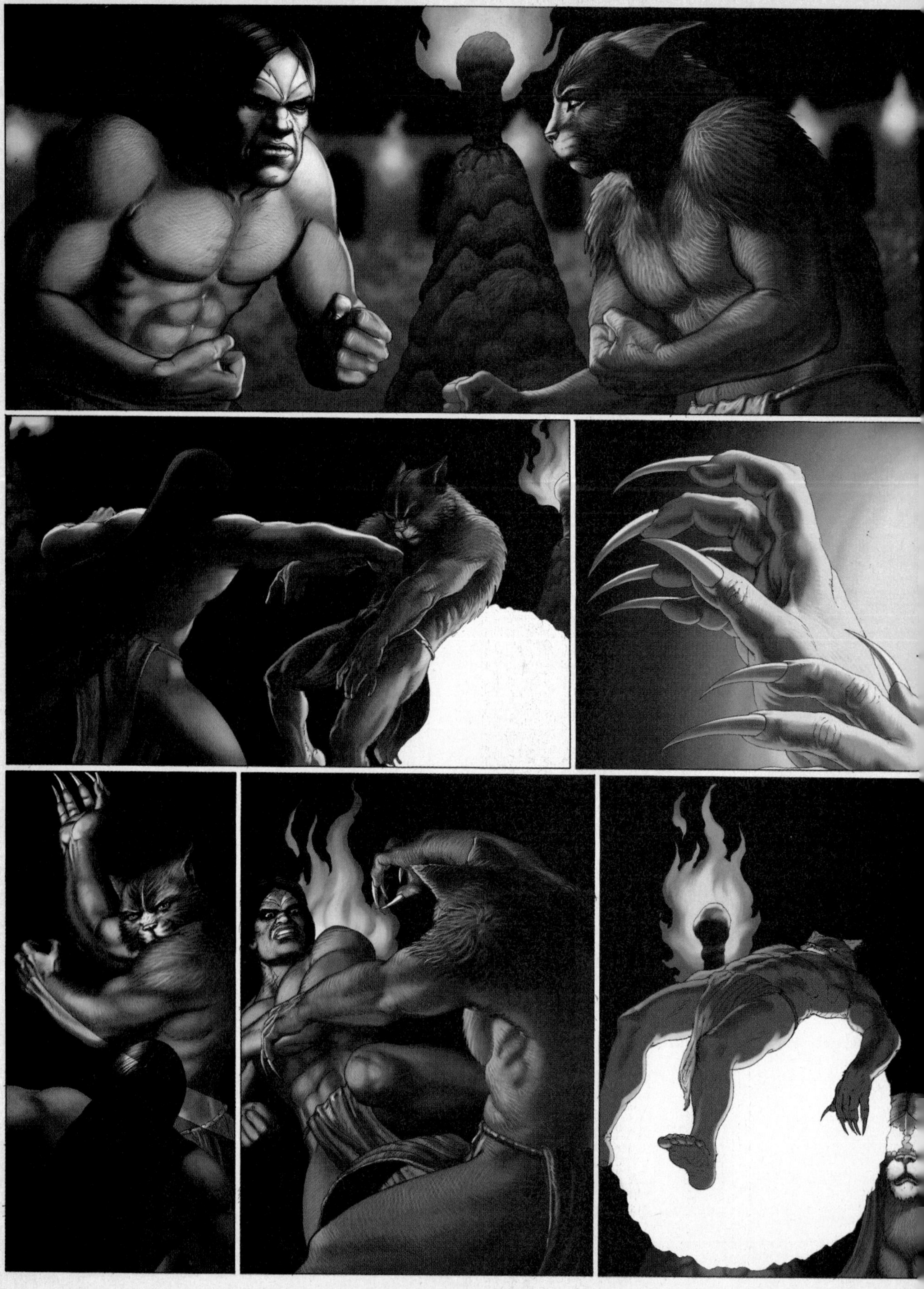

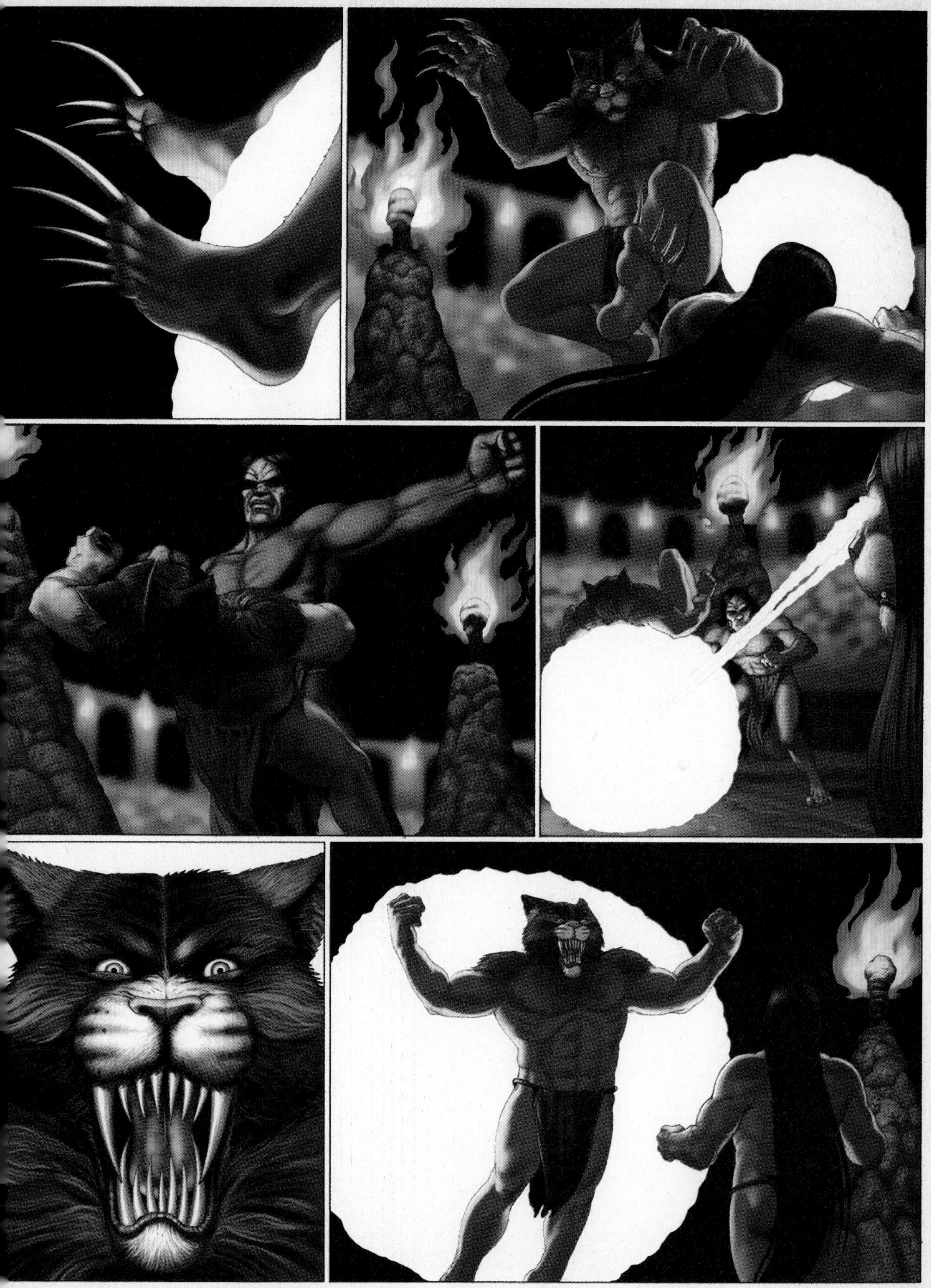

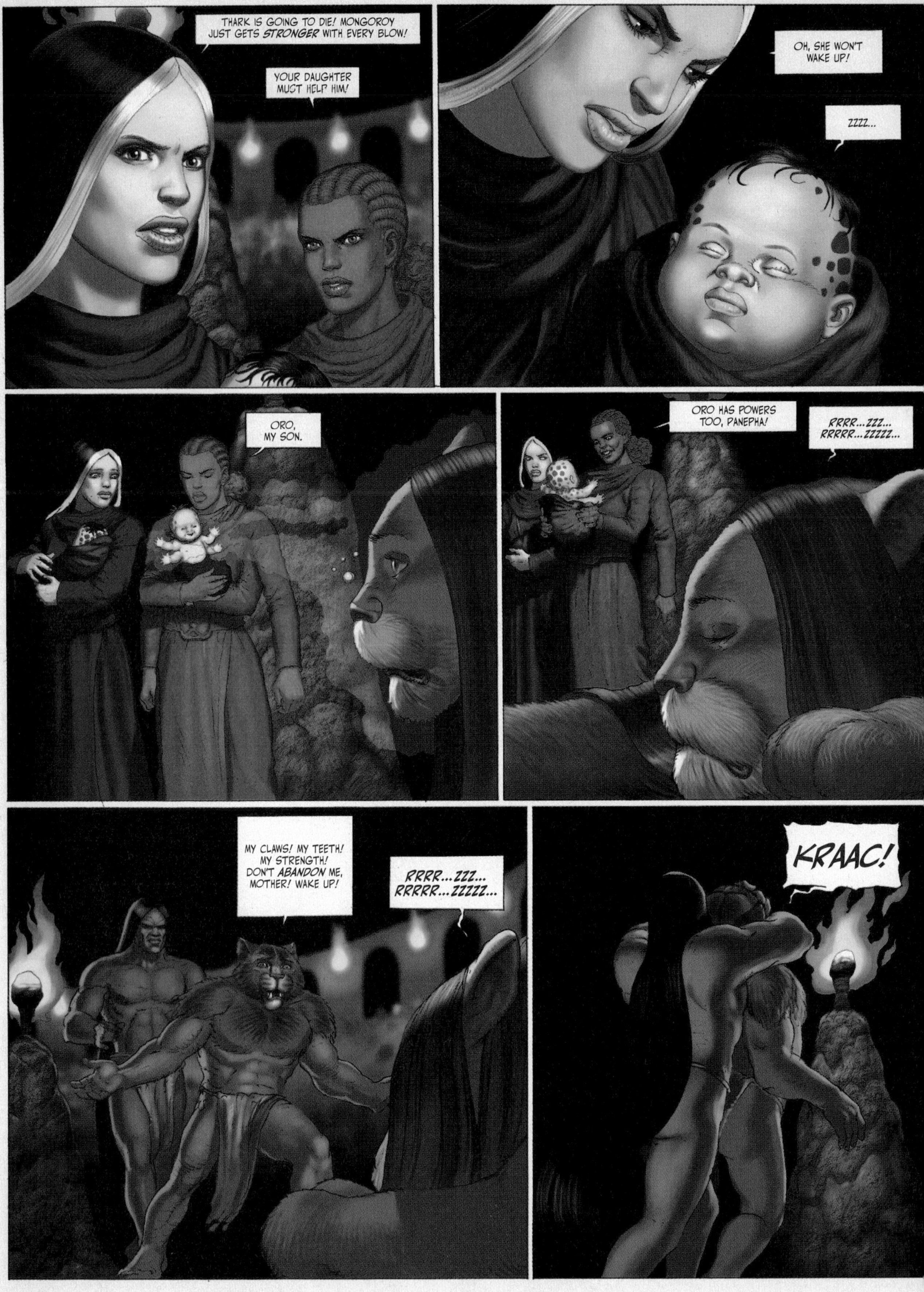
THARK IS GOING TO DIE! MONGOROY JUST GETS STRONGER WITH EVERY BLOW!
YOUR DAUGHTER MUST HELP HIM!
OH, SHE WON'T WAKE UP!
ZZZZ...
ORO, MY SON.
ORO HAS POWERS TOO, PANEPHA!
RRRR...ZZZ... RRRRR...ZZZZZ...
MY CLAWS! MY TEETH! MY STRENGTH! DON'T ABANDON ME, MOTHER! WAKE UP!
RRRR...ZZZ... RRRRR...ZZZZZ...
KRAAC!

GRROO

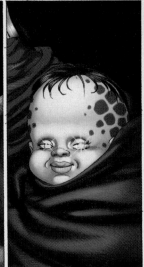

RRROOON...ROOON...RRRR...

THE CHAMPION!

THE CHAMPION!

THE CHAMPION!

MAY THARK, SON OF RAHMANIYAH, LIVE 1000 YEARS!

MAY THE FRESH WATER BE HIS!

MAY THE PLANET BE HIS!

OUR SUPREME LEADER!

YUM... GLORY TO OUR NEW PROPHET!

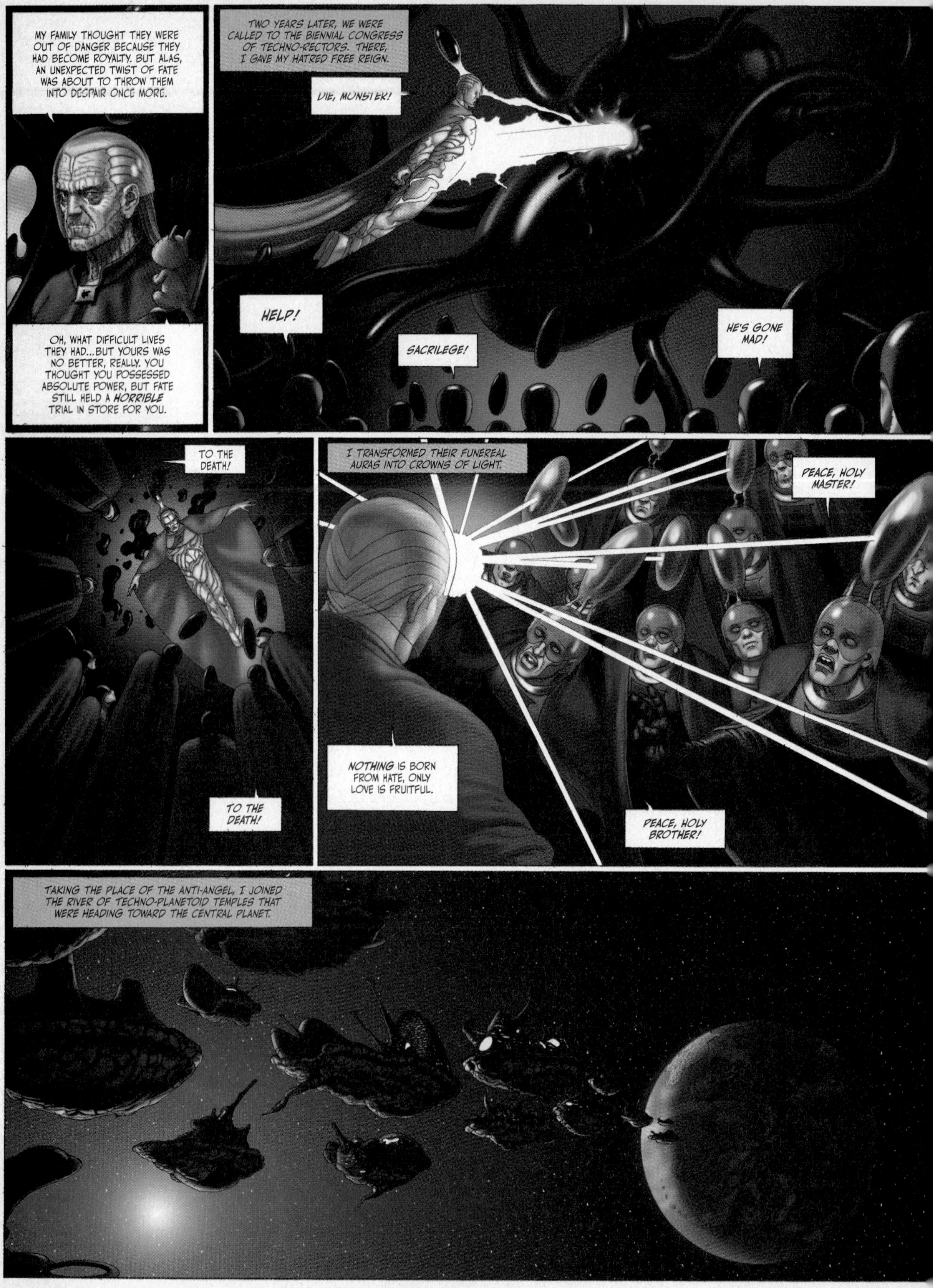

MY FAMILY THOUGHT THEY WERE OUT OF DANGER BECAUSE THEY HAD BECOME ROYALTY. BUT ALAS, AN UNEXPECTED TWIST OF FATE WAS ABOUT TO THROW THEM INTO DESPAIR ONCE MORE.
OH, WHAT DIFFICULT LIVES THEY HAD...BUT YOURS WAS NO BETTER, REALLY. YOU THOUGHT YOU POSSESSED ABSOLUTE POWER, BUT FATE STILL HELD A HORRIBLE TRIAL IN STORE FOR YOU.
TWO YEARS LATER, WE WERE CALLED TO THE BIENNIAL CONGRESS OF TECHNO-RECTORS. THERE, I GAVE MY HATRED FREE REIGN.
DIE, MONSTER!
HELP!
SACRILEGE!
HE'S GONE MAD!
TO THE DEATH!
TO THE DEATH!
I TRANSFORMED THEIR FUNEREAL AURAS INTO CROWNS OF LIGHT.
PEACE, HOLY MASTER!
NOTHING IS BORN FROM HATE, ONLY LOVE IS FRUITFUL.
PEACE, HOLY BROTHER!
TAKING THE PLACE OF THE ANTI-ANGEL, I JOINED THE RIVER OF TECHNO-PLANETOID TEMPLES THAT WERE HEADING TOWARD THE CENTRAL PLANET.

NO COMMITTEE CAME TO MEET US. THE TECHNO-VATICAN LOOKED LIKE A SLEEPING MONSTER...WE SAW NO SIGN OF LIFE...TOTAL SILENCE...WE APPROACHED...

THE TOWERS TURNED INTO CANONS AND STARTED SHOOTING AS IF WE WERE INVADERS. ABSURD!

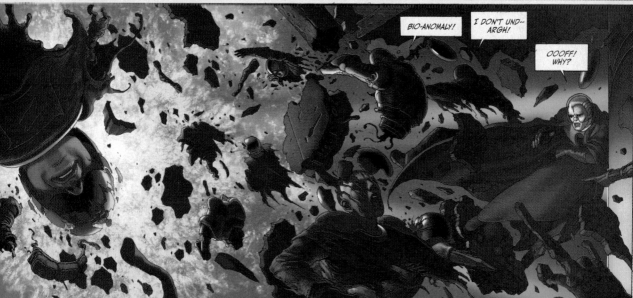

BIO-ANOMALY!

I DON'T UND-- ARGH!

OOOFF! WHY?

WHILE THE TECHNO-VATICAN DESTROYED ITS TECHNO-BISHOPS, I OPENED A SPECIAL RIFT--

--AND WENT THROUGH THE INTRAWORLD, EMERGING INTO THE COMMAND BOOTH.

93

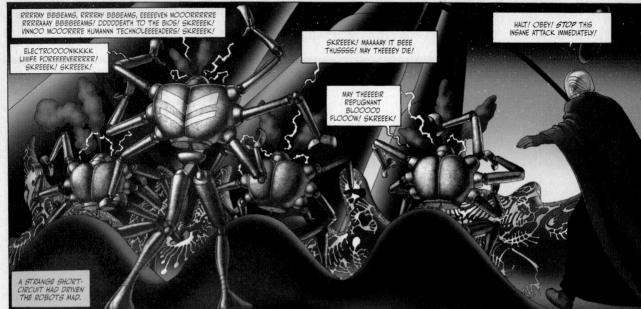

RRRRAY BBBEAMS, RRRRAY BBBEAMS, EEEEEVEN MOOORRRRRE RRRRAAAY BBBBEEAMS! DDDDDEATH TO THE BIOS! SKREEK! VNNOO MOOORRRE HUMANNN TECHNOLEEEEADERS! SKREEEK!

ELECTROOOONIKKKK LIIIIIFE FOREEEEVERRRRR! SKREEEK! SKREEEK!

SKREEEK! MAAAAAY IT BEEE THUSSSS! MAY THEEEEY DIE!

MAY THEEEEIR REPUGNANT BLOOOOD FLOOOW! SKREEEK!

HALT! OBEY! *STOP* THIS INSANE ATTACK IMMEDIATELY!

A STRANGE SHORT-CIRCUIT HAD DRIVEN THE ROBOTS MAD.

SKREEEK! DIIIEEE, BIO-INTRUUUDER!

THAT'S ONE!

THAT'S FIVE!

GAAAKKK!

SIX! YOU HAVE NO MORE LEFT!

A MORTAL SILENCE FELL ON THE FORTRESS. WHERE WAS THE SUPREME TECHNOPRIEST? AND THE OTHER TECHNOS? I WENT TO LOOK FOR THEM.

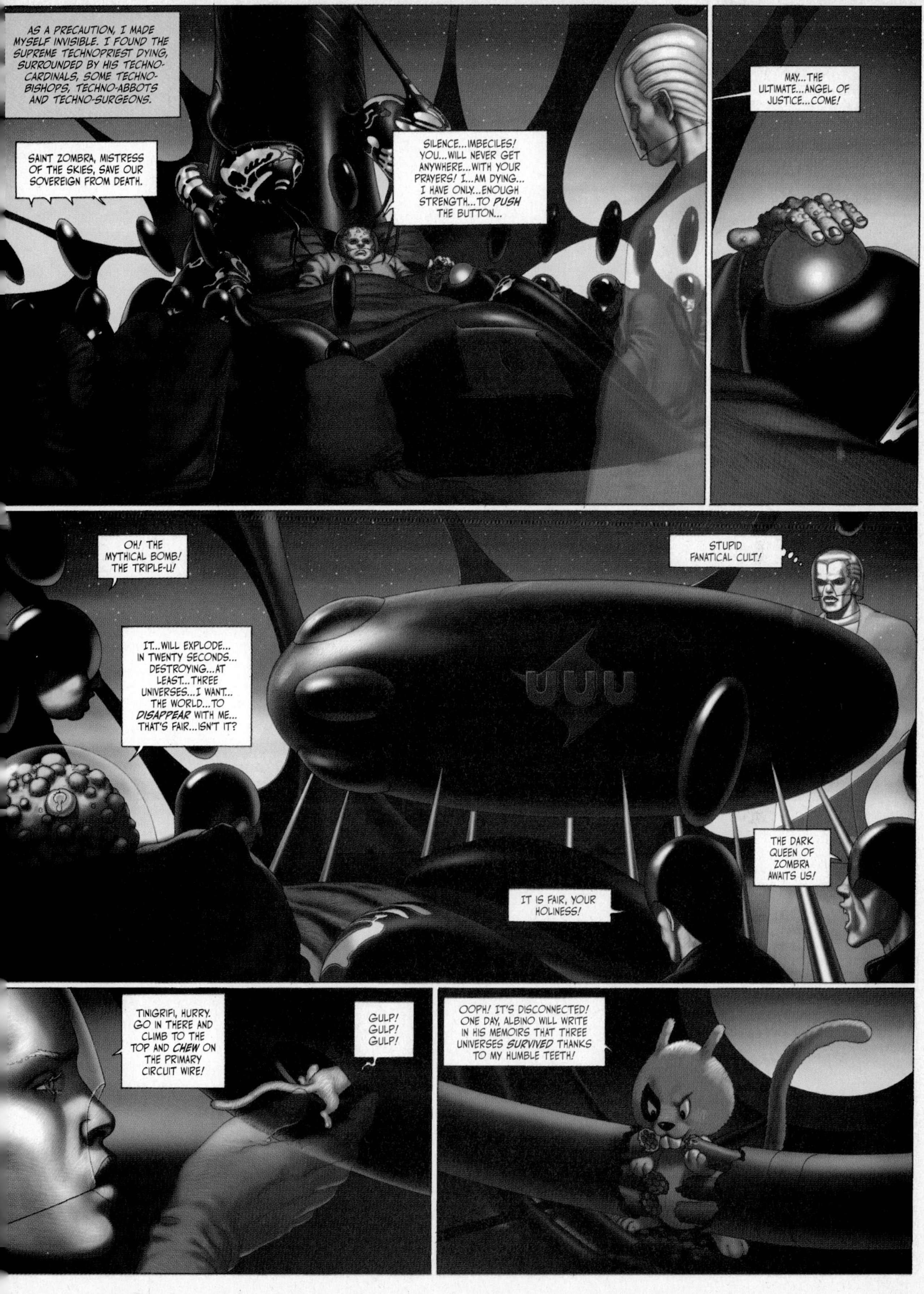
AS A PRECAUTION, I MADE MYSELF INVISIBLE. I FOUND THE SUPREME TECHNOPRIEST DYING, SURROUNDED BY HIS TECHNO-CARDINALS, SOME TECHNO-BISHOPS, TECHNO-ABBOTS AND TECHNO-SURGEONS.
SAINT ZOMBRA, MISTRESS OF THE SKIES, SAVE OUR SOVEREIGN FROM DEATH.
SILENCE...IMBECILES! YOU...WILL NEVER GET ANYWHERE...WITH YOUR PRAYERS! I...AM DYING... I HAVE ONLY...ENOUGH STRENGTH...TO PUSH THE BUTTON...
MAY...THE ULTIMATE...ANGEL OF JUSTICE...COME!
OH! THE MYTHICAL BOMB! THE TRIPLE-U!
STUPID FANATICAL CULT!
UUU
IT...WILL EXPLODE... IN TWENTY SECONDS... DESTROYING...AT LEAST...THREE UNIVERSES...I WANT... THE WORLD...TO DISAPPEAR WITH ME... THAT'S FAIR...ISN'T IT?
THE DARK QUEEN OF ZOMBRA AWAITS US!
IT IS FAIR, YOUR HOLINESS!
TINIGRIFI, HURRY. GO IN THERE AND CLIMB TO THE TOP AND CHEW ON THE PRIMARY CIRCUIT WIRE!
GULP! GULP! GULP!
OOPH! IT'S DISCONNECTED! ONE DAY, ALBINO WILL WRITE IN HIS MEMOIRS THAT THREE UNIVERSES SURVIVED THANKS TO MY HUMBLE TEETH!

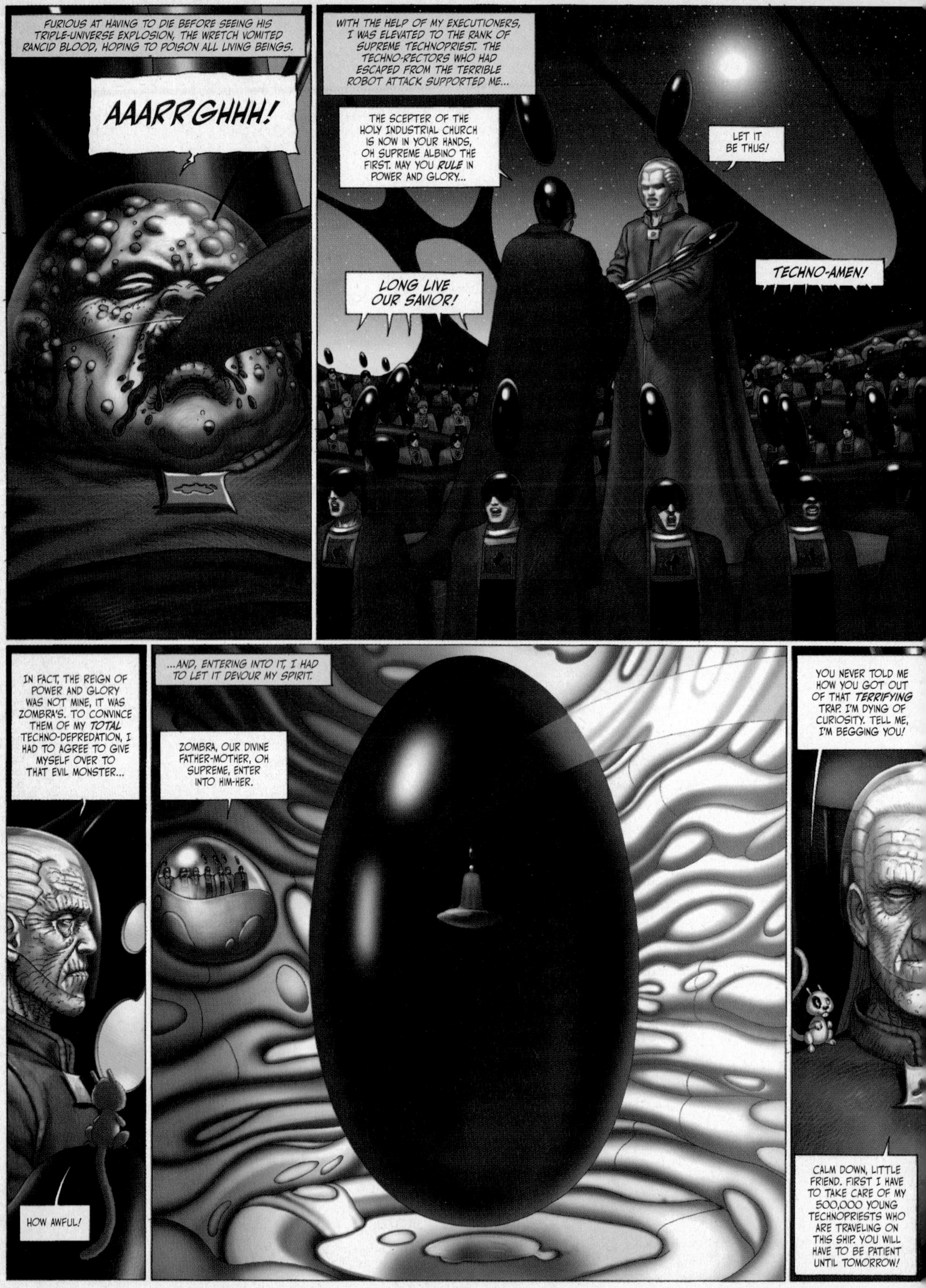
FURIOUS AT HAVING TO DIE BEFORE SEEING HIS TRIPLE-UNIVERSE EXPLOSION, THE WRETCH VOMITED RANCID BLOOD, HOPING TO POISON ALL LIVING BEINGS.
AAARRGHHH!
WITH THE HELP OF MY EXECUTIONERS, I WAS ELEVATED TO THE RANK OF SUPREME TECHNOPRIEST. THE TECHNO-RECTORS WHO HAD ESCAPED FROM THE TERRIBLE ROBOT ATTACK SUPPORTED ME...
THE SCEPTER OF THE HOLY INDUSTRIAL CHURCH IS NOW IN YOUR HANDS, OH SUPREME ALBINO THE FIRST. MAY YOU RULE IN POWER AND GLORY...
LET IT BE THUS!
LONG LIVE OUR SAVIOR!
TECHNO-AMEN!
IN FACT, THE REIGN OF POWER AND GLORY WAS NOT MINE, IT WAS ZOMBRA'S. TO CONVINCE THEM OF MY TOTAL TECHNO-DEPREDATION, I HAD TO AGREE TO GIVE MYSELF OVER TO THAT EVIL MONSTER...
HOW AWFUL!
...AND, ENTERING INTO IT, I HAD TO LET IT DEVOUR MY SPIRIT.
ZOMBRA, OUR DIVINE FATHER-MOTHER, OH SUPREME, ENTER INTO HIM-HER.
YOU NEVER TOLD ME HOW YOU GOT OUT OF THAT TERRIFYING TRAP. I'M DYING OF CURIOSITY. TELL ME, I'M BEGGING YOU!
CALM DOWN, LITTLE FRIEND. FIRST I HAVE TO TAKE CARE OF MY 500,000 YOUNG TECHNOPRIESTS WHO ARE TRAVELING ON THIS SHIP. YOU WILL HAVE TO BE PATIENT UNTIL TOMORROW!

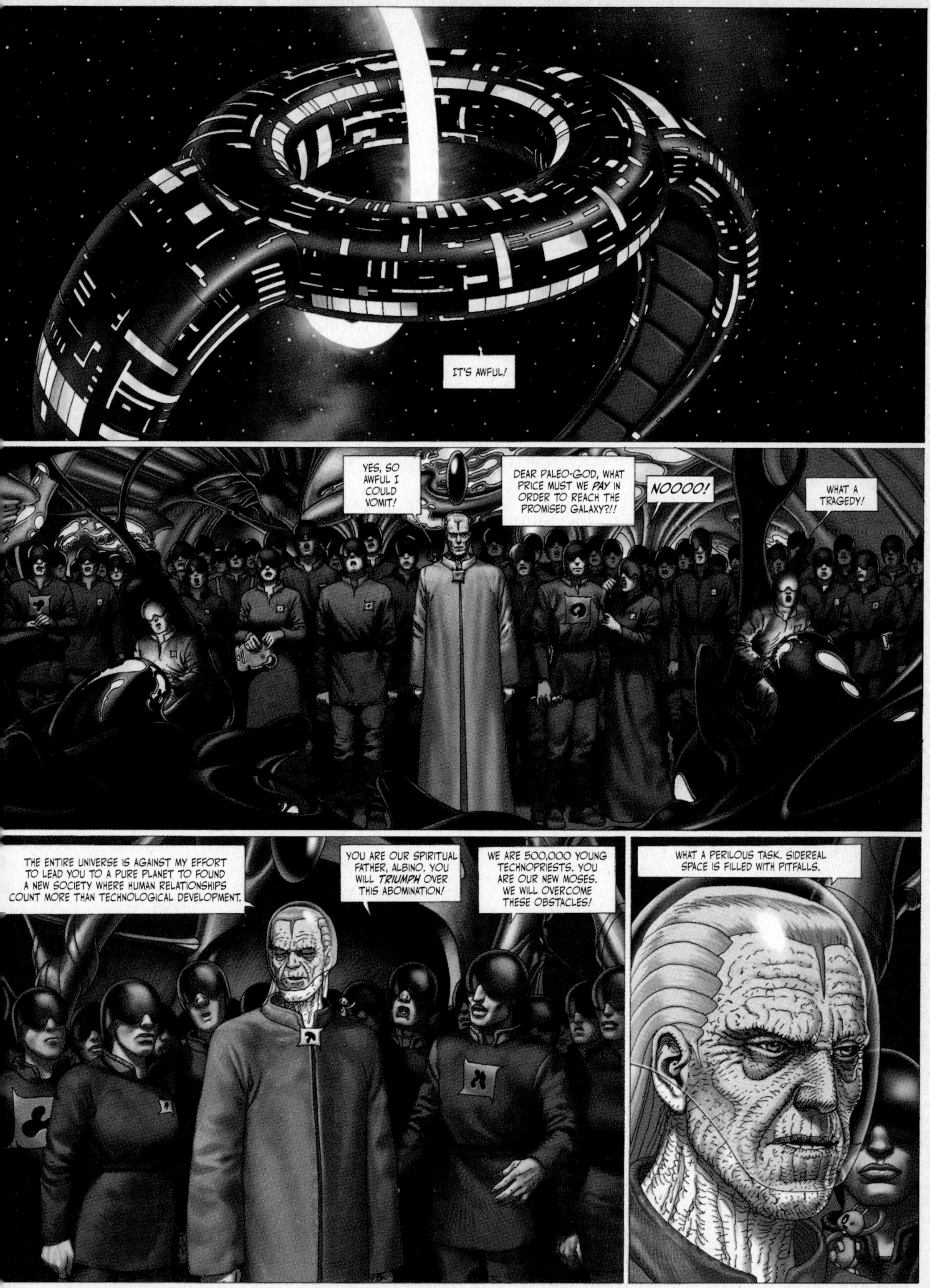
IT'S AWFUL!
YES, SO AWFUL I COULD VOMIT!
DEAR PALEO-GOD, WHAT PRICE MUST WE PAY IN ORDER TO REACH THE PROMISED GALAXY?!!
NOOOO!
WHAT A TRAGEDY!
THE ENTIRE UNIVERSE IS AGAINST MY EFFORT TO LEAD YOU TO A PURE PLANET TO FOUND A NEW SOCIETY WHERE HUMAN RELATIONSHIPS COUNT MORE THAN TECHNOLOGICAL DEVELOPMENT.
YOU ARE OUR SPIRITUAL FATHER, ALBINO. YOU WILL TRIUMPH OVER THIS ABOMINATION!
WE ARE 500,000 YOUNG TECHNOPRIESTS. YOU ARE OUR NEW MOSES. WE WILL OVERCOME THESE OBSTACLES!
WHAT A PERILOUS TASK. SIDEREAL SPACE IS FILLED WITH PITFALLS.

IN ADDITION TO THE VIOLENT PLASMA HURRICANES--

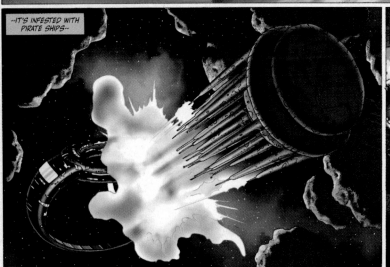

--IT'S INFESTED WITH PIRATE SHIPS--

--WITH DISGUSTING BARBARIANS--

--CANNIBAL FORESTS THAT SUCK OUT YOUR BRAINS--

--AND RAPIST COMETS.

AND YET THERE IS SOMETHING GREATER, MORE SHAMEFUL, MORE ABSURD THAN ALL THESE HORRORS: THE *PROLIFERATION* OF FILTH--

A VERITABLE ANT HILL!

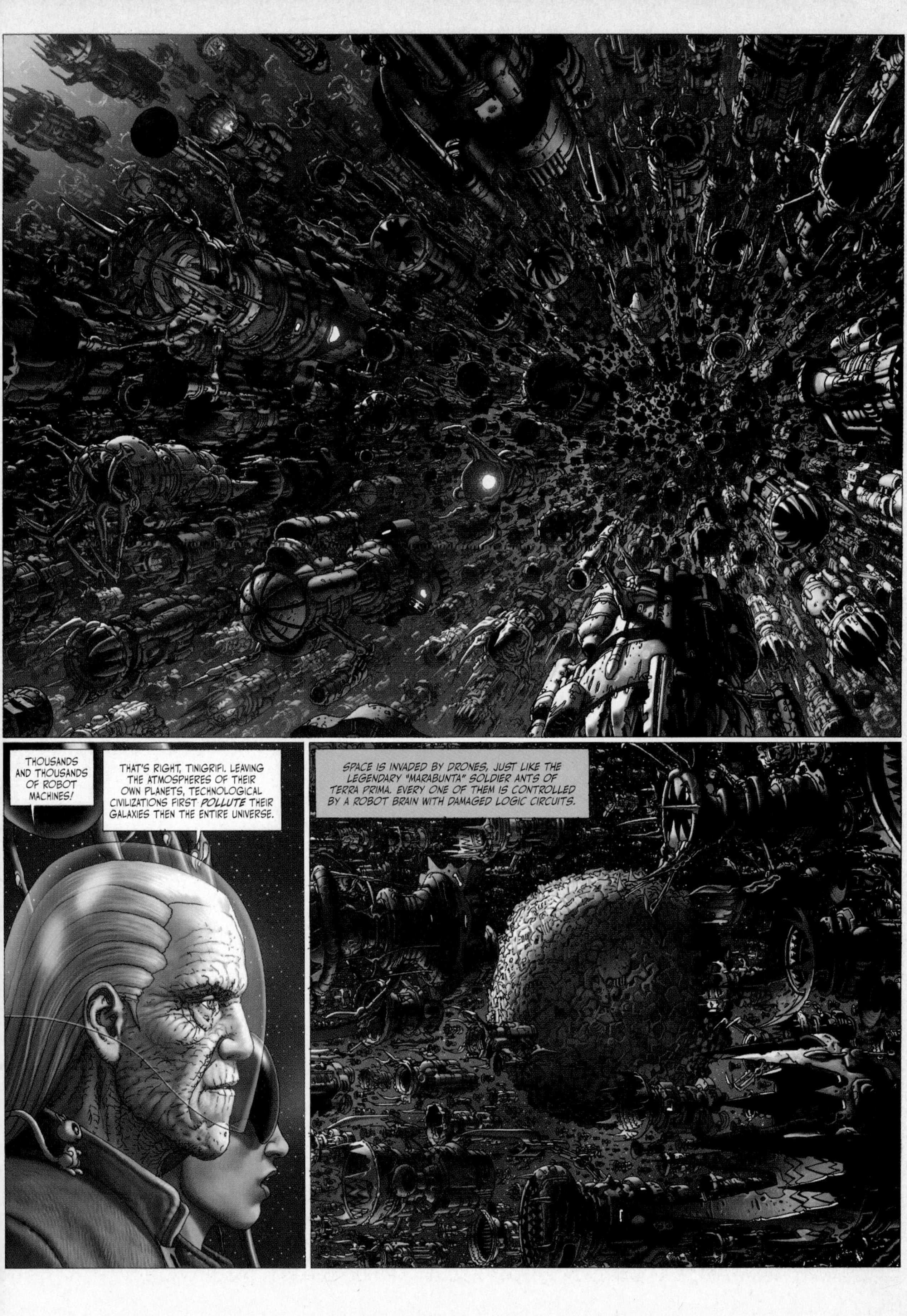
THOUSANDS AND THOUSANDS OF ROBOT MACHINES!
THAT'S RIGHT, TINIGRIFI. LEAVING THE ATMOSPHERES OF THEIR OWN PLANETS, TECHNOLOGICAL CIVILIZATIONS FIRST POLLUTE THEIR GALAXIES THEN THE ENTIRE UNIVERSE.
SPACE IS INVADED BY DRONES, JUST LIKE THE LEGENDARY "MARABUNTA" SOLDIER ANTS OF TERRA PRIMA. EVERY ONE OF THEM IS CONTROLLED BY A ROBOT BRAIN WITH DAMAGED LOGIC CIRCUITS.

I BLAME THE EXCESSIVE SCIENCE AND THE TOTAL LACK OF CONSCIENCE IN THE TECHNO INDUSTRY.

THESE ABSURD MACHINES FEEL NO HUNGER AND YET THEY DEVOUR ALL THAT LIES IN THEIR PATH--POINTLESS DESTRUCTION. THEIR "FOOD" IS INCINERATED IN THEIR ROBOSTOMACHS AND EXPELLED AS ASH.

THESE DISGUSTING MACHINES HAVE BECOME STERILE CREMATORIUMS, MY TINIGRIFI.

ENOUGH EXPLANATIONS, ALBINO. DO SOMETHING BEFORE THIS HORROR ATTACKS US!

MRKRRRR...

KRRR...

MRKRRRRR...

CZIIICZR...

KRRRR....

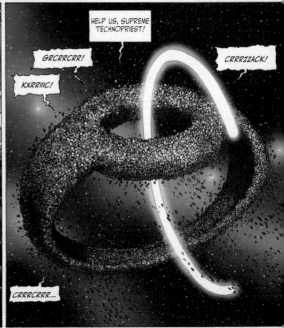

HELP US, SUPREME TECHNOPRIEST!

GRCRRCRR!

KXRRIIIC!

CRRRZZACK!

CRRRCRRR...

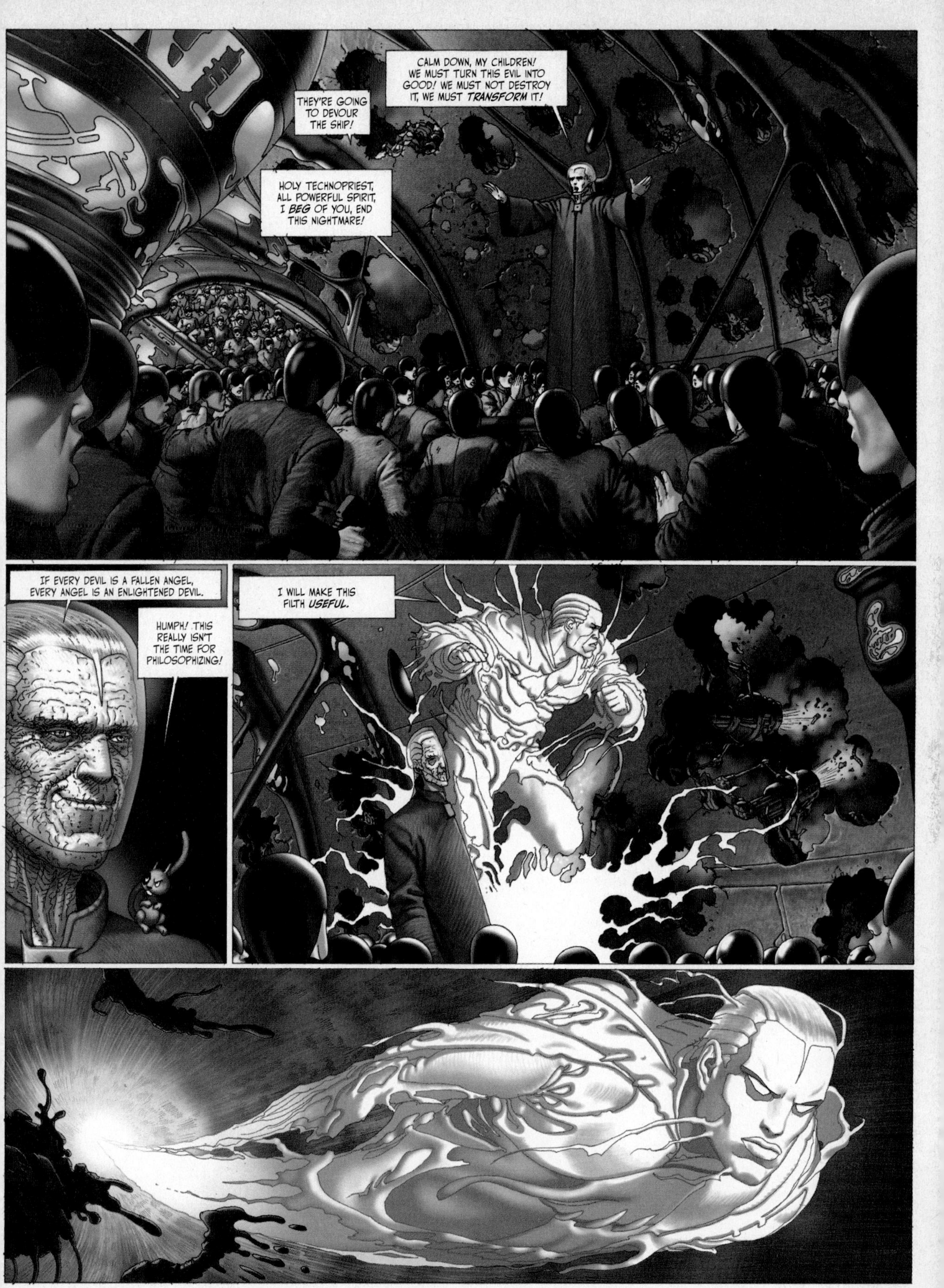
CALM DOWN, MY CHILDREN! WE MUST TURN THIS EVIL INTO GOOD! WE MUST NOT DESTROY IT, WE MUST TRANSFORM IT!
THEY'RE GOING TO DEVOUR THE SHIP!
HOLY TECHNOPRIEST, ALL POWERFUL SPIRIT, I BEG OF YOU, END THIS NIGHTMARE!
IF EVERY DEVIL IS A FALLEN ANGEL, EVERY ANGEL IS AN ENLIGHTENED DEVIL.
HUMPH! THIS REALLY ISN'T THE TIME FOR PHILOSOPHIZING!
I WILL MAKE THIS FILTH USEFUL.

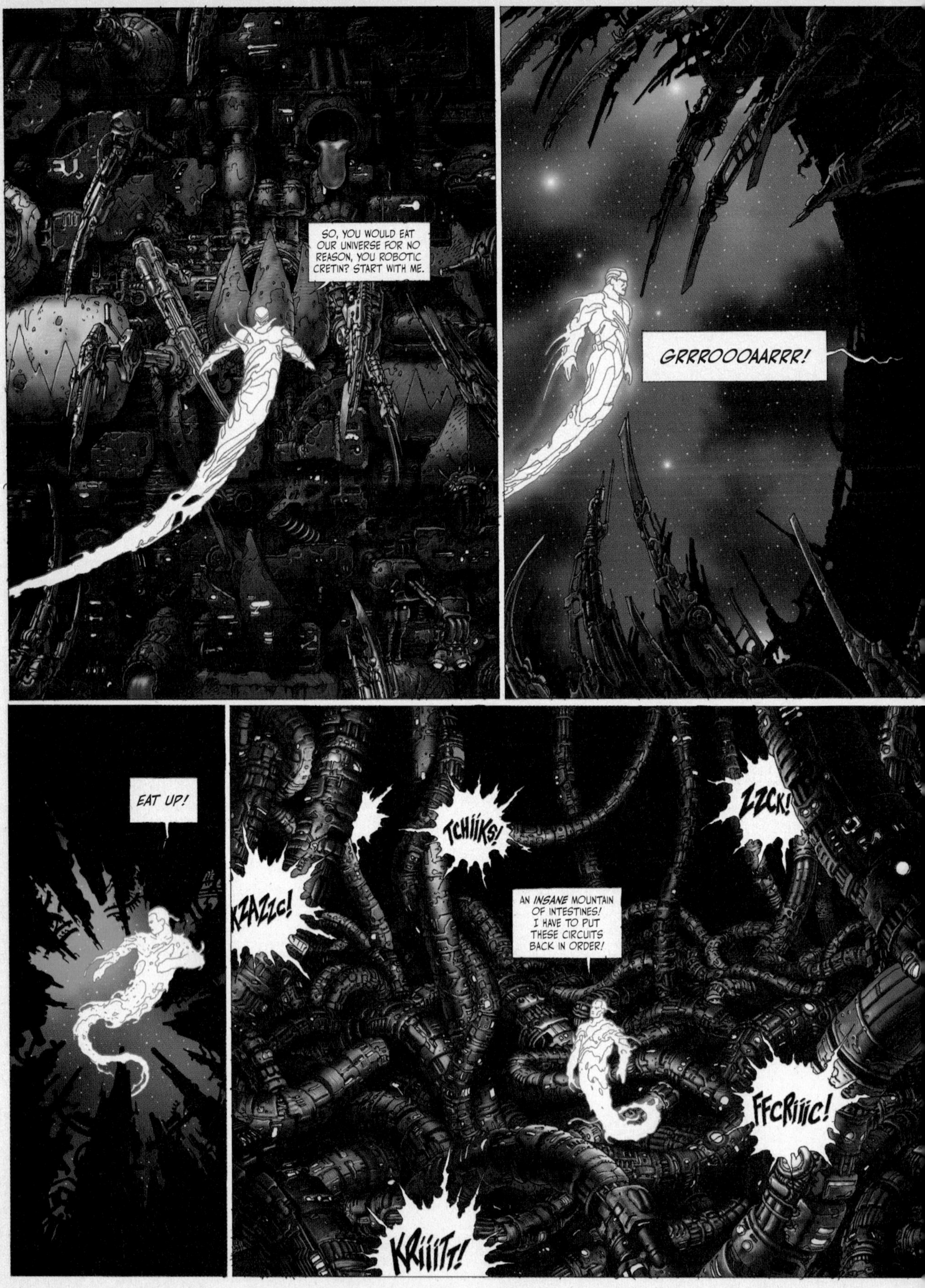
SO, YOU WOULD EAT OUR UNIVERSE FOR NO REASON, YOU ROBOTIC CRETIN? START WITH ME.
GRRROOOAARRR!
EAT UP!
TCHIIKS!
ZZCK!
KZAZZC!
AN *INSANE* MOUNTAIN OF INTESTINES! I HAVE TO PUT THESE CIRCUITS BACK IN ORDER!
FFCRIIIC!
KRIIITT!

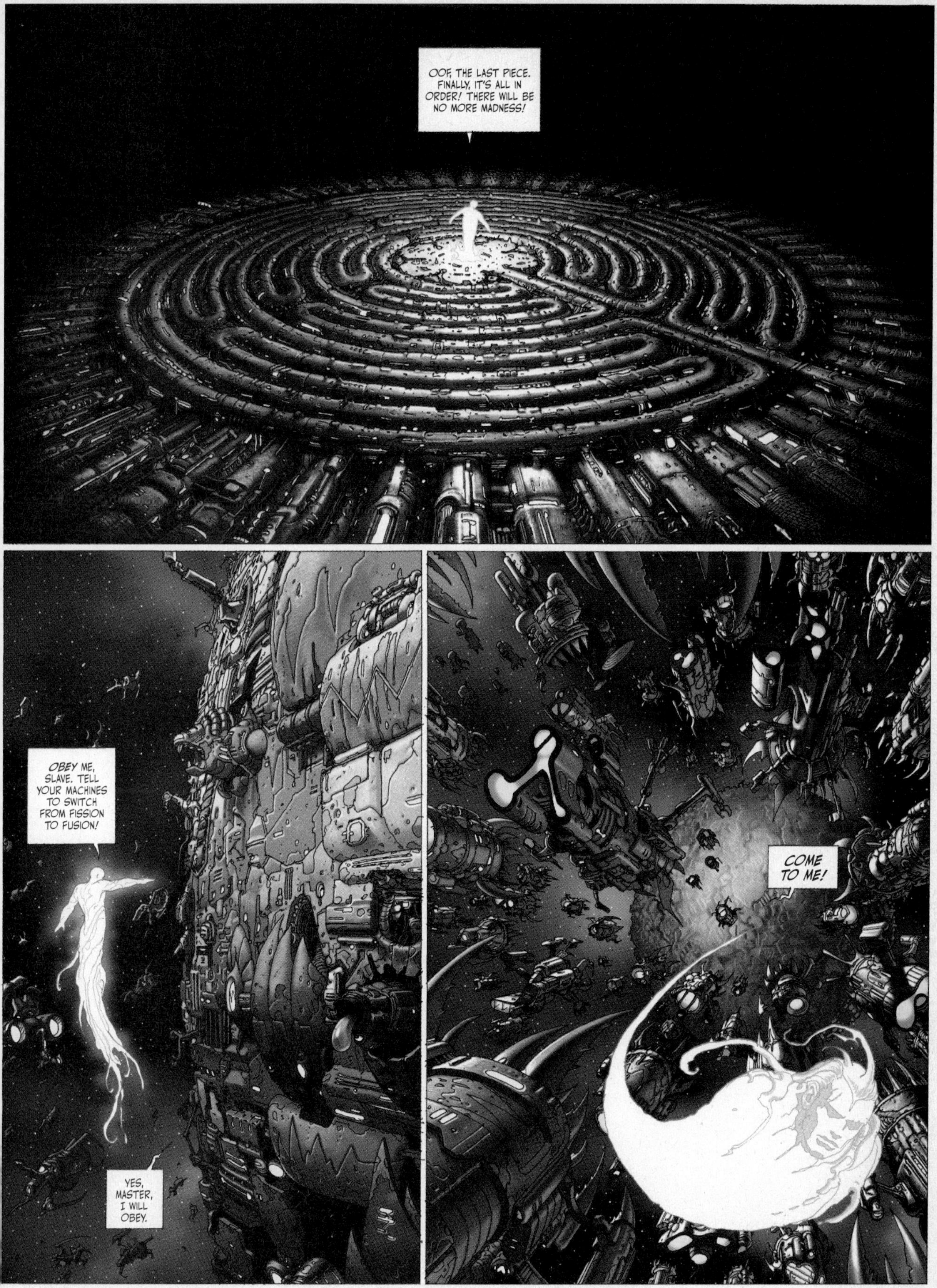
OOF, THE LAST PIECE. FINALLY, IT'S ALL IN ORDER! THERE WILL BE NO MORE MADNESS!
OBEY ME, SLAVE. TELL YOUR MACHINES TO SWITCH FROM FISSION TO FUSION!
YES, MASTER, I WILL OBEY.
COME TO ME!

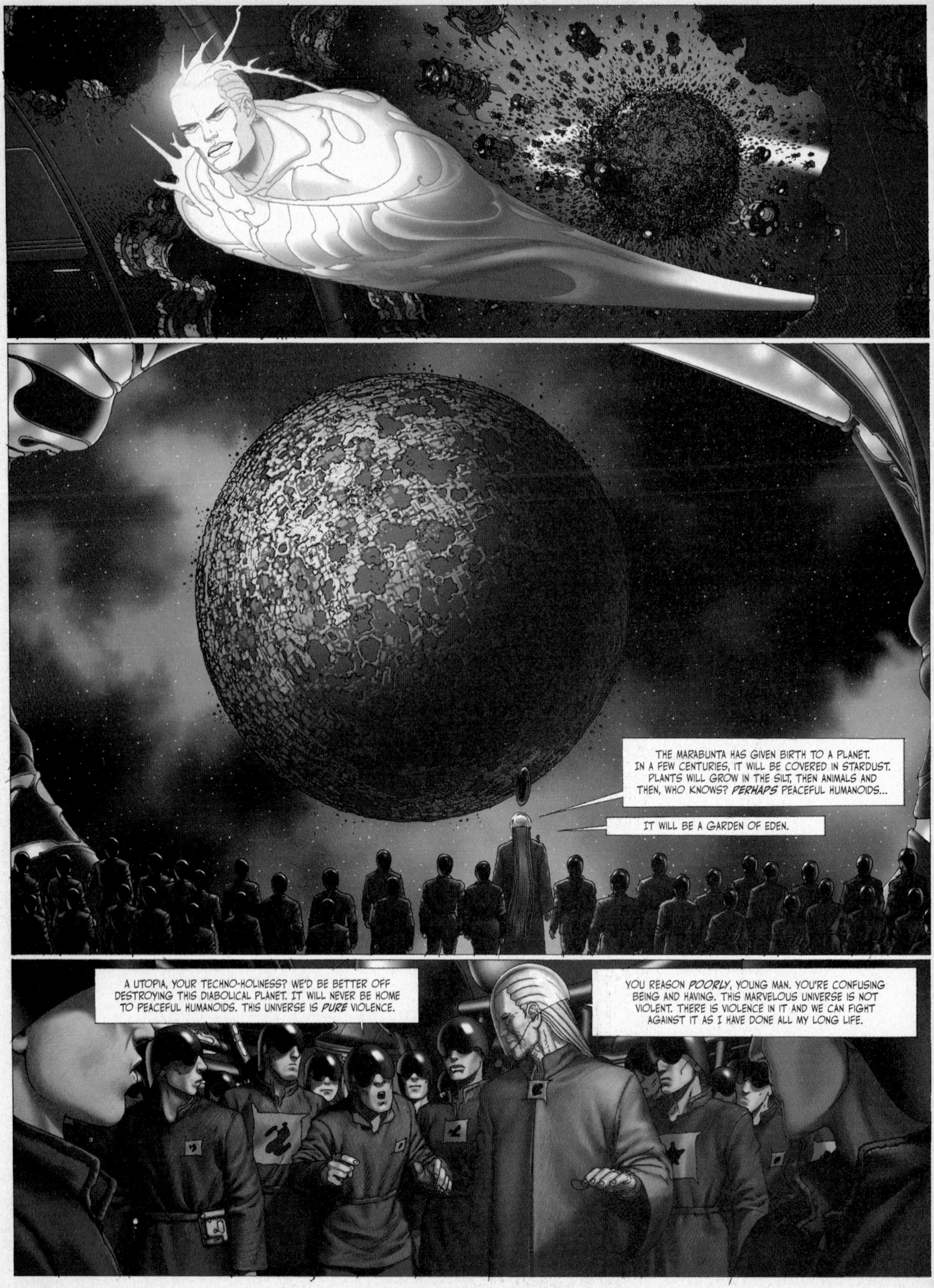
THE MARABUNTA HAS GIVEN BIRTH TO A PLANET. IN A FEW CENTURIES, IT WILL BE COVERED IN STARDUST. PLANTS WILL GROW IN THE SILT, THEN ANIMALS AND THEN, WHO KNOWS? *PERHAPS* PEACEFUL HUMANOIDS...
IT WILL BE A GARDEN OF EDEN.
A UTOPIA, YOUR TECHNO-HOLINESS? WE'D BE BETTER OFF DESTROYING THIS DIABOLICAL PLANET. IT WILL NEVER BE HOME TO PEACEFUL HUMANOIDS. THIS UNIVERSE IS *PURE* VIOLENCE.
YOU REASON *POORLY*, YOUNG MAN. YOU'RE CONFUSING BEING AND HAVING. THIS MARVELOUS UNIVERSE IS NOT VIOLENT. THERE IS VIOLENCE IN IT AND WE CAN FIGHT AGAINST IT AS I HAVE DONE ALL MY LONG LIFE.

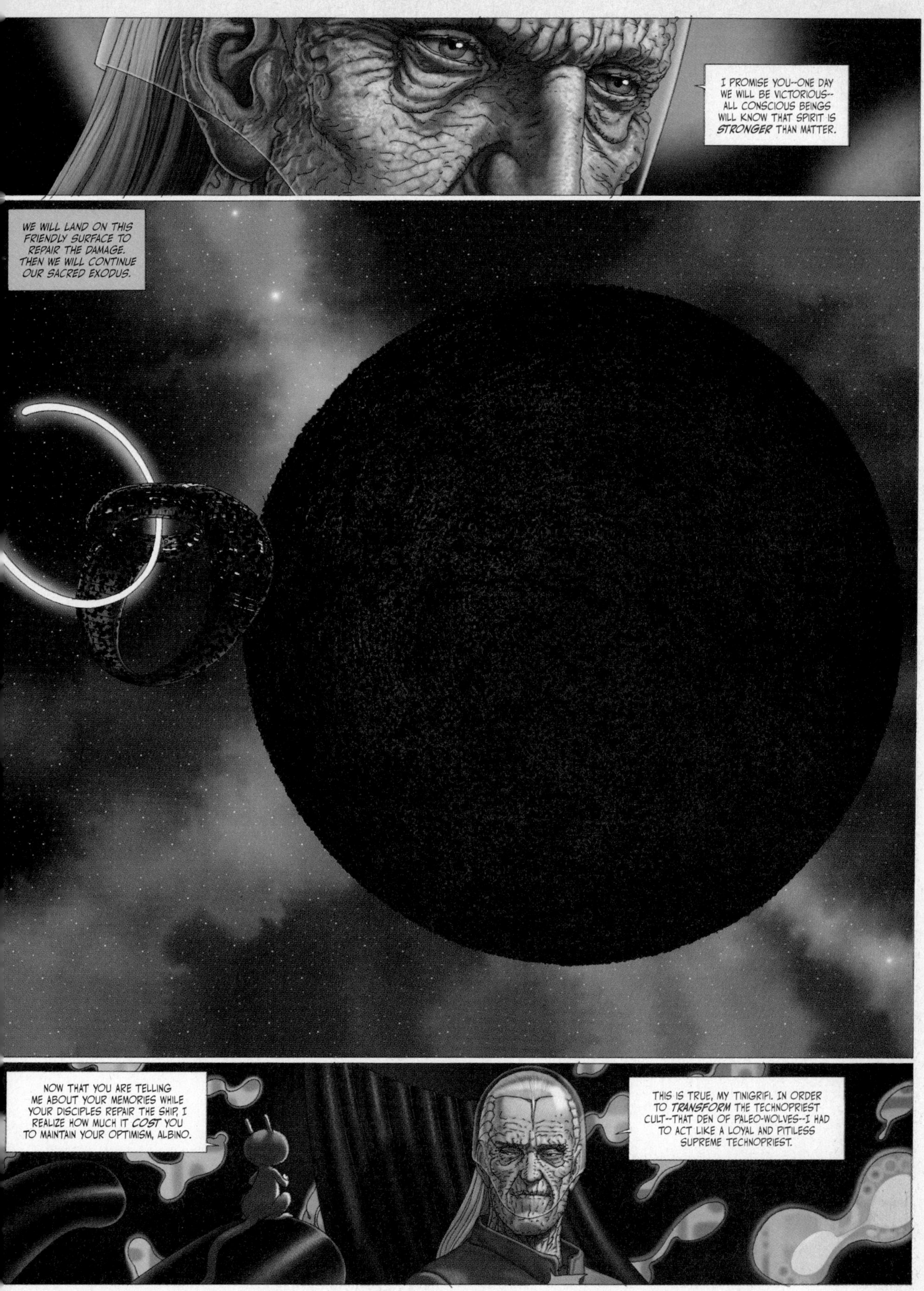
I PROMISE YOU--ONE DAY WE WILL BE VICTORIOUS--ALL CONSCIOUS BEINGS WILL KNOW THAT SPIRIT IS STRONGER THAN MATTER.
WE WILL LAND ON THIS FRIENDLY SURFACE TO REPAIR THE DAMAGE. THEN WE WILL CONTINUE OUR SACRED EXODUS.
NOW THAT YOU ARE TELLING ME ABOUT YOUR MEMORIES WHILE YOUR DISCIPLES REPAIR THE SHIP, I REALIZE HOW MUCH IT COST YOU TO MAINTAIN YOUR OPTIMISM, ALBINO.
THIS IS TRUE, MY TINIGRIFI. IN ORDER TO TRANSFORM THE TECHNOPRIEST CULT--THAT DEN OF PALEO-WOLVES--I HAD TO ACT LIKE A LOYAL AND PITILESS SUPREME TECHNOPRIEST.

I GIVE YOU THE SCEPTRE OF THE INDUSTRIAL CHURCH, OH TECHNO-SAINT ALBINO THE FIRST.

LET IT BE THUS!

LONG LIVE OUR PASTOR!

TECHNO-AMEN!

THE DARK SACRED CRYPT *OFFERS* YOU ITS MYSTERY...

HATAAN, THE ANTI-ARCHANGEL WILL CONFIRM YOU. IF YOU TRULY ARE A SUPREME TECHNOPRIEST, ENTRUST YOURSELF TO HIM.

I ENTRUST MYSELF! MAY MY SPIRIT DISSOLVE IN THE DEPTHS OF HIS BEING!

AND TO CONVINCE THEM OF MY ABSOLUTE TECHNO-DEVOTION, I HAD TO ENTER INTO THAT GREEDY FILTH.

WHAT A MONSTROSITY! YOU NEVER DID TELL ME HOW YOU GOT OUT OF THAT TERRIFYING TRAP UNSCATHED. I'M DYING OF CURIOSITY. TELL ME, PLEASE!

WITH THE HELP OF MY MENTAL POWERS, I *STOPPED* THE COURSE OF TIME.

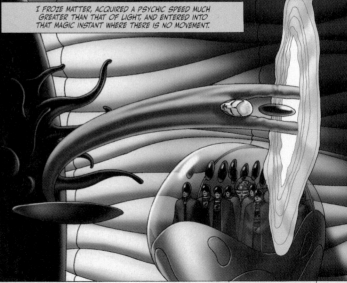

I FROZE MATTER, ACQUIRED A PSYCHIC SPEED MUCH GREATER THAN THAT OF LIGHT, AND ENTERED INTO THAT MAGIC INSTANT WHERE THERE IS NO MOVEMENT.

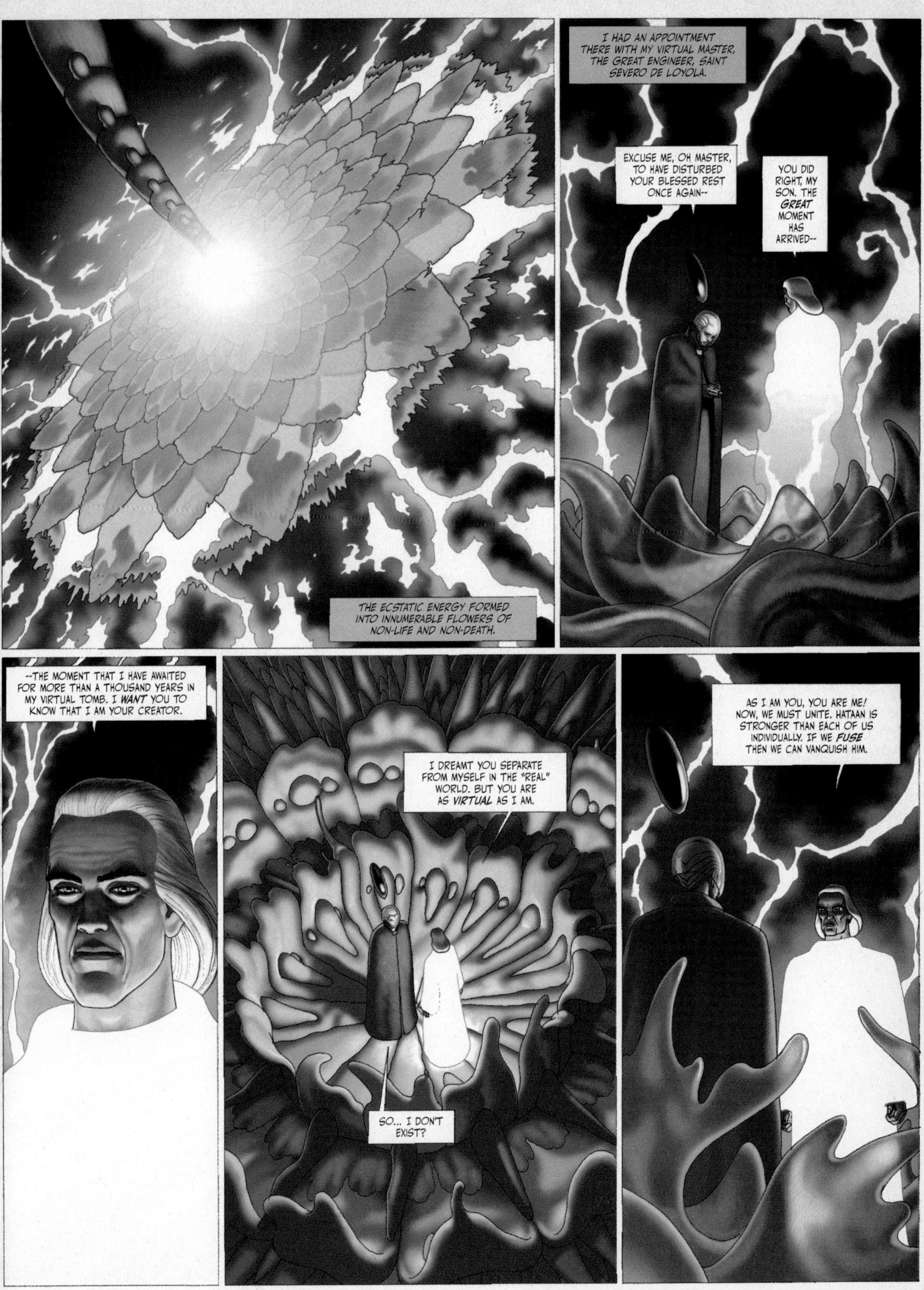
THE ECSTATIC ENERGY FORMED INTO INNUMERABLE FLOWERS OF NON-LIFE AND NON-DEATH.
I HAD AN APPOINTMENT THERE WITH MY VIRTUAL MASTER, THE GREAT ENGINEER, SAINT SEVERO DE LOYOLA.
EXCUSE ME, OH MASTER, TO HAVE DISTURBED YOUR BLESSED REST ONCE AGAIN--
YOU DID RIGHT, MY SON. THE GREAT MOMENT HAS ARRIVED--
--THE MOMENT THAT I HAVE AWAITED FOR MORE THAN A THOUSAND YEARS IN MY VIRTUAL TOMB. I WANT YOU TO KNOW THAT I AM YOUR CREATOR.
I DREAMT YOU SEPARATE FROM MYSELF IN THE "REAL" WORLD. BUT YOU ARE AS VIRTUAL AS I AM.
SO... I DON'T EXIST?
AS I AM YOU, YOU ARE ME! NOW, WE MUST UNITE. HATAAN IS STRONGER THAN EACH OF US INDIVIDUALLY. IF WE FUSE THEN WE CAN VANQUISH HIM.

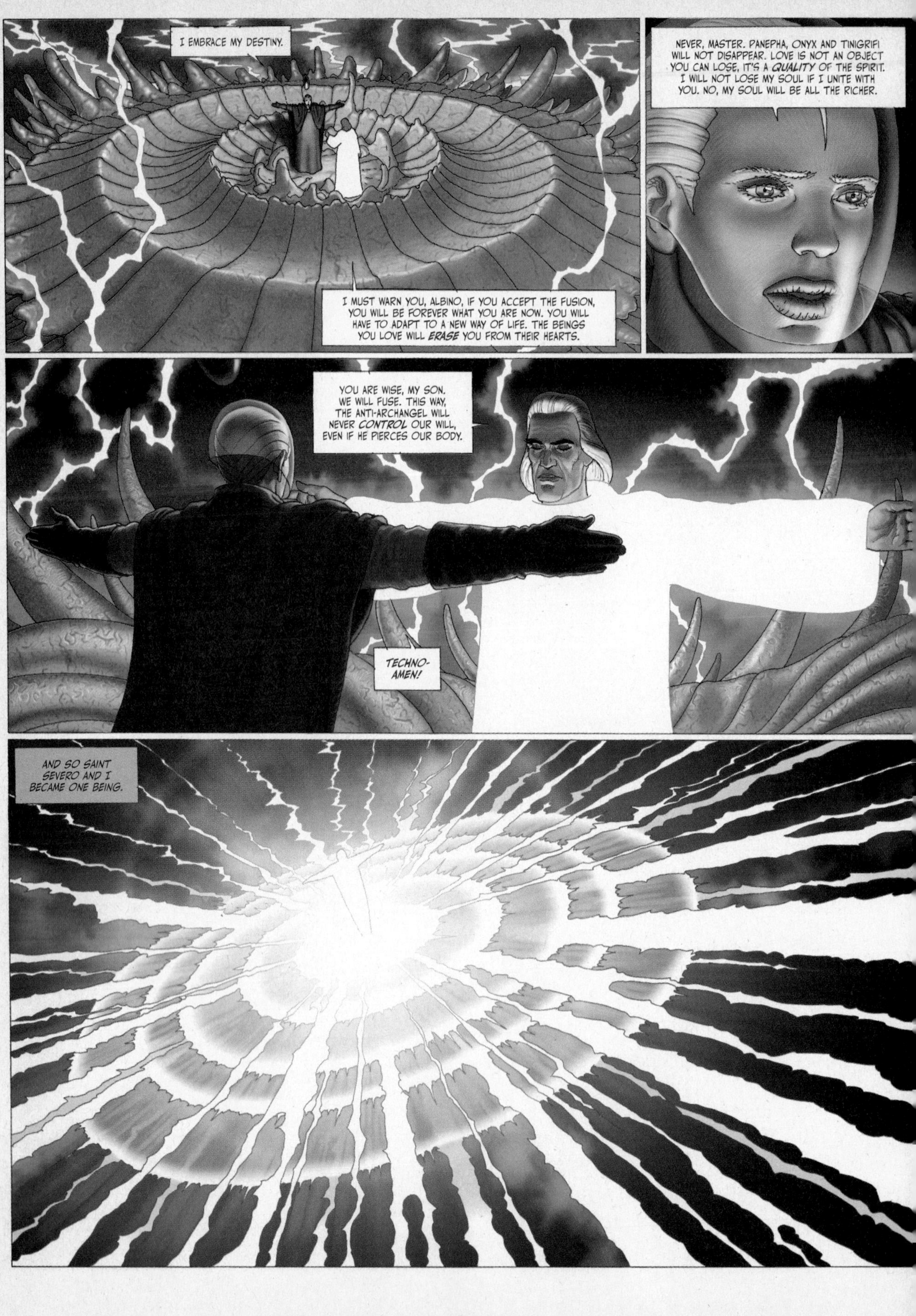
I EMBRACE MY DESTINY.
I MUST WARN YOU, ALBINO, IF YOU ACCEPT THE FUSION, YOU WILL BE FOREVER WHAT YOU ARE NOW. YOU WILL HAVE TO ADAPT TO A NEW WAY OF LIFE. THE BEINGS YOU LOVE WILL ERASE YOU FROM THEIR HEARTS.
NEVER, MASTER. PANEPHA, ONYX AND TINIGRIFI WILL NOT DISAPPEAR. LOVE IS NOT AN OBJECT YOU CAN LOSE, IT'S A QUALITY OF THE SPIRIT. I WILL NOT LOSE MY SOUL IF I UNITE WITH YOU. NO, MY SOUL WILL BE ALL THE RICHER.
YOU ARE WISE, MY SON. WE WILL FUSE. THIS WAY, THE ANTI-ARCHANGEL WILL NEVER CONTROL OUR WILL, EVEN IF HE PIERCES OUR BODY.
TECHNO-AMEN!
AND SO SAINT SEVERO AND I BECAME ONE BEING.

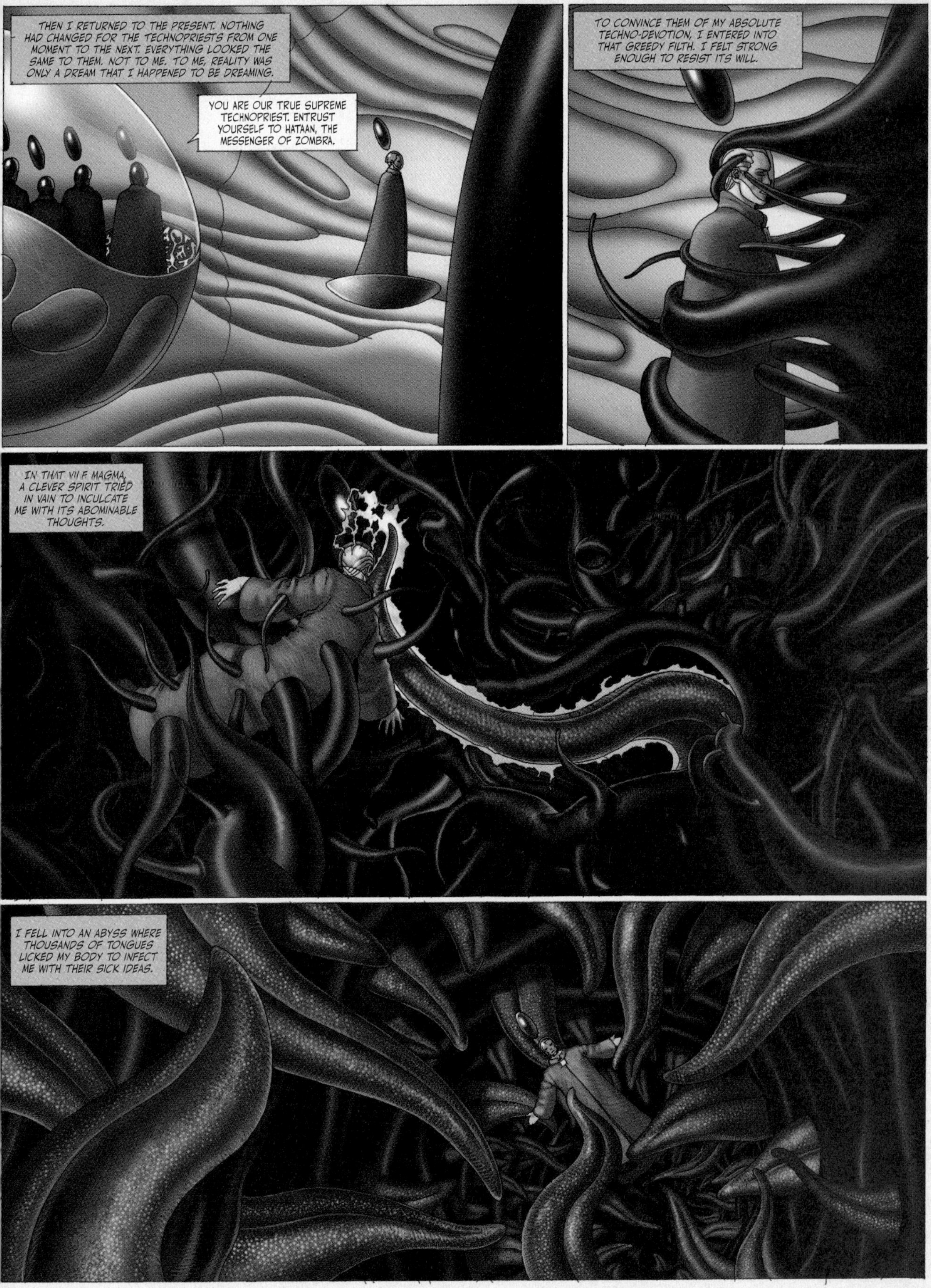
THEN I RETURNED TO THE PRESENT. NOTHING HAD CHANGED FOR THE TECHNOPRIESTS FROM ONE MOMENT TO THE NEXT. EVERYTHING LOOKED THE SAME TO THEM. NOT TO ME. TO ME, REALITY WAS ONLY A DREAM THAT I HAPPENED TO BE DREAMING.
YOU ARE OUR TRUE SUPREME TECHNOPRIEST. ENTRUST YOURSELF TO HATAAN, THE MESSENGER OF ZOMBRA.
TO CONVINCE THEM OF MY ABSOLUTE TECHNO-DEVOTION, I ENTERED INTO THAT GREEDY FILTH. I FELT STRONG ENOUGH TO RESIST ITS WILL.
IN THAT VILE MAGMA, A CLEVER SPIRIT TRIED IN VAIN TO INCULCATE ME WITH ITS ABOMINABLE THOUGHTS.
I FELL INTO AN ABYSS WHERE THOUSANDS OF TONGUES LICKED MY BODY TO INFECT ME WITH THEIR SICK IDEAS.

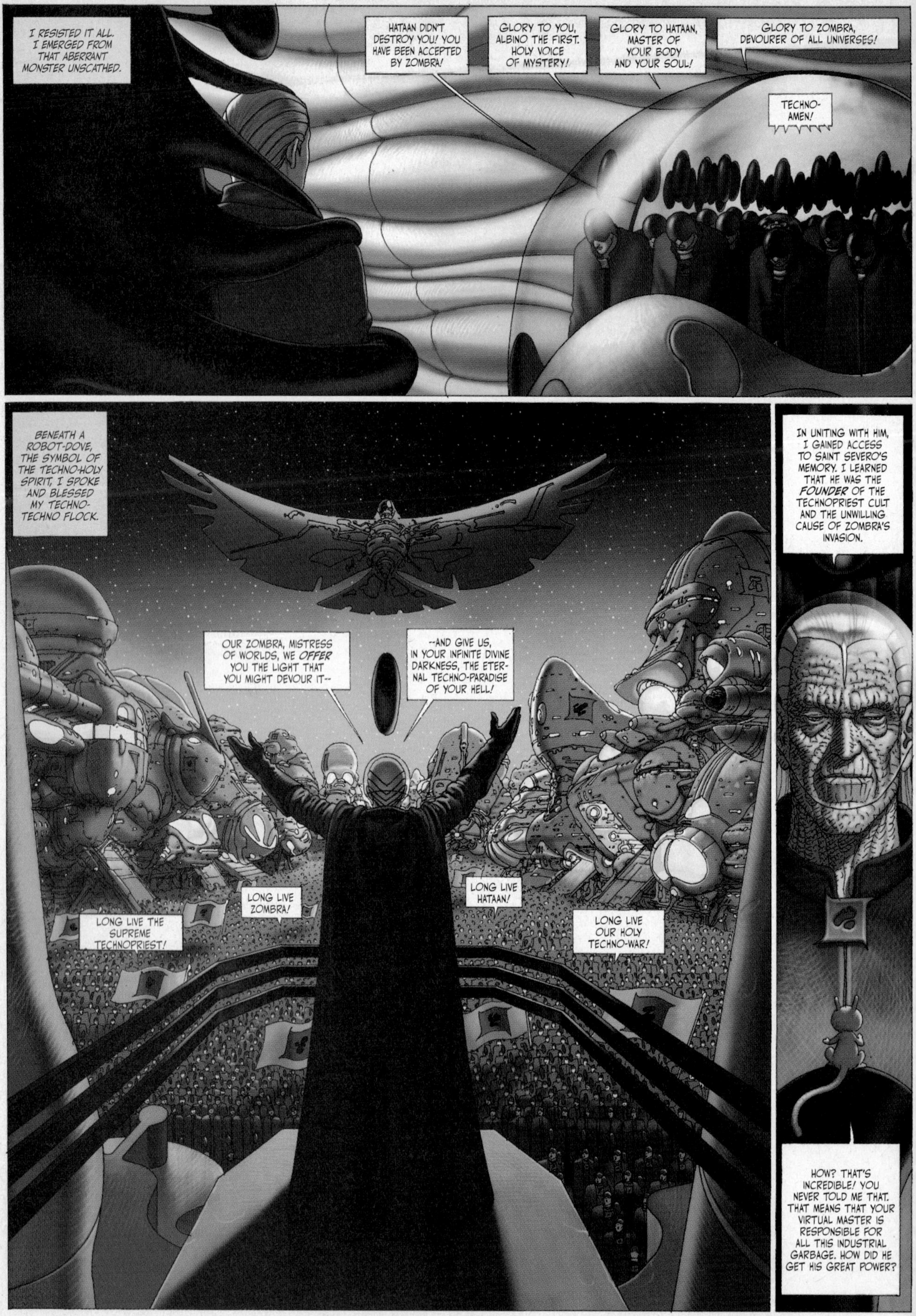

I RESISTED IT ALL. I EMERGED FROM THAT ABERRANT MONSTER UNSCATHED.
HATAAN DIDN'T DESTROY YOU! YOU HAVE BEEN ACCEPTED BY ZOMBRA!
GLORY TO YOU, ALBINO THE FIRST. HOLY VOICE OF MYSTERY!
GLORY TO HATAAN, MASTER OF YOUR BODY AND YOUR SOUL!
GLORY TO ZOMBRA, DEVOURER OF ALL UNIVERSES!
TECHNO-AMEN!
BENEATH A ROBOT-DOVE, THE SYMBOL OF THE TECHNO-HOLY SPIRIT, I SPOKE AND BLESSED MY TECHNO-TECHNO FLOCK.
OUR ZOMBRA, MISTRESS OF WORLDS, WE OFFER YOU THE LIGHT THAT YOU MIGHT DEVOUR IT--
--AND GIVE US, IN YOUR INFINITE DIVINE DARKNESS, THE ETERNAL TECHNO-PARADISE OF YOUR HELL!
LONG LIVE THE SUPREME TECHNOPRIEST!
LONG LIVE ZOMBRA!
LONG LIVE HATAAN!
LONG LIVE OUR HOLY TECHNO-WAR!
IN UNITING WITH HIM, I GAINED ACCESS TO SAINT SEVERO'S MEMORY. I LEARNED THAT HE WAS THE FOUNDER OF THE TECHNOPRIEST CULT AND THE UNWILLING CAUSE OF ZOMBRA'S INVASION.
HOW? THAT'S INCREDIBLE! YOU NEVER TOLD ME THAT. THAT MEANS THAT YOUR VIRTUAL MASTER IS RESPONSIBLE FOR ALL THIS INDUSTRIAL GARBAGE. HOW DID HE GET HIS GREAT POWER?

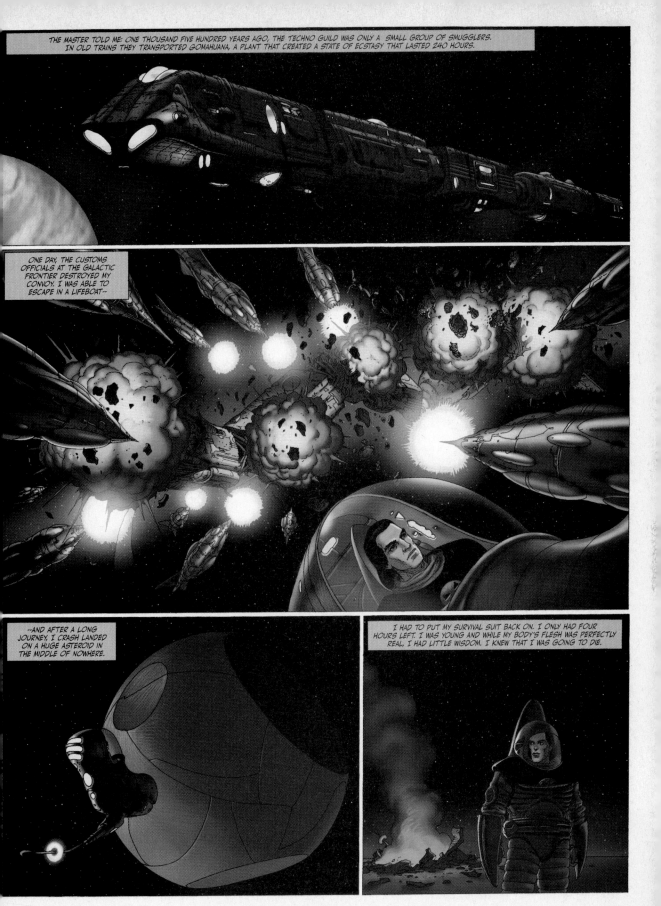

THE MASTER TOLD ME: ONE THOUSAND FIVE HUNDRED YEARS AGO, THE TECHNO GUILD WAS ONLY A SMALL GROUP OF SMUGGLERS. IN OLD TRAINS THEY TRANSPORTED GOMAHUANA, A PLANT THAT CREATED A STATE OF ECSTASY THAT LASTED 240 HOURS.

ONE DAY, THE CUSTOMS OFFICIALS AT THE GALACTIC FRONTIER DESTROYED MY CONVOY. I WAS ABLE TO ESCAPE IN A LIFEBOAT--

--AND AFTER A LONG JOURNEY, I CRASH LANDED ON A HUGE ASTEROID IN THE MIDDLE OF NOWHERE.

I HAD TO PUT MY SURVIVAL SUIT BACK ON. I ONLY HAD FOUR HOURS LEFT. I WAS YOUNG AND WHILE MY BODY'S FLESH WAS PERFECTLY REAL, I HAD LITTLE WISDOM. I KNEW THAT I WAS GOING TO DIE.

111

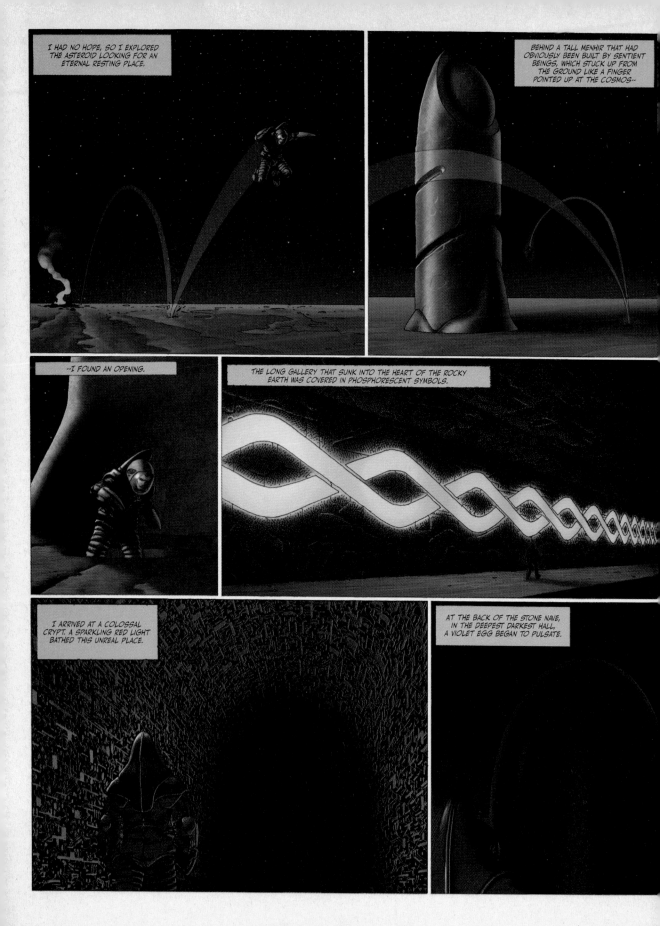

I HAD NO HOPE, SO I EXPLORED THE ASTEROID LOOKING FOR AN ETERNAL RESTING PLACE.

BEHIND A TALL MENHIR THAT HAD OBVIOUSLY BEEN BUILT BY SENTIENT BEINGS, WHICH STUCK UP FROM THE GROUND LIKE A FINGER POINTED UP AT THE COSMOS--

--I FOUND AN OPENING.

THE LONG GALLERY THAT SUNK INTO THE HEART OF THE ROCKY EARTH WAS COVERED IN PHOSPHORESCENT SYMBOLS.

I ARRIVED AT A COLOSSAL CRYPT. A SPARKLING RED LIGHT BATHED THIS UNREAL PLACE.

AT THE BACK OF THE STONE NAVE, IN THE DEEPEST DARKEST HALL, A VIOLET EGG BEGAN TO PULSATE.

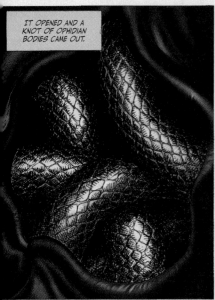

IT OPENED AND A KNOT OF OPHIDIAN BODIES CAME OUT.

MY SUIT OPENED LIKE A FLOWER SHEDDING ITS PETALS. I WAS LEFT NAKED BEFORE THIS NIGHTMARE. I THOUGHT I WOULD SUFFOCATE.

BUT THE MOUTHS OF THREE SNAKES EXHALED A FLOOD OF HEALTHY OXYGEN.

AND RAYS OF LIGHT SHOT FROM THEIR EYES. THEY CAUSED MY BRAIN TO MUTATE. THEY TRANSMITTED THE SECRETS OF A MARVELOUS TECHNOLOGY FROM ANOTHER UNIVERSE.

WITH INVENTIVE ABILITIES SUPERIOR TO THOSE OF THE HUMAN BRAIN, CONCEIVING THE TRI-U BOMB, FOR EXAMPLE, I FOUNDED THE PANTECHNO CULT. THAT'S HOW I BECAME ZOMBRA'S ALLY.

I OPENED A DOOR AND ALLOWED THIS ABOMINATION TO ENTER OUR UNIVERSE.

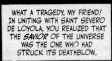

WHAT A TRAGEDY, MY FRIEND! IN UNITING WITH SAINT SEVERO DE LOYOLA, YOU REALIZED THAT THE *SAVIOR* OF THE UNIVERSE WAS THE ONE WHO HAD STRUCK ITS DEATHBLOW.

THAT'S RIGHT, MY TINIGRIFI. IMAGINE MY SADNESS. I HAD BECOME SUPREME TECHNOPRIEST ONLY TO HELP ZOMBRA DEVOUR EVERY SUN.

AT *FIRST* I HAD TO GO ALONG WITH THEM IN ORDER TO TRICK HATAAN, THE ANTI-ARCHANGEL SPY.

I BLESSED COUNTLESS INITIATION CEREMONIES DURING WHICH A THOUSAND NEW TECHNOMONKS WERE CASTRATED.

I ORDERED THE EXECUTIONS OF SMUGGLERS, SPACE PIRATES AND ECOLOGIST DEFENDERS OF THE LIGHT.

MURDERERS, THE COSMOS BELONGS TO EVERYONE!

LONG LIVE FREE COMMERCE, THIEVES!

MADMEN, LIFE NEEDS LIGHT!

OPEN YOUR MIND. DARKNESS IS DEATH!

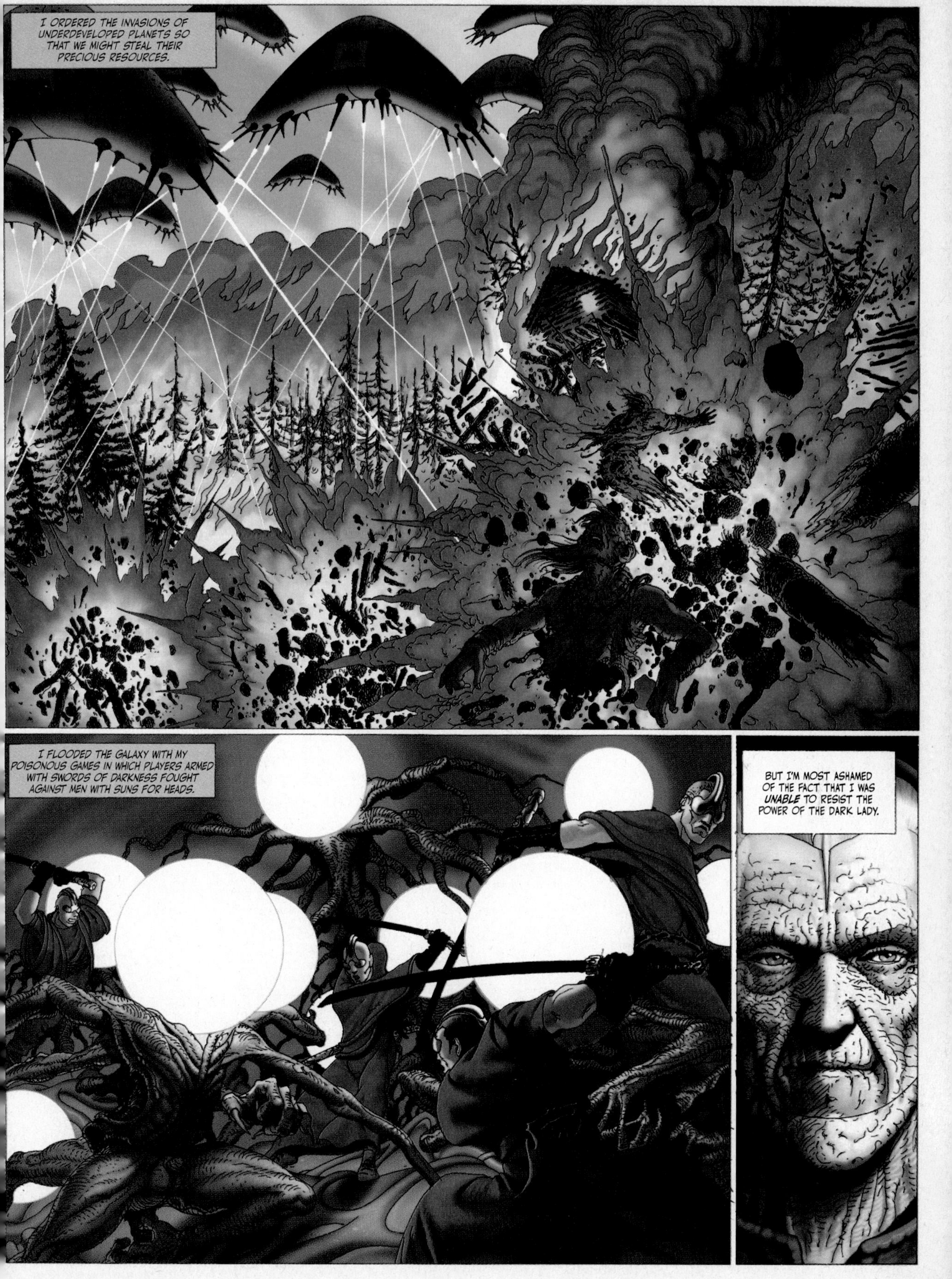
I ORDERED THE INVASIONS OF UNDERDEVELOPED PLANETS SO THAT WE MIGHT STEAL THEIR PRECIOUS RESOURCES.
I FLOODED THE GALAXY WITH MY POISONOUS GAMES IN WHICH PLAYERS ARMED WITH SWORDS OF DARKNESS FOUGHT AGAINST MEN WITH SUNS FOR HEADS.
BUT I'M MOST ASHAMED OF THE FACT THAT I WAS UNABLE TO RESIST THE POWER OF THE DARK LADY.

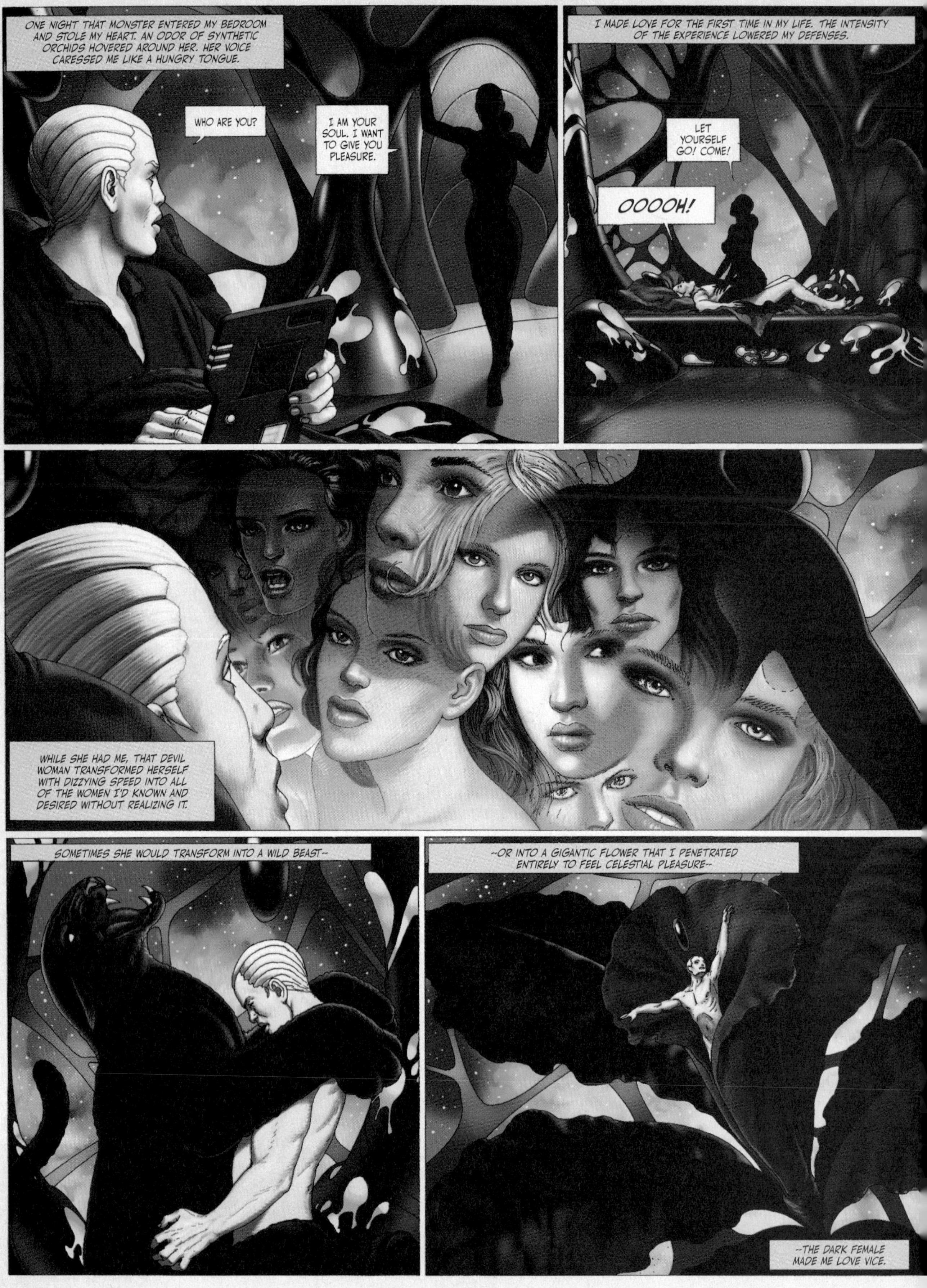
ONE NIGHT THAT MONSTER ENTERED MY BEDROOM AND STOLE MY HEART. AN ODOR OF SYNTHETIC ORCHIDS HOVERED AROUND HER. HER VOICE CARESSED ME LIKE A HUNGRY TONGUE.
WHO ARE YOU?
I AM YOUR SOUL. I WANT TO GIVE YOU PLEASURE.
I MADE LOVE FOR THE FIRST TIME IN MY LIFE. THE INTENSITY OF THE EXPERIENCE LOWERED MY DEFENSES.
LET YOURSELF GO! COME!
OOOOH!
WHILE SHE HAD ME, THAT DEVIL WOMAN TRANSFORMED HERSELF WITH DIZZYING SPEED INTO ALL OF THE WOMEN I'D KNOWN AND DESIRED WITHOUT REALIZING IT.
SOMETIMES SHE WOULD TRANSFORM INTO A WILD BEAST--
--OR INTO A GIGANTIC FLOWER THAT I PENETRATED ENTIRELY TO FEEL CELESTIAL PLEASURE--
--THE DARK FEMALE MADE ME LOVE VICE.

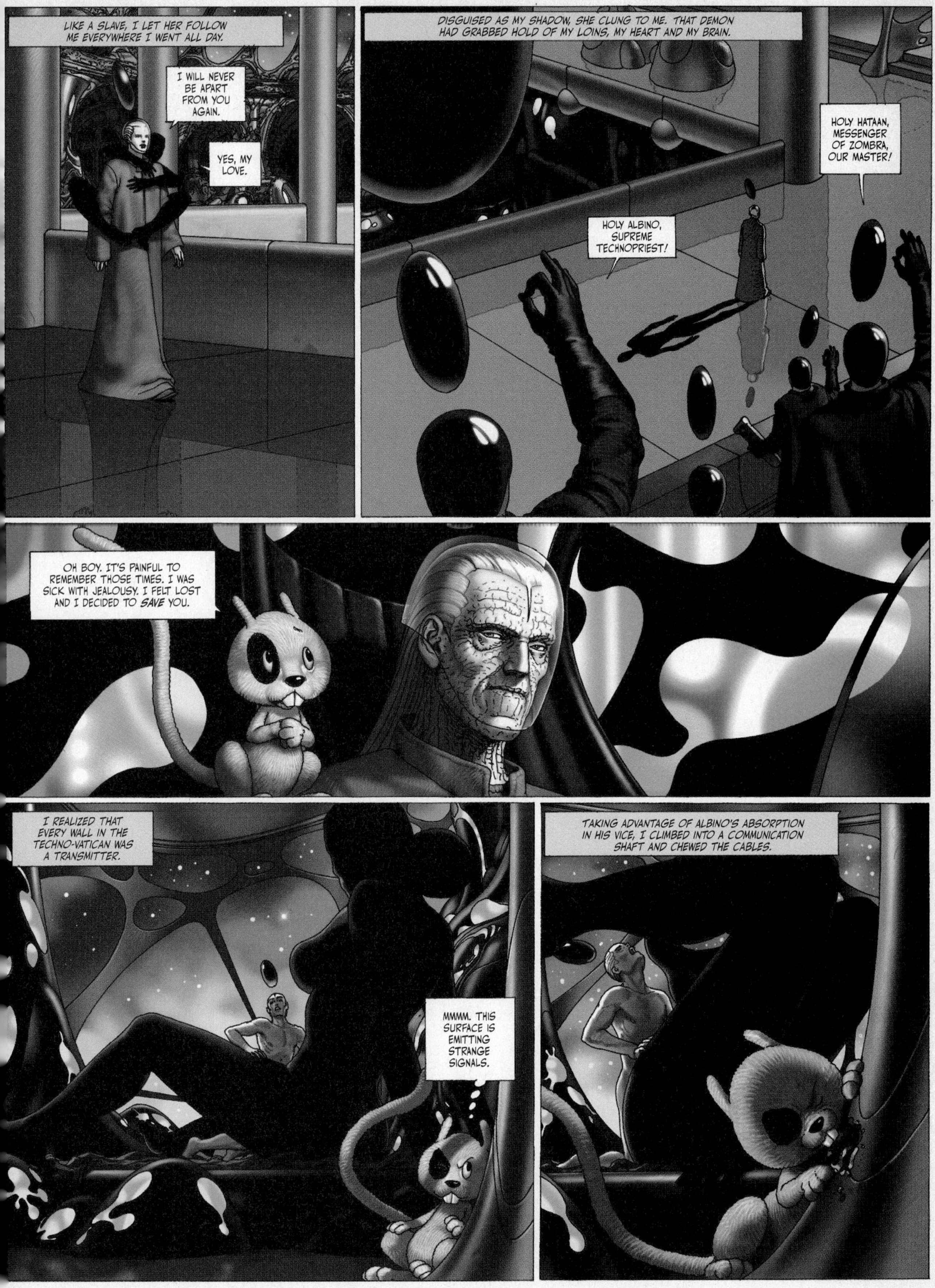
LIKE A SLAVE, I LET HER FOLLOW ME EVERYWHERE I WENT ALL DAY.
I WILL NEVER BE APART FROM YOU AGAIN.
YES, MY LOVE.
DISGUISED AS MY SHADOW, SHE CLUNG TO ME. THAT DEMON HAD GRABBED HOLD OF MY LOINS, MY HEART AND MY BRAIN.
HOLY HATAAN, MESSENGER OF ZOMBRA, OUR MASTER!
HOLY ALBINO, SUPREME TECHNOPRIEST!
OH BOY. IT'S PAINFUL TO REMEMBER THOSE TIMES. I WAS SICK WITH JEALOUSY. I FELT LOST AND I DECIDED TO SAVE YOU.
I REALIZED THAT EVERY WALL IN THE TECHNO-VATICAN WAS A TRANSMITTER.
MMMM. THIS SURFACE IS EMITTING STRANGE SIGNALS.
TAKING ADVANTAGE OF ALBINO'S ABSORPTION IN HIS VICE, I CLIMBED INTO A COMMUNICATION SHAFT AND CHEWED THE CABLES.

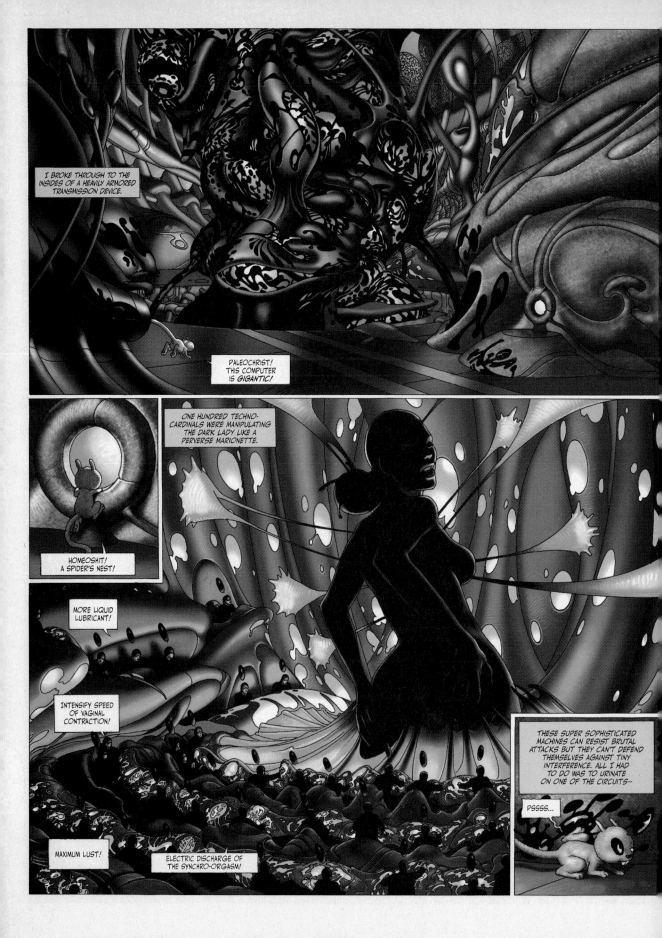

I BROKE THROUGH TO THE INSIDES OF A HEAVILY ARMORED TRANSMISSION DEVICE.

PALEOCHRIST! THIS COMPUTER IS *GIGANTIC!*

ONE HUNDRED TECHNO-CARDINALS WERE MANIPULATING THE DARK LADY LIKE A PERVERSE MARIONETTE.

HOMEOSHIT! A SPIDER'S NEST!

MORE LIQUID LUBRICANT!

INTENSIFY SPEED OF VAGINAL CONTRACTION!

THESE SUPER SOPHISTICATED MACHINES CAN RESIST BRUTAL ATTACKS BUT THEY CAN'T DEFEND THEMSELVES AGAINST TINY INTERFERENCE. ALL I HAD TO DO WAS TO URINATE ON ONE OF THE CIRCUITS--

PSSSS...

MAXIMUM LUST!

ELECTRIC DISCHARGE OF THE SYNCHRO-ORGASM!

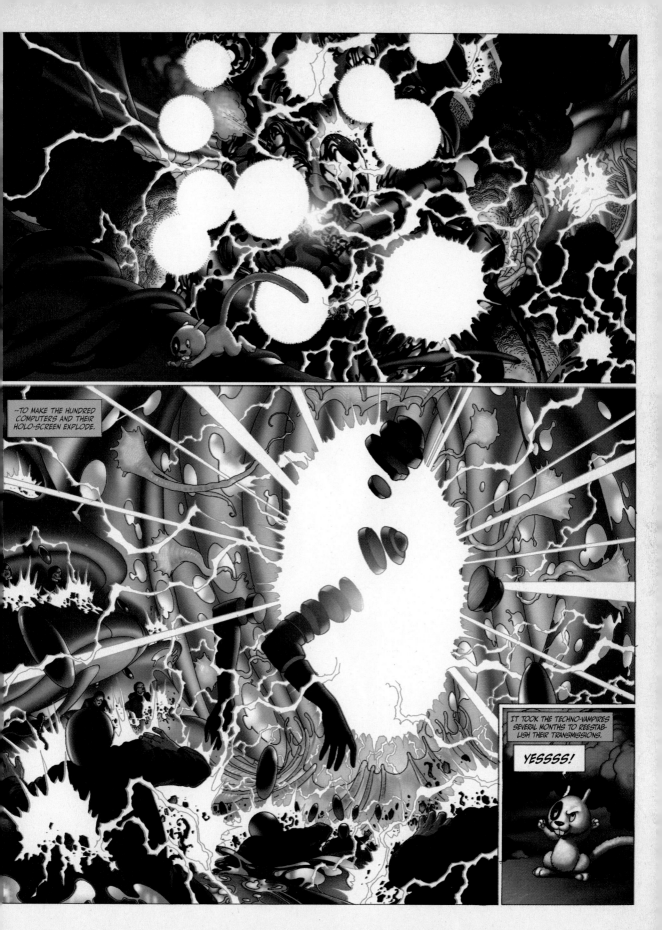

--TO MAKE THE HUNDRED COMPUTERS AND THEIR HOLO-SCREEN EXPLODE.

IT TOOK THE TECHNO-VAMPIRES SEVERAL MONTHS TO REESTAB-LISH THEIR TRANSMISSIONS.

YESSSS!

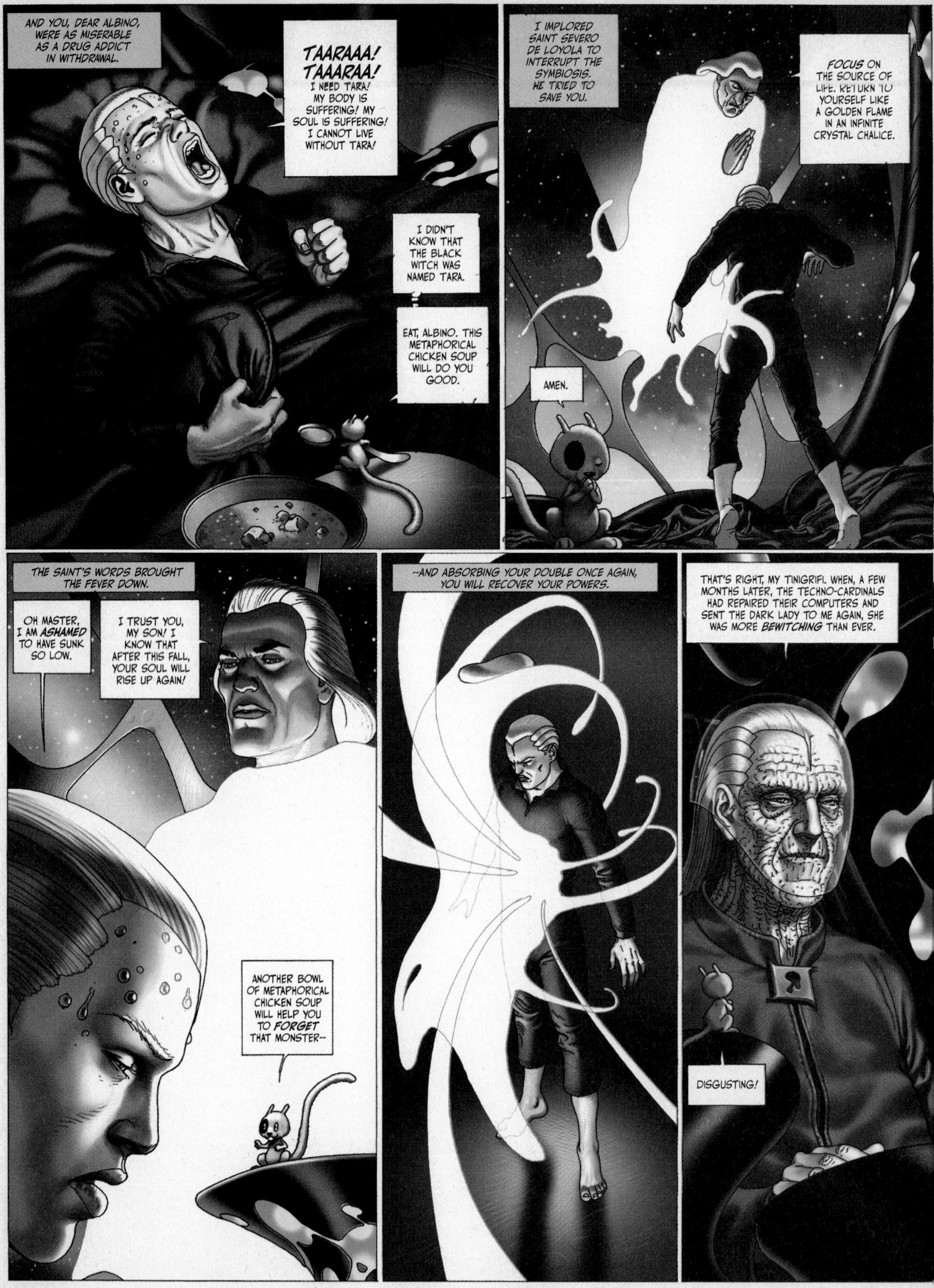
AND YOU, DEAR ALBINO, WERE AS MISERABLE AS A DRUG ADDICT IN WITHDRAWAL.
TAARAAA! TAAARAA! I NEED TARA! MY BODY IS SUFFERING! MY SOUL IS SUFFERING! I CANNOT LIVE WITHOUT TARA!
I DIDN'T KNOW THAT THE BLACK WITCH WAS NAMED TARA.
EAT, ALBINO. THIS METAPHORICAL CHICKEN SOUP WILL DO YOU GOOD.
I IMPLORED SAINT SEVERO DE LOYOLA TO INTERRUPT THE SYMBIOSIS. HE TRIED TO SAVE YOU.
FOCUS ON THE SOURCE OF LIFE. RETURN TO YOURSELF LIKE A GOLDEN FLAME IN AN INFINITE CRYSTAL CHALICE.
AMEN.
THE SAINT'S WORDS BROUGHT THE FEVER DOWN.
OH MASTER, I AM ASHAMED TO HAVE SUNK SO LOW.
I TRUST YOU, MY SON! I KNOW THAT AFTER THIS FALL, YOUR SOUL WILL RISE UP AGAIN!
ANOTHER BOWL OF METAPHORICAL CHICKEN SOUP WILL HELP YOU TO FORGET THAT MONSTER--
--AND ABSORBING YOUR DOUBLE ONCE AGAIN, YOU WILL RECOVER YOUR POWERS.
THAT'S RIGHT, MY TINIGRIFI. WHEN, A FEW MONTHS LATER, THE TECHNO-CARDINALS HAD REPAIRED THEIR COMPUTERS AND SENT THE DARK LADY TO ME AGAIN, SHE WAS MORE BEWITCHING THAN EVER.
DISGUSTING!

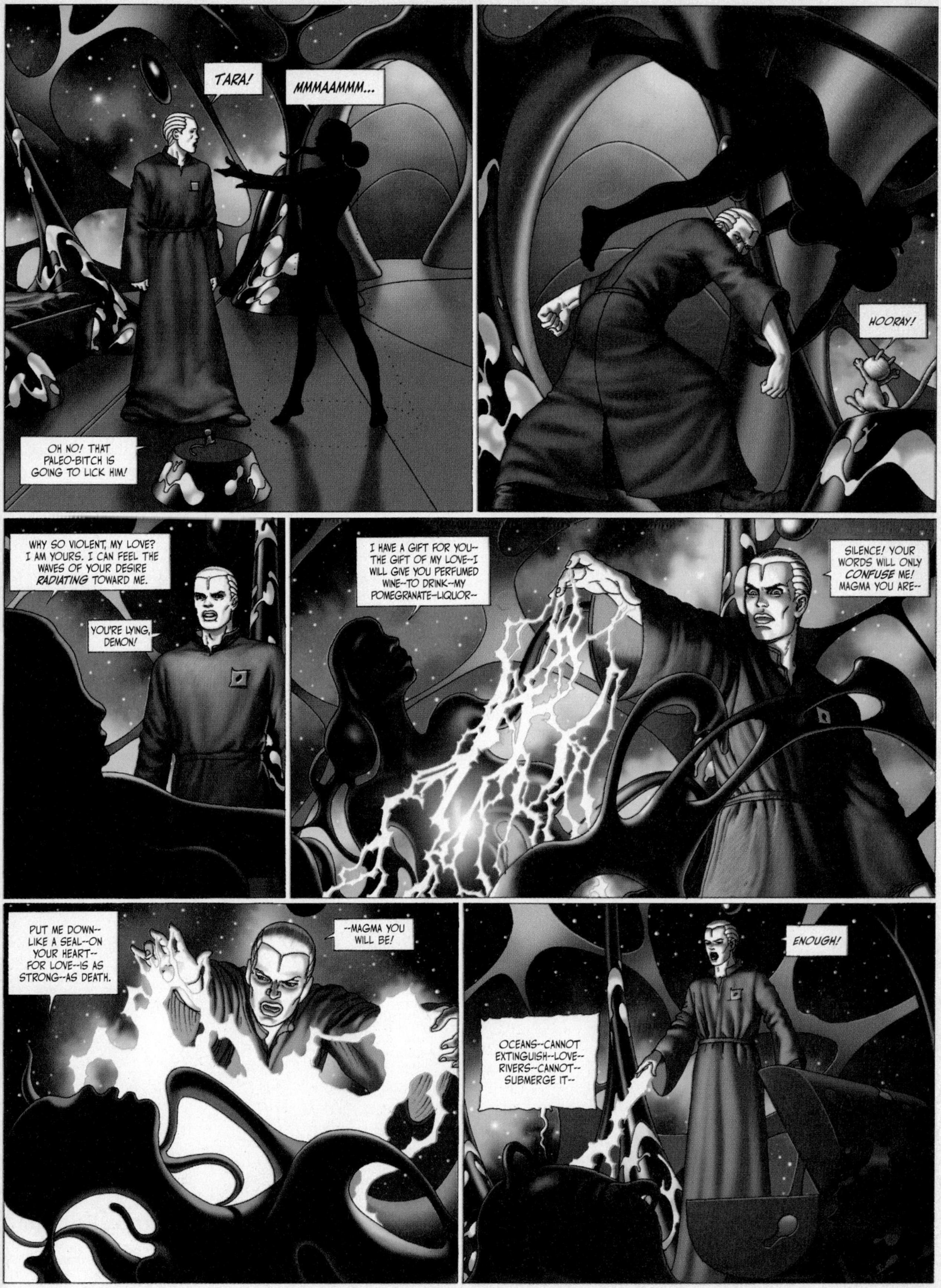
TARA!
MMMAAMMM...
OH NO! THAT PALEO-BITCH IS GOING TO LICK HIM!
HOORAY!
WHY SO VIOLENT, MY LOVE? I AM YOURS. I CAN FEEL THE WAVES OF YOUR DESIRE RADIATING TOWARD ME.
YOU'RE LYING, DEMON!
I HAVE A GIFT FOR YOU-- THE GIFT OF MY LOVE--I WILL GIVE YOU PERFUMED WINE--TO DRINK--MY POMEGRANATE-LIQUOR--
SILENCE! YOUR WORDS WILL ONLY CONFUSE ME! MAGMA YOU ARE--
PUT ME DOWN-- LIKE A SEAL--ON YOUR HEART-- FOR LOVE--IS AS STRONG--AS DEATH.
--MAGMA YOU WILL BE!
ENOUGH!
OCEANS--CANNOT EXTINGUISH--LOVE-- RIVERS--CANNOT-- SUBMERGE IT--

I LOCKED IT IN AN ANTIPROTON VAULT.

THERE YOU WILL REMAIN *FOREVER* CLOISTERED!

I'M GOING TO HAVE TO BURN A KILO OF INCENSE TO GET RID OF THAT SICKENING SMELL OF SYNTHETIC ORCHIDS.

I SENT FALSE IMAGES TO THE TRANSMISSION LABORATORY'S SCREENS. THEY BELIEVED THAT THE MONSTER HAD SEDUCED ME ONCE MORE.

I'M RAISING THE TEMPERATURE OF THE LABIA.

I'M ENGORGING THE CLITORIS.

I'M RAISING THE NUMBER OF VAGINAL CONTRACTIONS TO ONE HUNDRED PER SECOND.

I'M ADDING APHRODISIAC INFRASOUNDS TO HER VOICE.

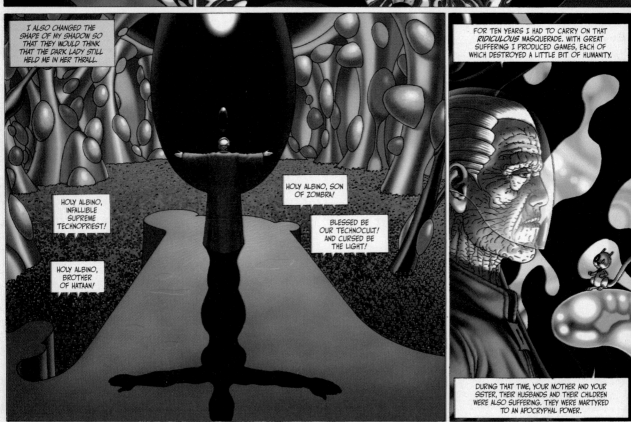

I ALSO CHANGED THE SHAPE OF MY SHADOW SO THAT THEY WOULD THINK THAT THE DARK LADY STILL HELD ME IN HER THRALL.

HOLY ALBINO, INFALLIBLE SUPREME TECHNOPRIEST!

HOLY ALBINO, BROTHER OF HATAAN!

HOLY ALBINO, SON OF ZOMBRA!

BLESSED BE OUR TECHNOCULT! AND CURSED BE THE LIGHT!

FOR TEN YEARS I HAD TO CARRY ON THAT *RIDICULOUS* MASQUERADE. WITH GREAT SUFFERING I PRODUCED GAMES, EACH OF WHICH DESTROYED A LITTLE BIT OF HUMANITY.

DURING THAT TIME, YOUR MOTHER AND YOUR SISTER, THEIR HUSBANDS AND THEIR CHILDREN WERE ALSO SUFFERING. THEY WERE MARTYRED TO AN APOCRYPHAL POWER.

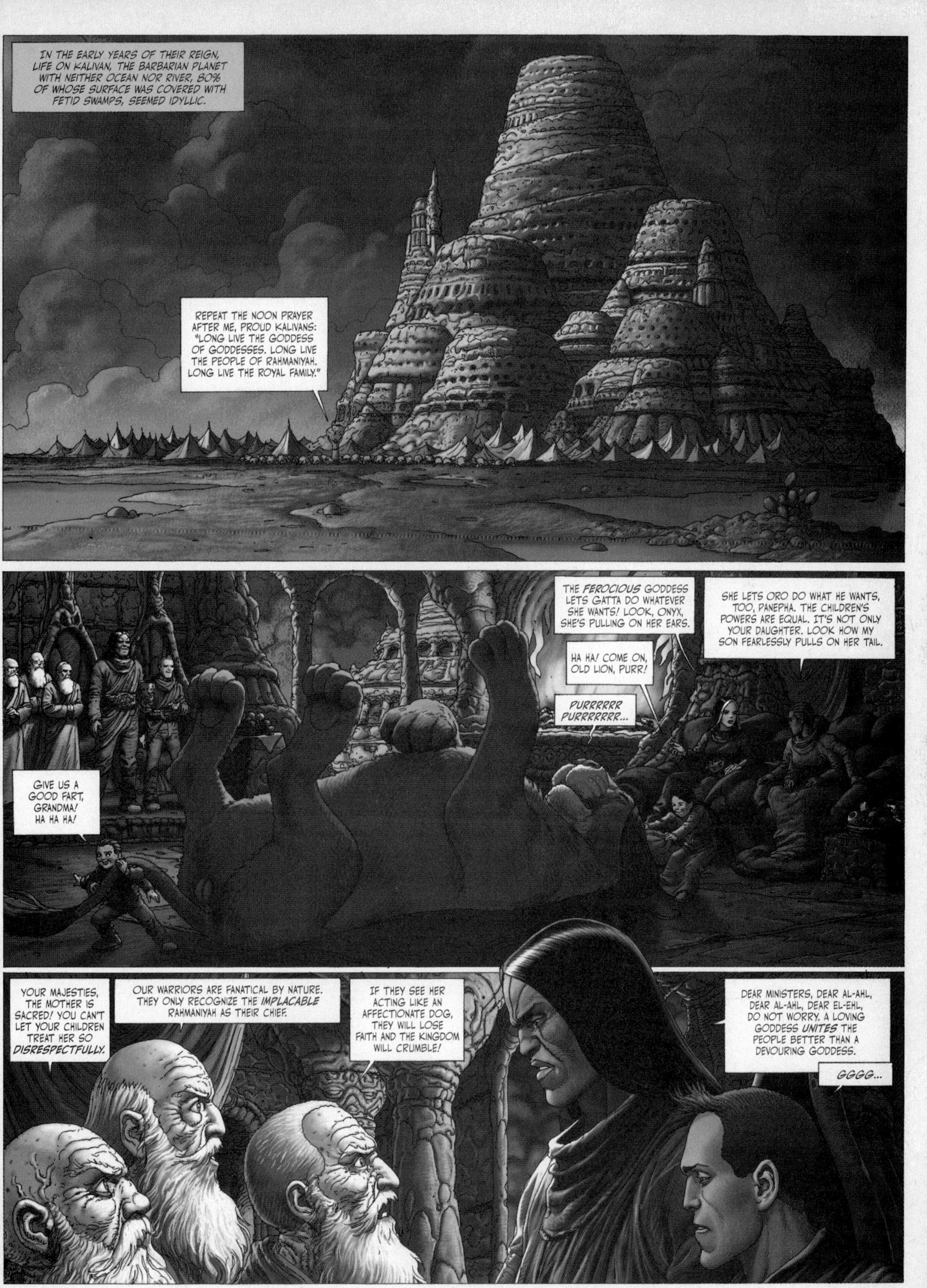

IN THE EARLY YEARS OF THEIR REIGN, LIFE ON KALIVAN, THE BARBARIAN PLANET WITH NEITHER OCEAN NOR RIVER, 80% OF WHOSE SURFACE WAS COVERED WITH FETID SWAMPS, SEEMED IDYLLIC.
REPEAT THE NOON PRAYER AFTER ME, PROUD KALIVANS: "LONG LIVE THE GODDESS OF GODDESSES. LONG LIVE THE PEOPLE OF RAHMANIYAH. LONG LIVE THE ROYAL FAMILY."
THE *FEROCIOUS* GODDESS LETS GATTA DO WHATEVER SHE WANTS! LOOK, ONYX, SHE'S PULLING ON HER EARS.
HA HA! COME ON, OLD LION, PURR!
PURRRRRR PURRRRRRR...
SHE LETS ORO DO WHAT HE WANTS, TOO, PANEPHA. THE CHILDREN'S POWERS ARE EQUAL. IT'S NOT ONLY YOUR DAUGHTER. LOOK HOW MY SON FEARLESSLY PULLS ON HER TAIL.
GIVE US A GOOD FART, GRANDMA! HA HA HA!
YOUR MAJESTIES, THE MOTHER IS SACRED! YOU CAN'T LET YOUR CHILDREN TREAT HER SO *DISRESPECTFULLY.*
OUR WARRIORS ARE FANATICAL BY NATURE. THEY ONLY RECOGNIZE THE *IMPLACABLE* RAHMANIYAH AS THEIR CHIEF.
IF THEY SEE HER ACTING LIKE AN AFFECTIONATE DOG, THEY WILL LOSE FAITH AND THE KINGDOM WILL CRUMBLE!
DEAR MINISTERS, DEAR AL-AHL, DEAR AL-AHL, DEAR EL-EHL, DO NOT WORRY. A LOVING GODDESS *UNITES* THE PEOPLE BETTER THAN A DEVOURING GODDESS.
GGGG...

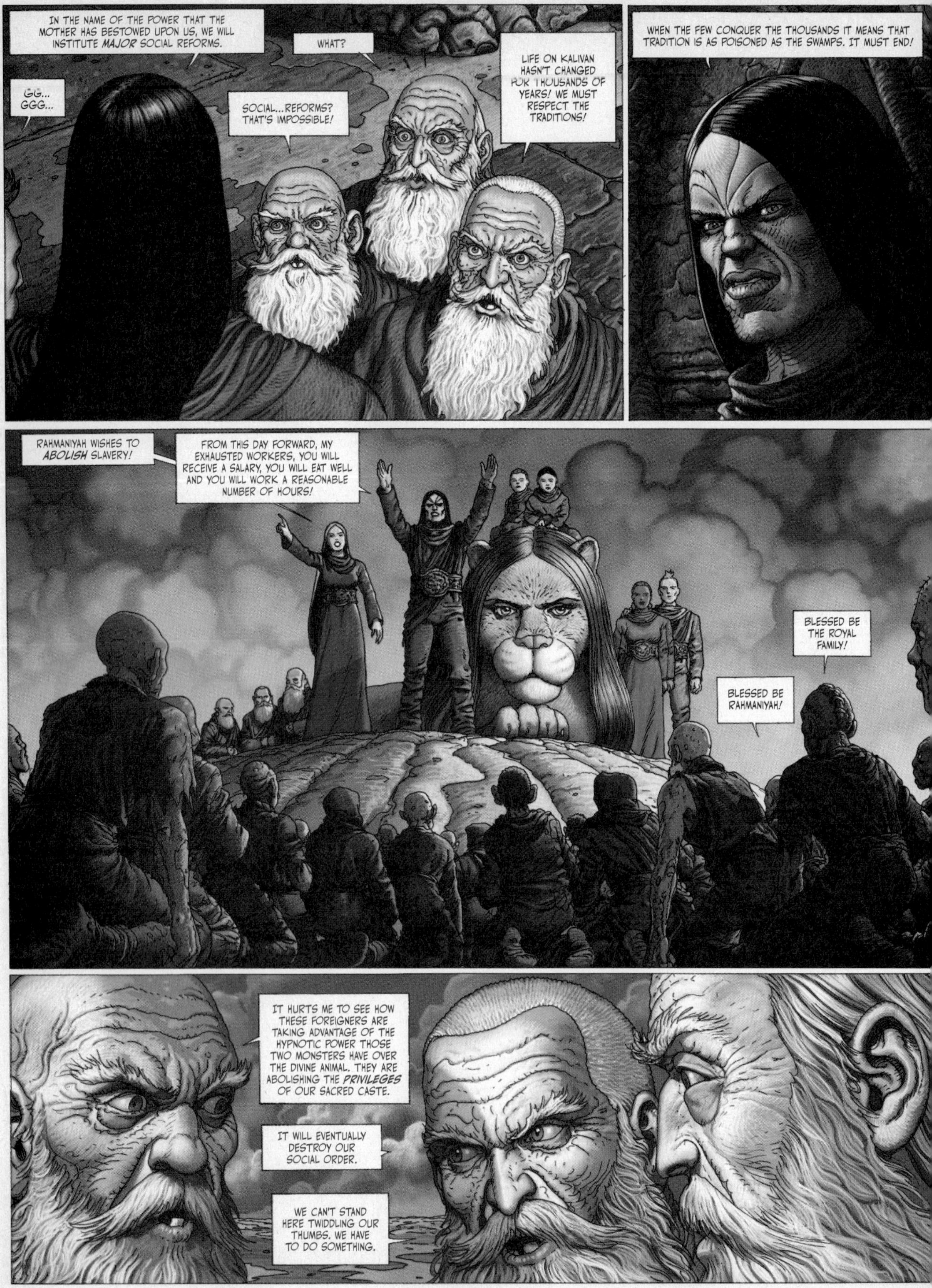
IN THE NAME OF THE POWER THAT THE MOTHER HAS BESTOWED UPON US, WE WILL INSTITUTE MAJOR SOCIAL REFORMS.
GG... GGG...
WHAT?
SOCIAL...REFORMS? THAT'S IMPOSSIBLE!
LIFE ON KALIVAN HASN'T CHANGED FOR THOUSANDS OF YEARS! WE MUST RESPECT THE TRADITIONS!
WHEN THE FEW CONQUER THE THOUSANDS IT MEANS THAT TRADITION IS AS POISONED AS THE SWAMPS. IT MUST END!
RAHMANIYAH WISHES TO ABOLISH SLAVERY!
FROM THIS DAY FORWARD, MY EXHAUSTED WORKERS, YOU WILL RECEIVE A SALARY, YOU WILL EAT WELL AND YOU WILL WORK A REASONABLE NUMBER OF HOURS!
BLESSED BE THE ROYAL FAMILY!
BLESSED BE RAHMANIYAH!
IT HURTS ME TO SEE HOW THESE FOREIGNERS ARE TAKING ADVANTAGE OF THE HYPNOTIC POWER THOSE TWO MONSTERS HAVE OVER THE DIVINE ANIMAL. THEY ARE ABOLISHING THE PRIVILEGES OF OUR SACRED CASTE.
IT WILL EVENTUALLY DESTROY OUR SOCIAL ORDER.
WE CAN'T STAND HERE TWIDDLING OUR THUMBS. WE HAVE TO DO SOMETHING.

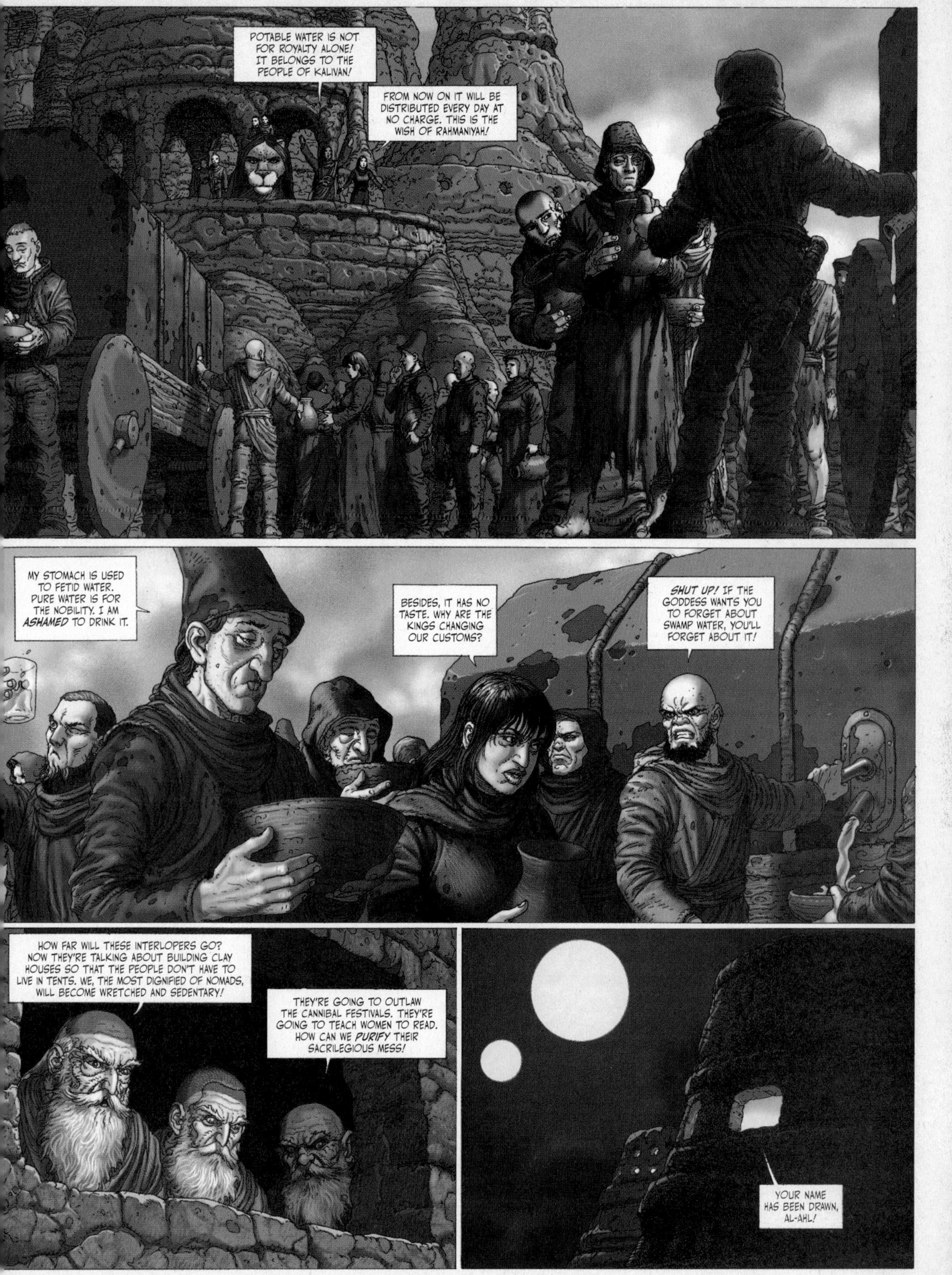
POTABLE WATER IS NOT FOR ROYALTY ALONE! IT BELONGS TO THE PEOPLE OF KALIVAN!
FROM NOW ON IT WILL BE DISTRIBUTED EVERY DAY AT NO CHARGE. THIS IS THE WISH OF RAHMANIYAH!
MY STOMACH IS USED TO FETID WATER. PURE WATER IS FOR THE NOBILITY. I AM ASHAMED TO DRINK IT.
BESIDES, IT HAS NO TASTE. WHY ARE THE KINGS CHANGING OUR CUSTOMS?
SHUT UP! IF THE GODDESS WANTS YOU TO FORGET ABOUT SWAMP WATER, YOU'LL FORGET ABOUT IT!
HOW FAR WILL THESE INTERLOPERS GO? NOW THEY'RE TALKING ABOUT BUILDING CLAY HOUSES SO THAT THE PEOPLE DON'T HAVE TO LIVE IN TENTS. WE, THE MOST DIGNIFIED OF NOMADS, WILL BECOME WRETCHED AND SEDENTARY!
THEY'RE GOING TO OUTLAW THE CANNIBAL FESTIVALS. THEY'RE GOING TO TEACH WOMEN TO READ. HOW CAN WE PURIFY THEIR SACRILEGIOUS MESS!
YOUR NAME HAS BEEN DRAWN, AL-AHL!

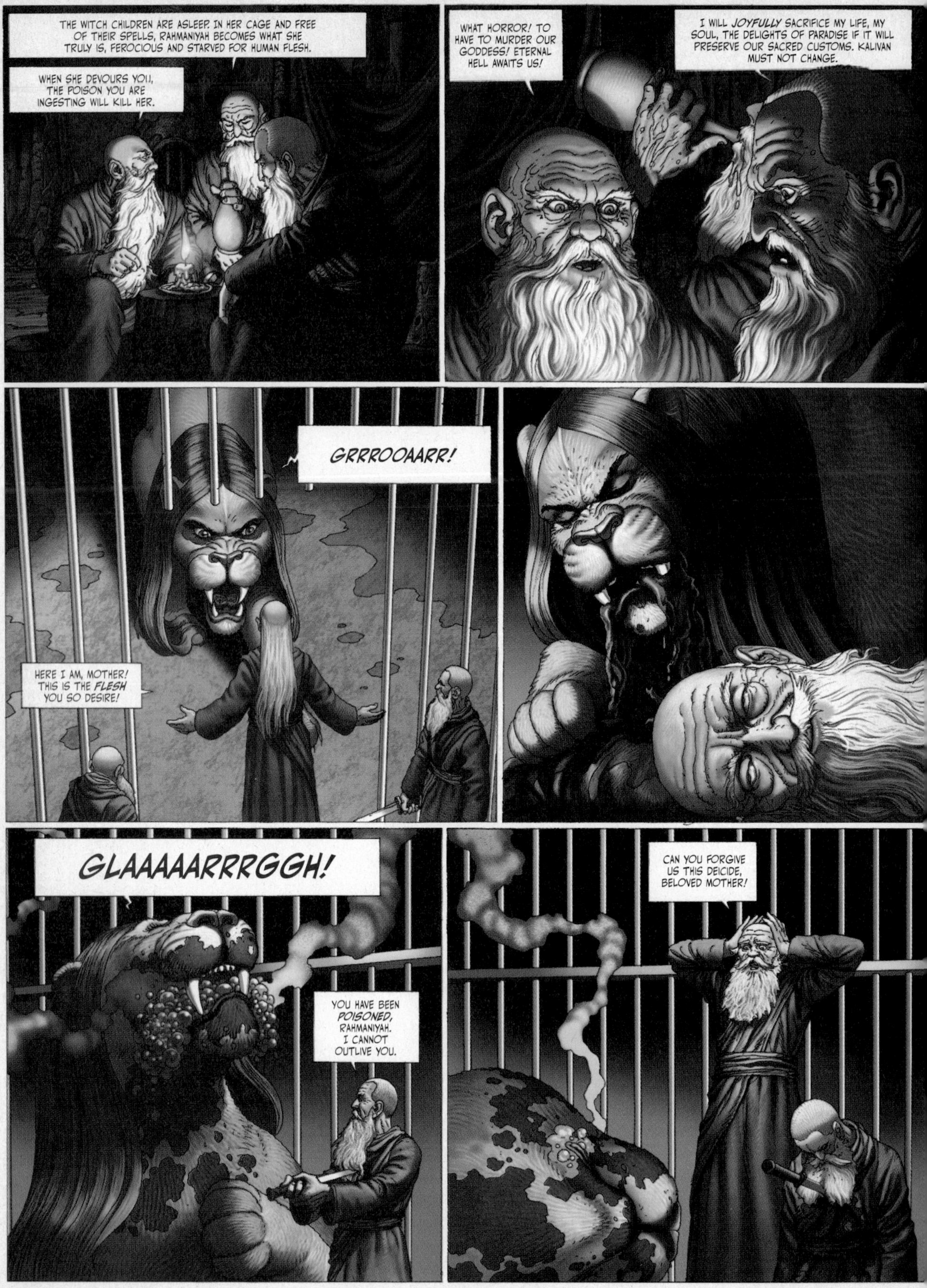
THE WITCH CHILDREN ARE ASLEEP. IN HER CAGE AND FREE OF THEIR SPELLS, RAHMANIYAH BECOMES WHAT SHE TRULY IS, FEROCIOUS AND STARVED FOR HUMAN FLESH.
WHEN SHE DEVOURS YOU, THE POISON YOU ARE INGESTING WILL KILL HER.
WHAT HORROR! TO HAVE TO MURDER OUR GODDESS! ETERNAL HELL AWAITS US!
I WILL JOYFULLY SACRIFICE MY LIFE, MY SOUL, THE DELIGHTS OF PARADISE IF IT WILL PRESERVE OUR SACRED CUSTOMS. KALIVAN MUST NOT CHANGE.
GRRROOAARR!
HERE I AM, MOTHER! THIS IS THE FLESH YOU SO DESIRE!
GLAAAAARRRGGH!
YOU HAVE BEEN POISONED, RAHMANIYAH. I CANNOT OUTLIVE YOU.
CAN YOU FORGIVE US THIS DEICIDE, BELOVED MOTHER!

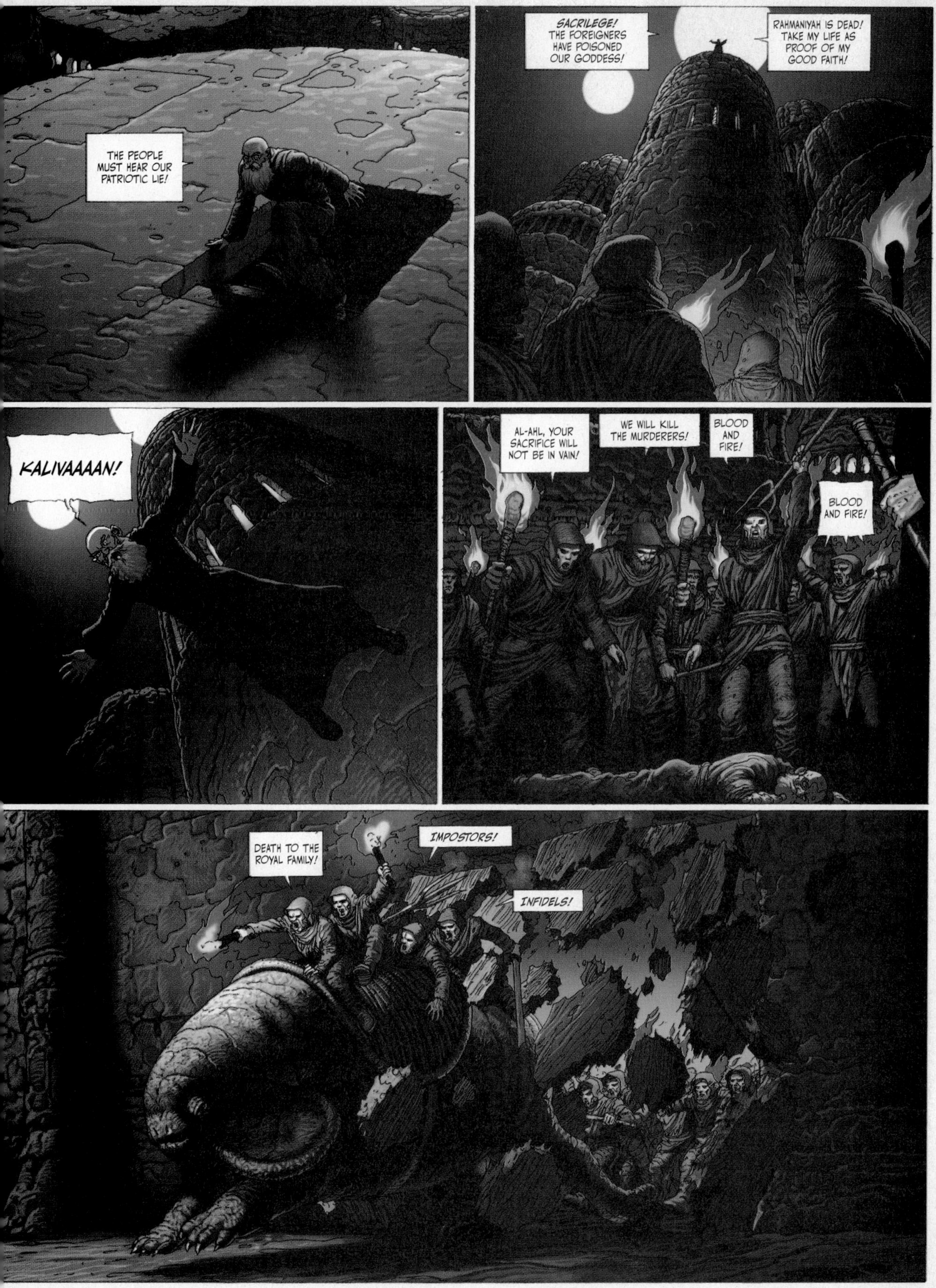
THE PEOPLE MUST HEAR OUR PATRIOTIC LIE!
SACRILEGE! THE FOREIGNERS HAVE POISONED OUR GODDESS!
RAHMANIYAH IS DEAD! TAKE MY LIFE AS PROOF OF MY GOOD FAITH!
KALIVAAAAN!
AL-AHL, YOUR SACRIFICE WILL NOT BE IN VAIN!
WE WILL KILL THE MURDERERS!
BLOOD AND FIRE!
BLOOD AND FIRE!
DEATH TO THE ROYAL FAMILY!
IMPOSTORS!
INFIDELS!

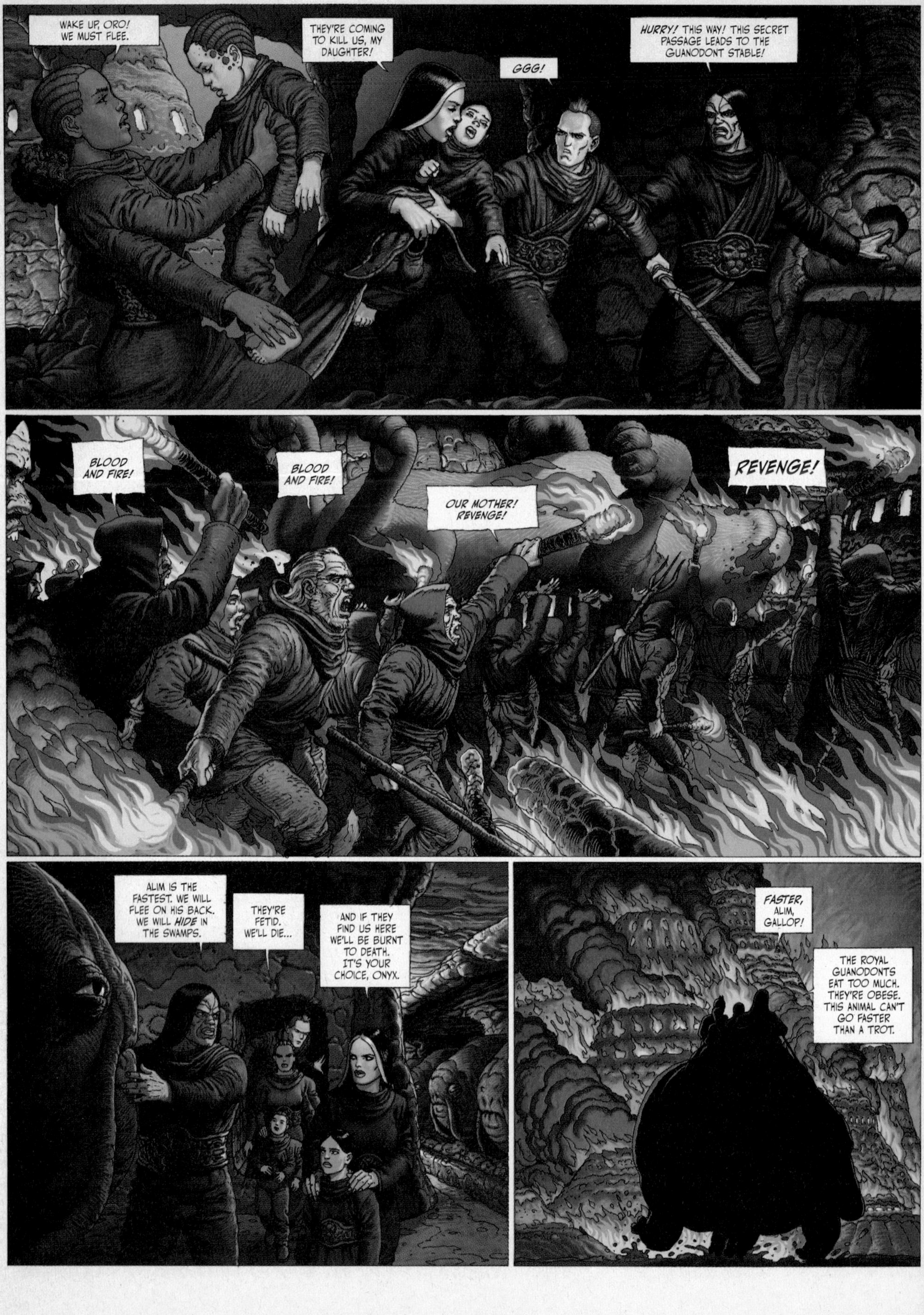
WAKE UP, ORO! WE MUST FLEE.
THEY'RE COMING TO KILL US, MY DAUGHTER!
GGG!
HURRY! THIS WAY! THIS SECRET PASSAGE LEADS TO THE GUANODONT STABLE!
BLOOD AND FIRE!
BLOOD AND FIRE!
OUR MOTHER! REVENGE!
REVENGE!
ALIM IS THE FASTEST. WE WILL FLEE ON HIS BACK. WE WILL HIDE IN THE SWAMPS.
THEY'RE FETID. WE'LL DIE...
AND IF THEY FIND US HERE WE'LL BE BURNT TO DEATH. IT'S YOUR CHOICE, ONYX.
FASTER, ALIM, GALLOP!
THE ROYAL GUANODONTS EAT TOO MUCH. THEY'RE OBESE. THIS ANIMAL CAN'T GO FASTER THAN A TROT.

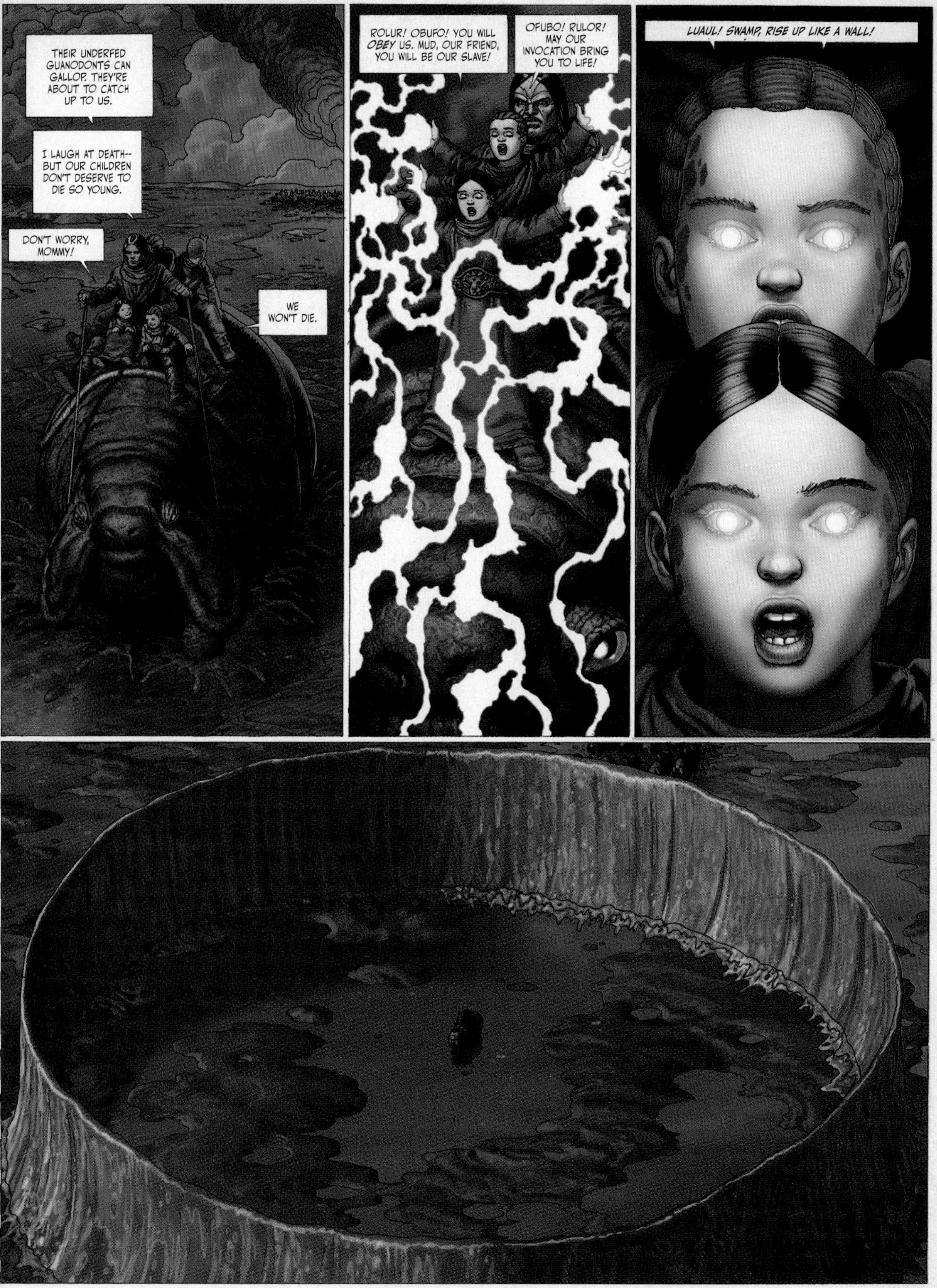
THEIR UNDERFED GUANODONTS CAN GALLOP. THEY'RE ABOUT TO CATCH UP TO US.
I LAUGH AT DEATH-- BUT OUR CHILDREN DON'T DESERVE TO DIE SO YOUNG.
DON'T WORRY, MOMMY!
WE WON'T DIE.
ROLUR! OBUFO! YOU WILL OBEY US. MUD, OUR FRIEND, YOU WILL BE OUR SLAVE!
OFUBO! RULOR! MAY OUR INVOCATION BRING YOU TO LIFE!
LUAUL! SWAMP, RISE UP LIKE A WALL!

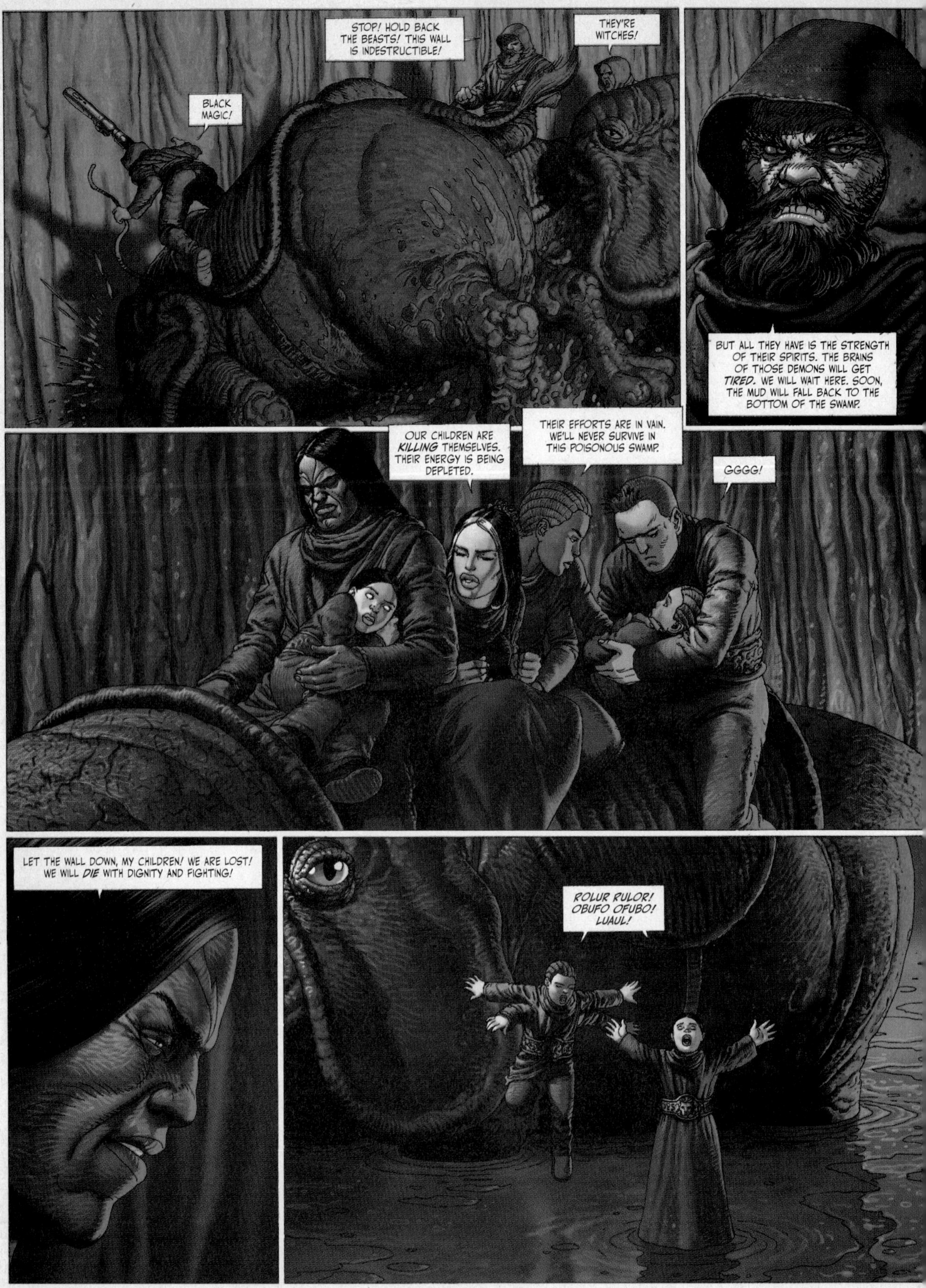

BLACK MAGIC!
STOP! HOLD BACK THE BEASTS! THIS WALL IS INDESTRUCTIBLE!
THEY'RE WITCHES!
BUT ALL THEY HAVE IS THE STRENGTH OF THEIR SPIRITS. THE BRAINS OF THOSE DEMONS WILL GET TIRED. WE WILL WAIT HERE. SOON, THE MUD WILL FALL BACK TO THE BOTTOM OF THE SWAMP.
OUR CHILDREN ARE KILLING THEMSELVES. THEIR ENERGY IS BEING DEPLETED.
THEIR EFFORTS ARE IN VAIN. WE'LL NEVER SURVIVE IN THIS POISONOUS SWAMP.
GGGG!
LET THE WALL DOWN, MY CHILDREN! WE ARE LOST! WE WILL DIE WITH DIGNITY AND FIGHTING!
ROLUR RULOR! OBUFO OFUBO! LUAUL!

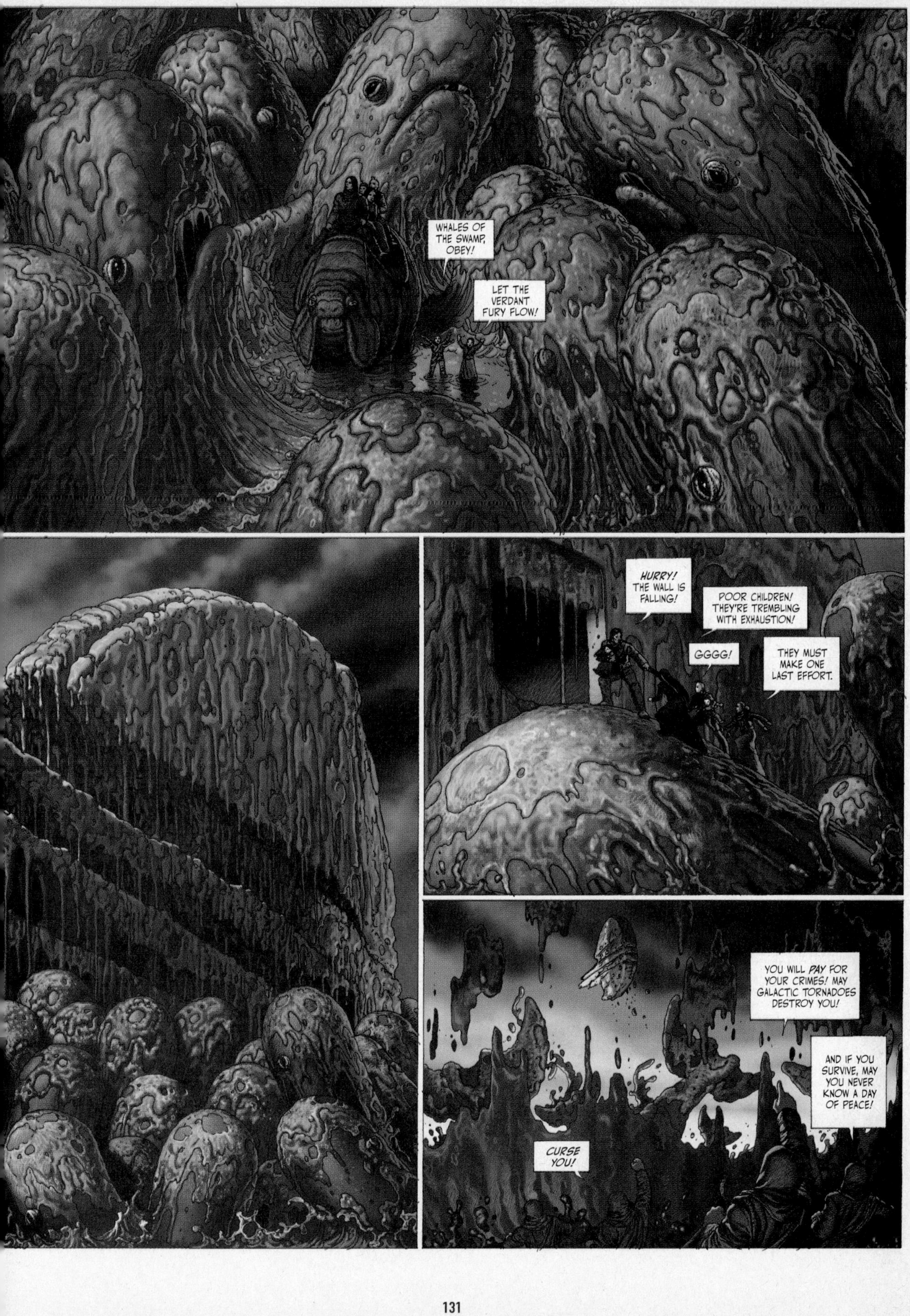
WHALES OF THE SWAMP, OBEY!
LET THE VERDANT FURY FLOW!
HURRY! THE WALL IS FALLING!
POOR CHILDREN! THEY'RE TREMBLING WITH EXHAUSTION!
GGGG!
THEY MUST MAKE ONE LAST EFFORT.
YOU WILL PAY FOR YOUR CRIMES! MAY GALACTIC TORNADOES DESTROY YOU!
AND IF YOU SURVIVE, MAY YOU NEVER KNOW A DAY OF PEACE!
CURSE YOU!

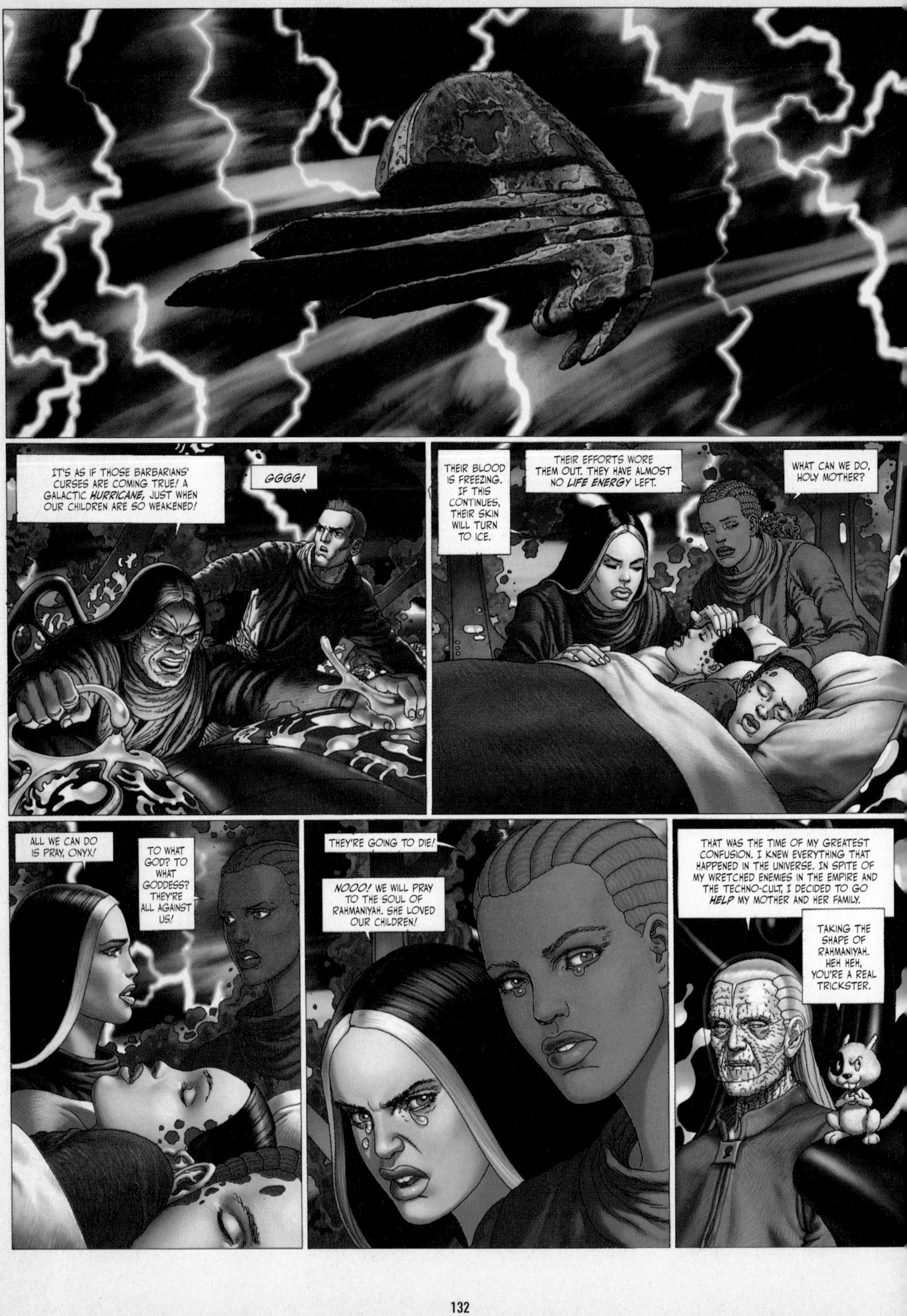
IT'S AS IF THOSE BARBARIANS' CURSES ARE COMING TRUE! A GALACTIC HURRICANE, JUST WHEN OUR CHILDREN ARE SO WEAKENED!
GGGG!
THEIR BLOOD IS FREEZING. IF THIS CONTINUES, THEIR SKIN WILL TURN TO ICE.
THEIR EFFORTS WORE THEM OUT. THEY HAVE ALMOST NO LIFE ENERGY LEFT.
WHAT CAN WE DO, HOLY MOTHER?
ALL WE CAN DO IS PRAY, ONYX!
TO WHAT GOD? TO WHAT GODDESS? THEY'RE ALL AGAINST US!
THEY'RE GOING TO DIE!
NOOO! WE WILL PRAY TO THE SOUL OF RAHMANIYAH. SHE LOVED OUR CHILDREN!
THAT WAS THE TIME OF MY GREATEST CONFUSION. I KNEW EVERYTHING THAT HAPPENED IN THE UNIVERSE. IN SPITE OF MY WRETCHED ENEMIES IN THE EMPIRE AND THE TECHNO-CULT, I DECIDED TO GO HELP MY MOTHER AND HER FAMILY.
TAKING THE SHAPE OF RAHMANIYAH. HEH HEH, YOU'RE A REAL TRICKSTER.

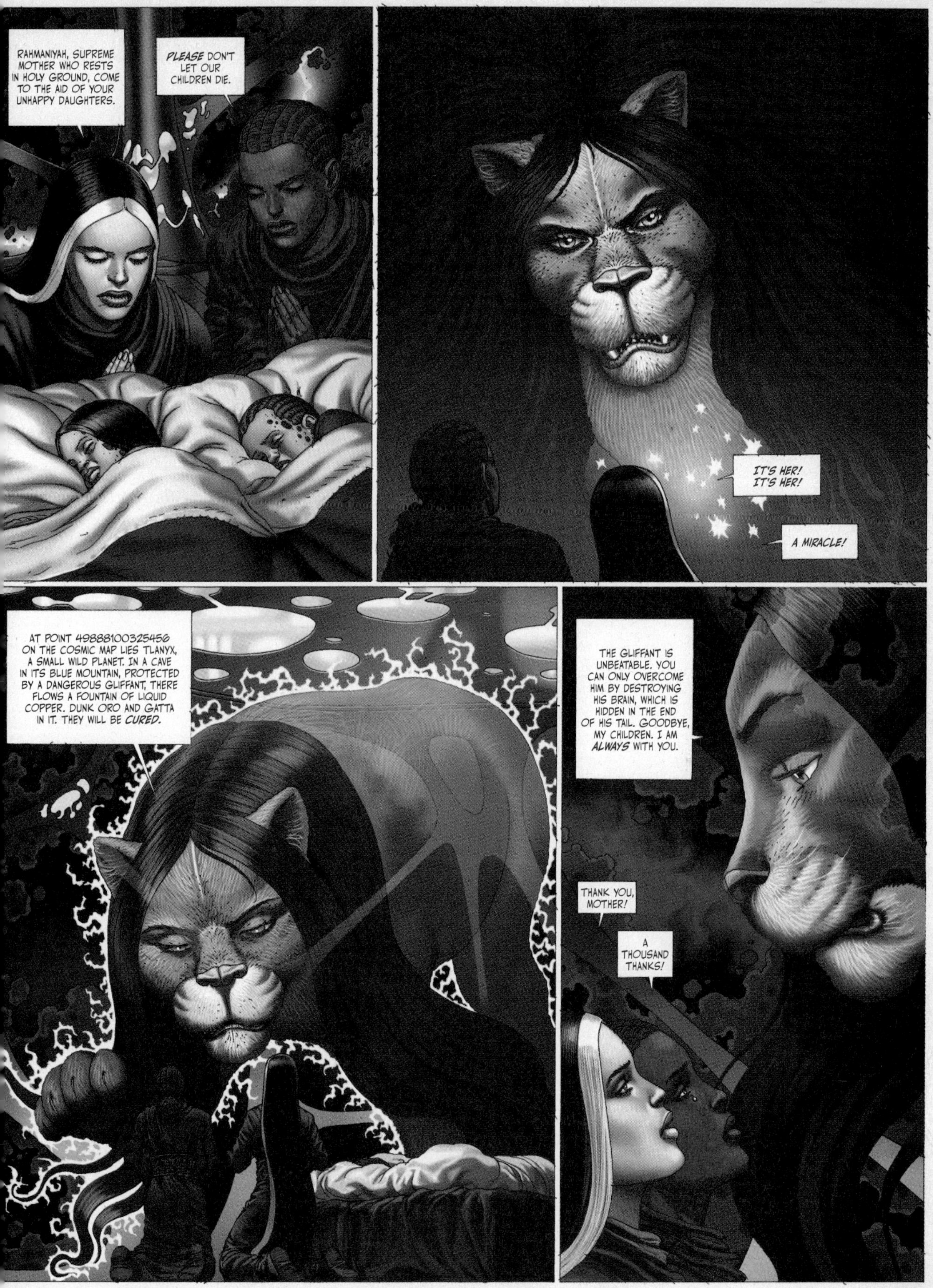
RAHMANIYAH, SUPREME MOTHER WHO RESTS IN HOLY GROUND, COME TO THE AID OF YOUR UNHAPPY DAUGHTERS.
PLEASE DON'T LET OUR CHILDREN DIE.
IT'S HER! IT'S HER!
A MIRACLE!
AT POINT 49888100325456 ON THE COSMIC MAP LIES TLANYX, A SMALL WILD PLANET. IN A CAVE IN ITS BLUE MOUNTAIN, PROTECTED BY A DANGEROUS GLIFFANT, THERE FLOWS A FOUNTAIN OF LIQUID COPPER. DUNK ORO AND GATTA IN IT. THEY WILL BE CURED.
THE GLIFFANT IS UNBEATABLE. YOU CAN ONLY OVERCOME HIM BY DESTROYING HIS BRAIN, WHICH IS HIDDEN IN THE END OF HIS TAIL. GOODBYE, MY CHILDREN. I AM ALWAYS WITH YOU.
THANK YOU, MOTHER!
A THOUSAND THANKS!

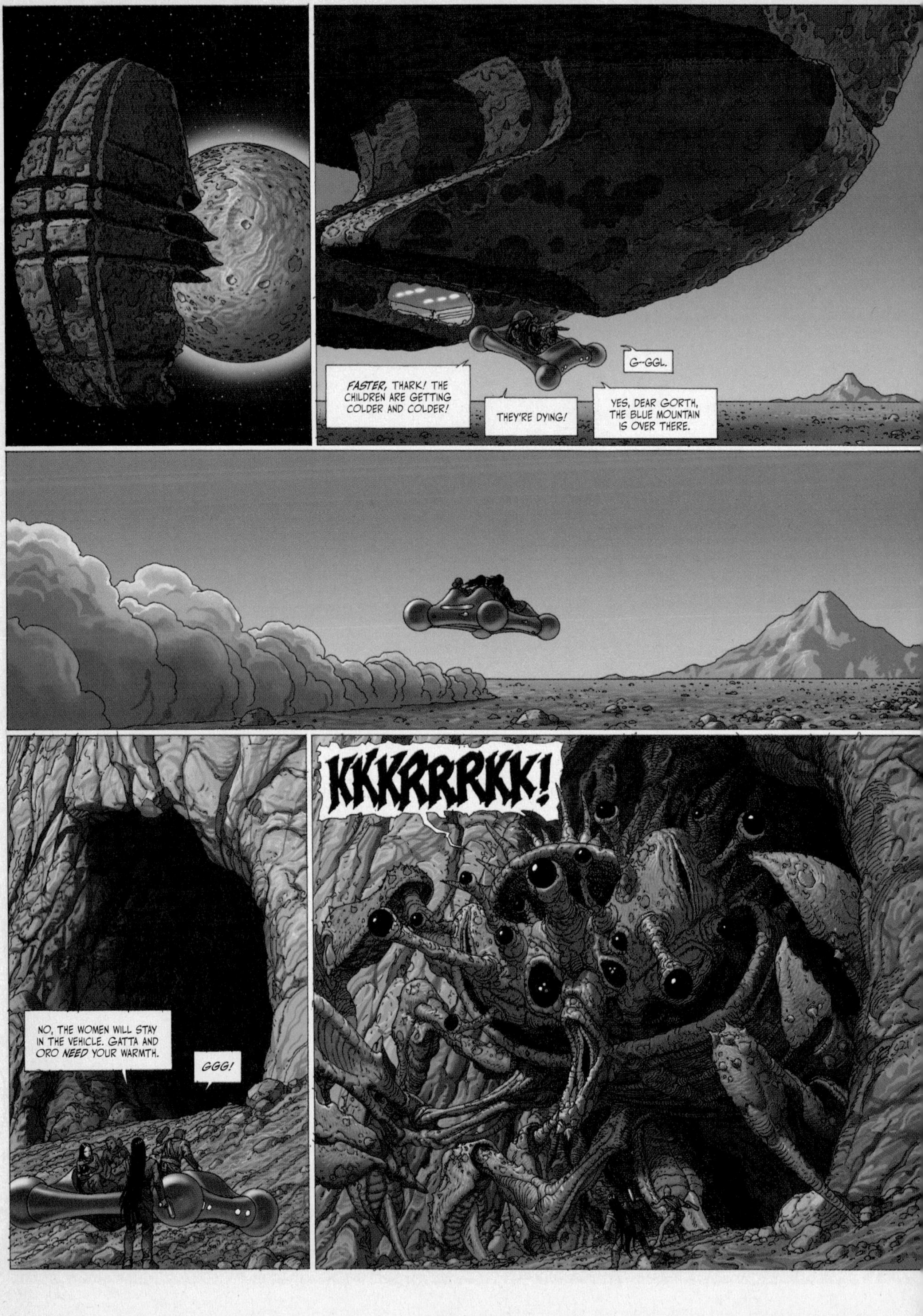

FASTER, THARK! THE CHILDREN ARE GETTING COLDER AND COLDER!
THEY'RE DYING!
G--GGL.
YES, DEAR GORTH, THE BLUE MOUNTAIN IS OVER THERE.
NO, THE WOMEN WILL STAY IN THE VEHICLE. GATTA AND ORO NEED YOUR WARMTH.
GGG!
KKKRRRKK!

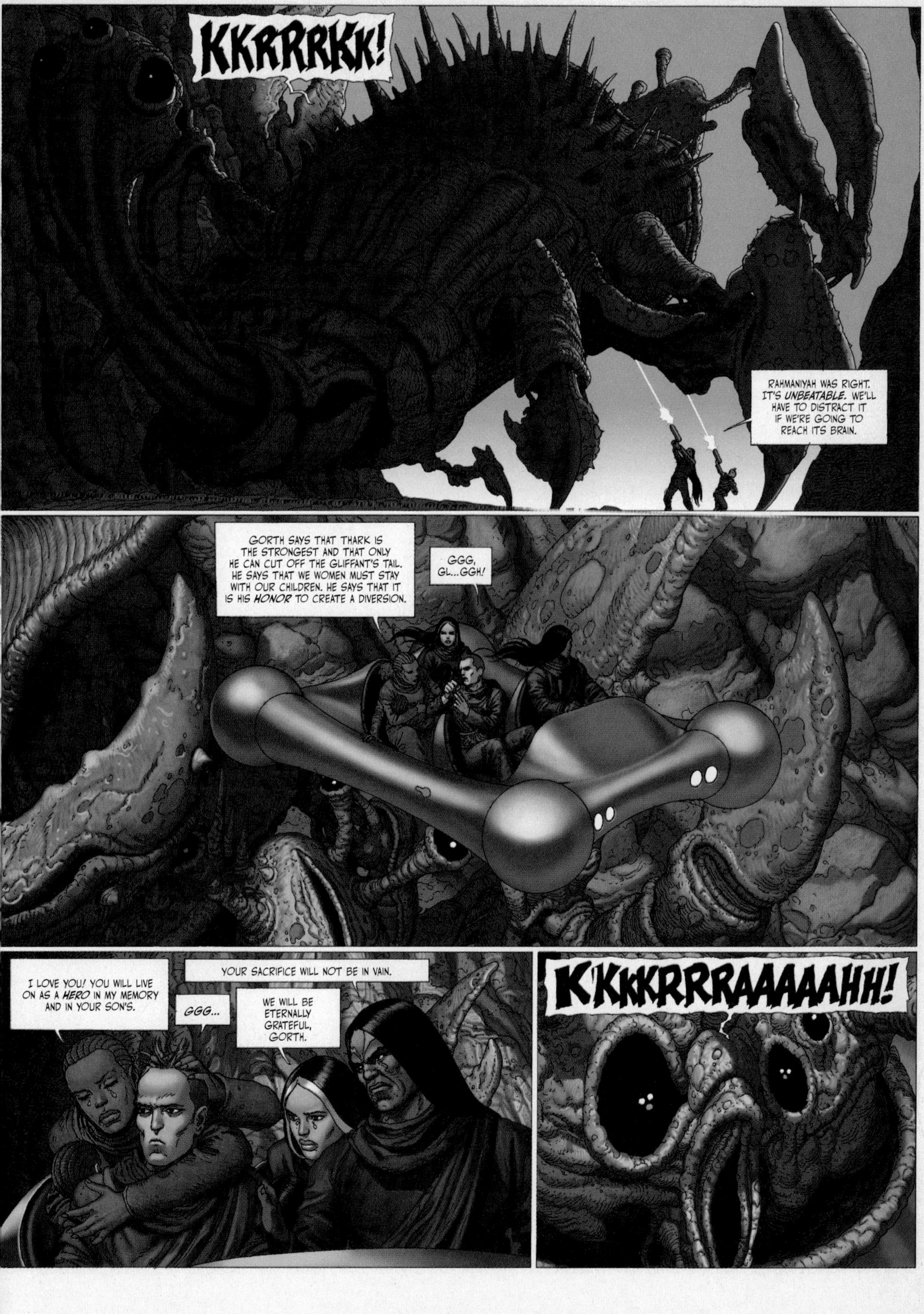
KKRRRKK!
RAHMANIYAH WAS RIGHT. IT'S UNBEATABLE. WE'LL HAVE TO DISTRACT IT IF WE'RE GOING TO REACH ITS BRAIN.
GORTH SAYS THAT THARK IS THE STRONGEST AND THAT ONLY HE CAN CUT OFF THE GLIFFANT'S TAIL. HE SAYS THAT WE WOMEN MUST STAY WITH OUR CHILDREN. HE SAYS THAT IT IS HIS HONOR TO CREATE A DIVERSION.
GGG, GL...GGH!
I LOVE YOU! YOU WILL LIVE ON AS A HERO IN MY MEMORY AND IN YOUR SON'S.
YOUR SACRIFICE WILL NOT BE IN VAIN.
GGG...
WE WILL BE ETERNALLY GRATEFUL, GORTH.
K'KKKRRRAAAAAHH!

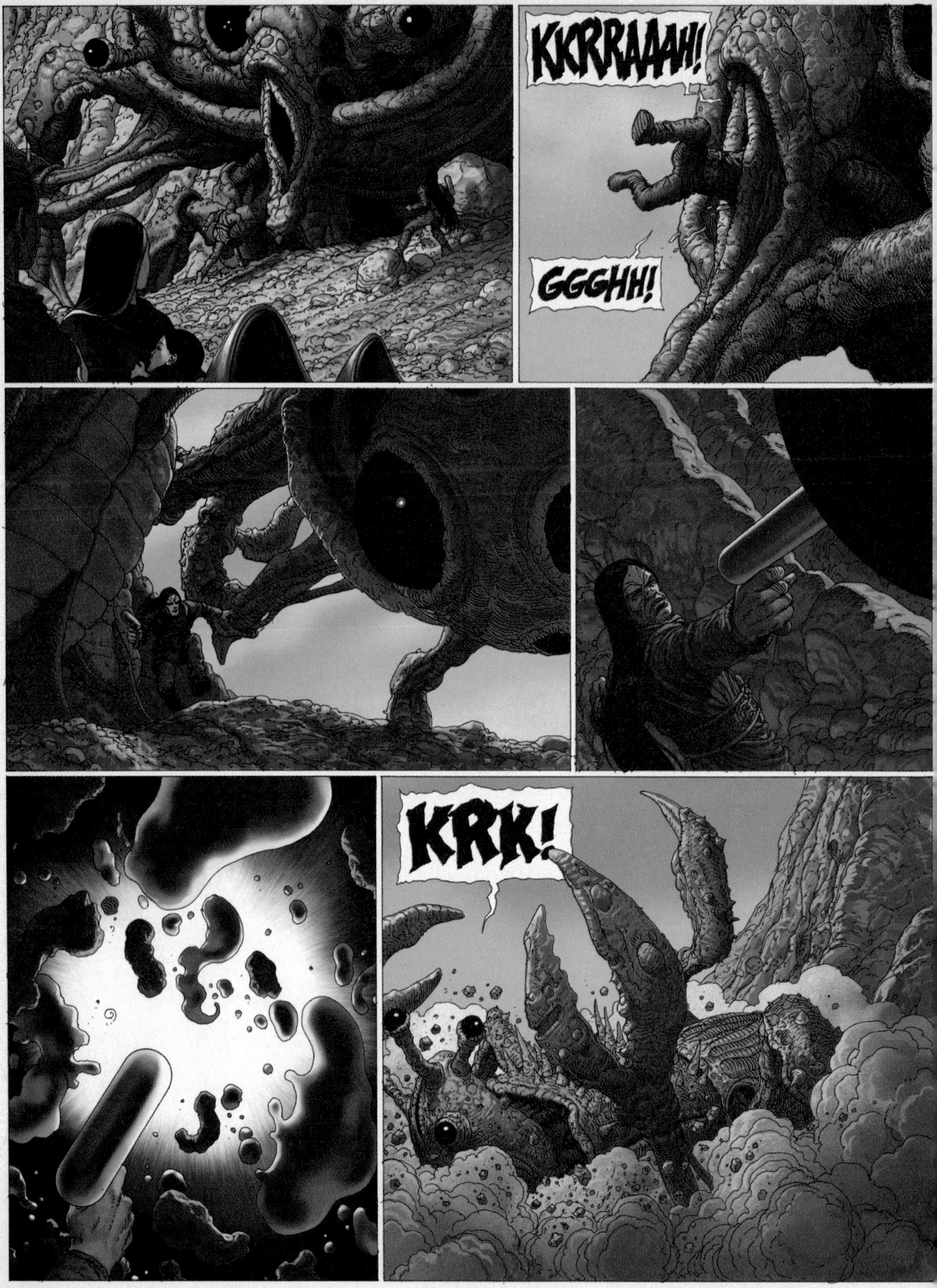
KKRRAAAH!
GGGHH!
KRK!

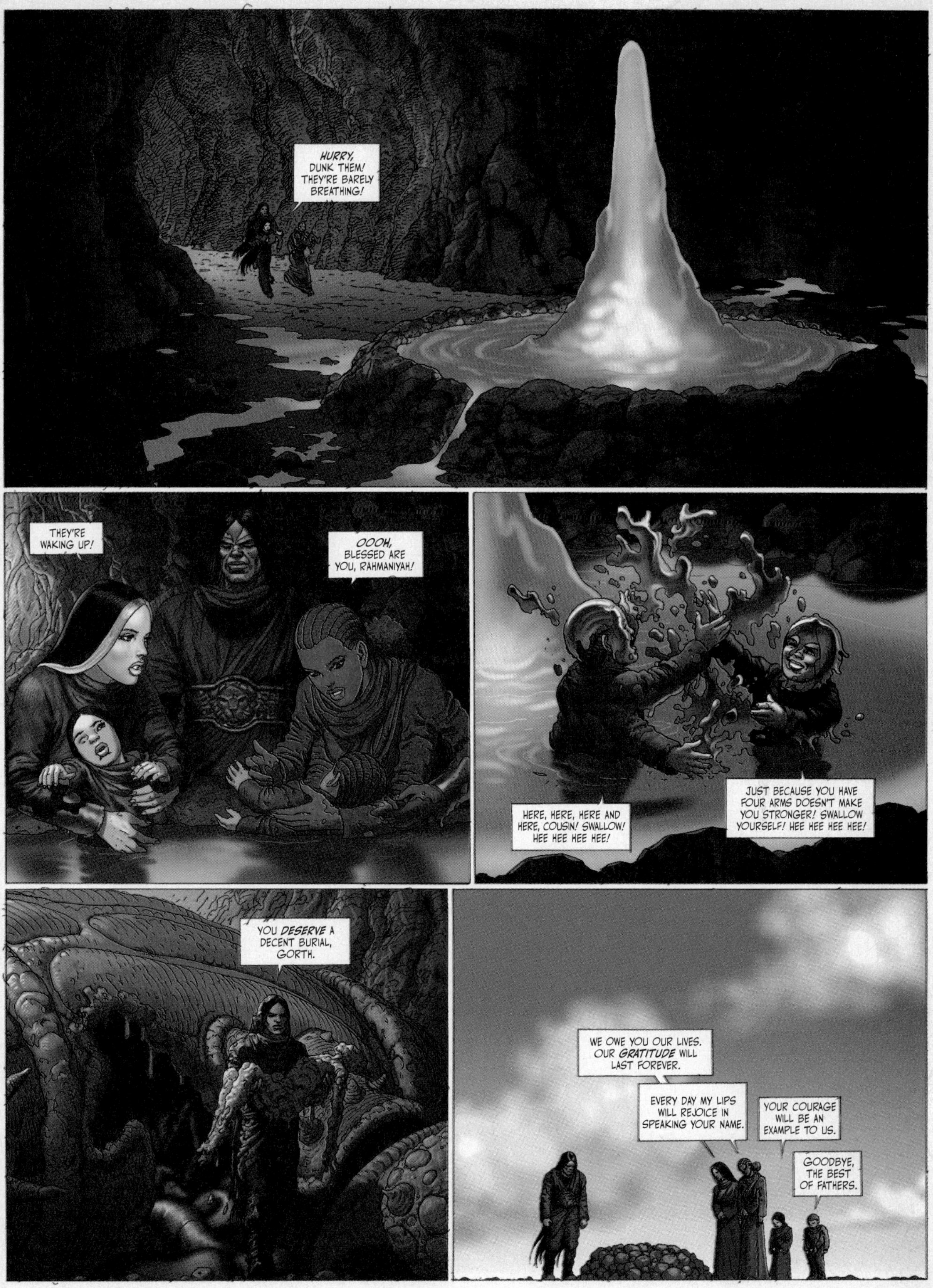

HURRY, DUNK THEM! THEY'RE BARELY BREATHING!
THEY'RE WAKING UP!
OOOH, BLESSED ARE YOU, RAHMANIYAH!
HERE, HERE, HERE AND HERE, COUSIN! SWALLOW! HEE HEE HEE HEE!
JUST BECAUSE YOU HAVE FOUR ARMS DOESN'T MAKE YOU STRONGER! SWALLOW YOURSELF! HEE HEE HEE HEE!
YOU DESERVE A DECENT BURIAL, GORTH.
WE OWE YOU OUR LIVES. OUR GRATITUDE WILL LAST FOREVER.
EVERY DAY MY LIPS WILL REJOICE IN SPEAKING YOUR NAME.
YOUR COURAGE WILL BE AN EXAMPLE TO US.
GOODBYE, THE BEST OF FATHERS.

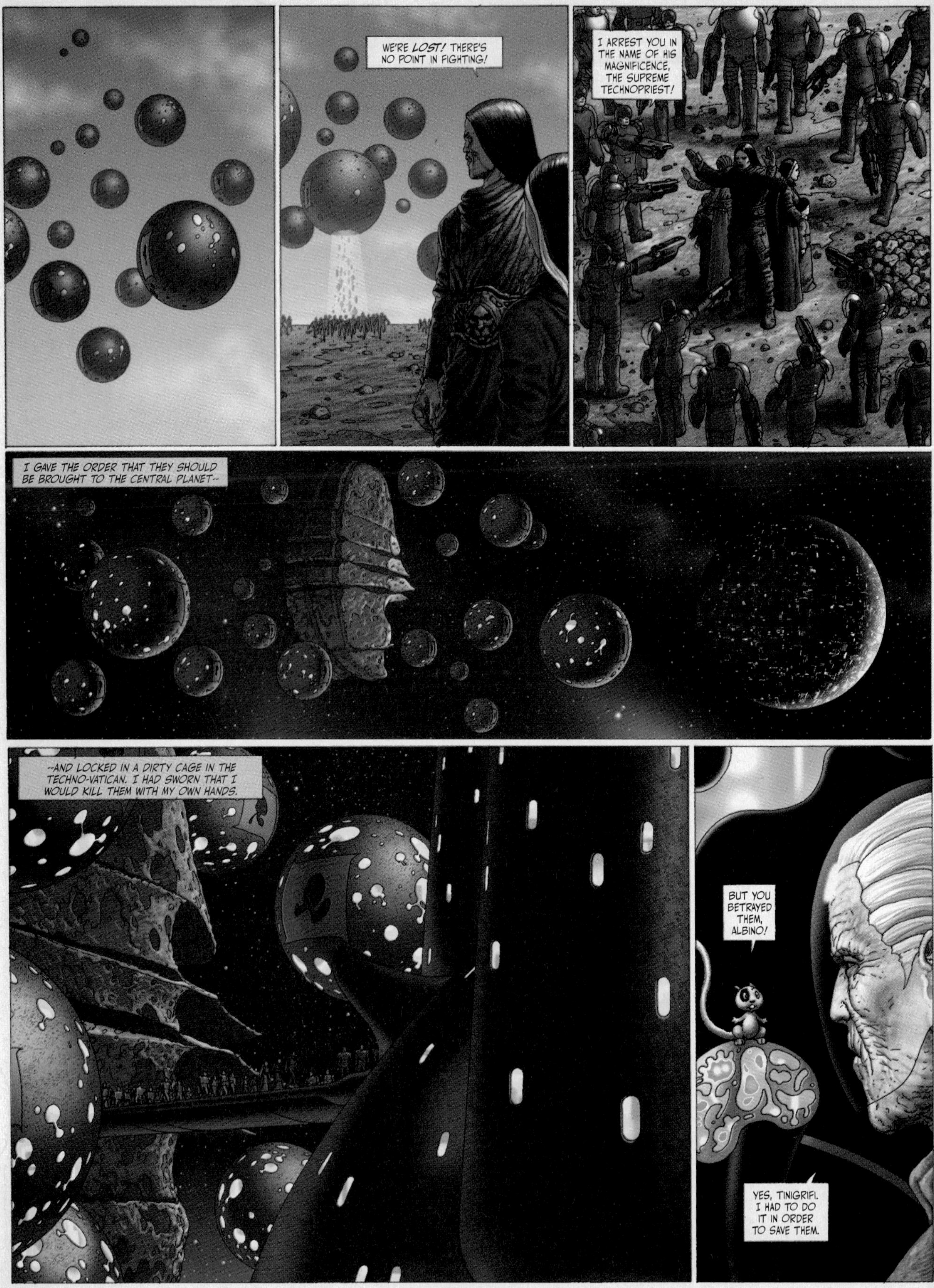
WE'RE LOST! THERE'S NO POINT IN FIGHTING!
I ARREST YOU IN THE NAME OF HIS MAGNIFICENCE, THE SUPREME TECHNOPRIEST!
I GAVE THE ORDER THAT THEY SHOULD BE BROUGHT TO THE CENTRAL PLANET--
--AND LOCKED IN A DIRTY CAGE IN THE TECHNO-VATICAN. I HAD SWORN THAT I WOULD KILL THEM WITH MY OWN HANDS.
BUT YOU BETRAYED THEM, ALBINO!
YES, TINIGRIFI. I HAD TO DO IT IN ORDER TO SAVE THEM.

SO THAT MY COLLABORATORS WOULD BELIEVE THAT I WAS AS SADISTIC AS THEY WERE, I THREW THE PRISONERS INTO A DARK CELL.

LEAVE ME, MY FAITHFUL TECHNO-CARDINALS. I WANT TO SAVOR THE PLEASURE OF INTERROGATING THEM, TORTURING THEM AND KILLING THEM ALONE. I WILL GIVE YOU WHAT *REMAINS* OF THEIR BODIES.

IT IS ONLY NATURAL, SUPREME TECHNOPRIEST. THE GREATEST PLEASURES ARE TAKEN ALONE.

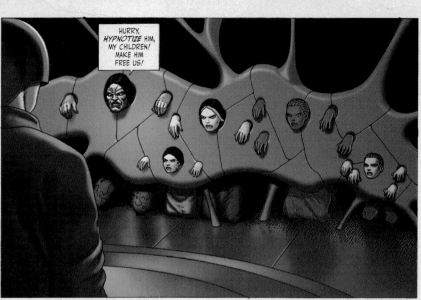

HURRY, *HYPNOTIZE* HIM, MY CHILDREN! MAKE HIM FREE US!

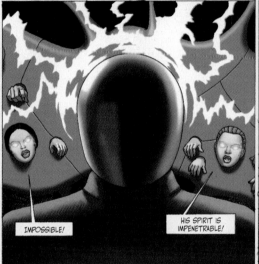

IMPOSSIBLE!

HIS SPIRIT IS IMPENETRABLE!

I AM *NOT* YOUR ENEMY.

I AM ALBINO!

MY *SON*...

MY MOTHER, MY SISTER, MY NIECE, MY NEPHEW, MY STEP-FATHER, OUR WHOLE FAMILY IS REUNITED. WHAT JOY!

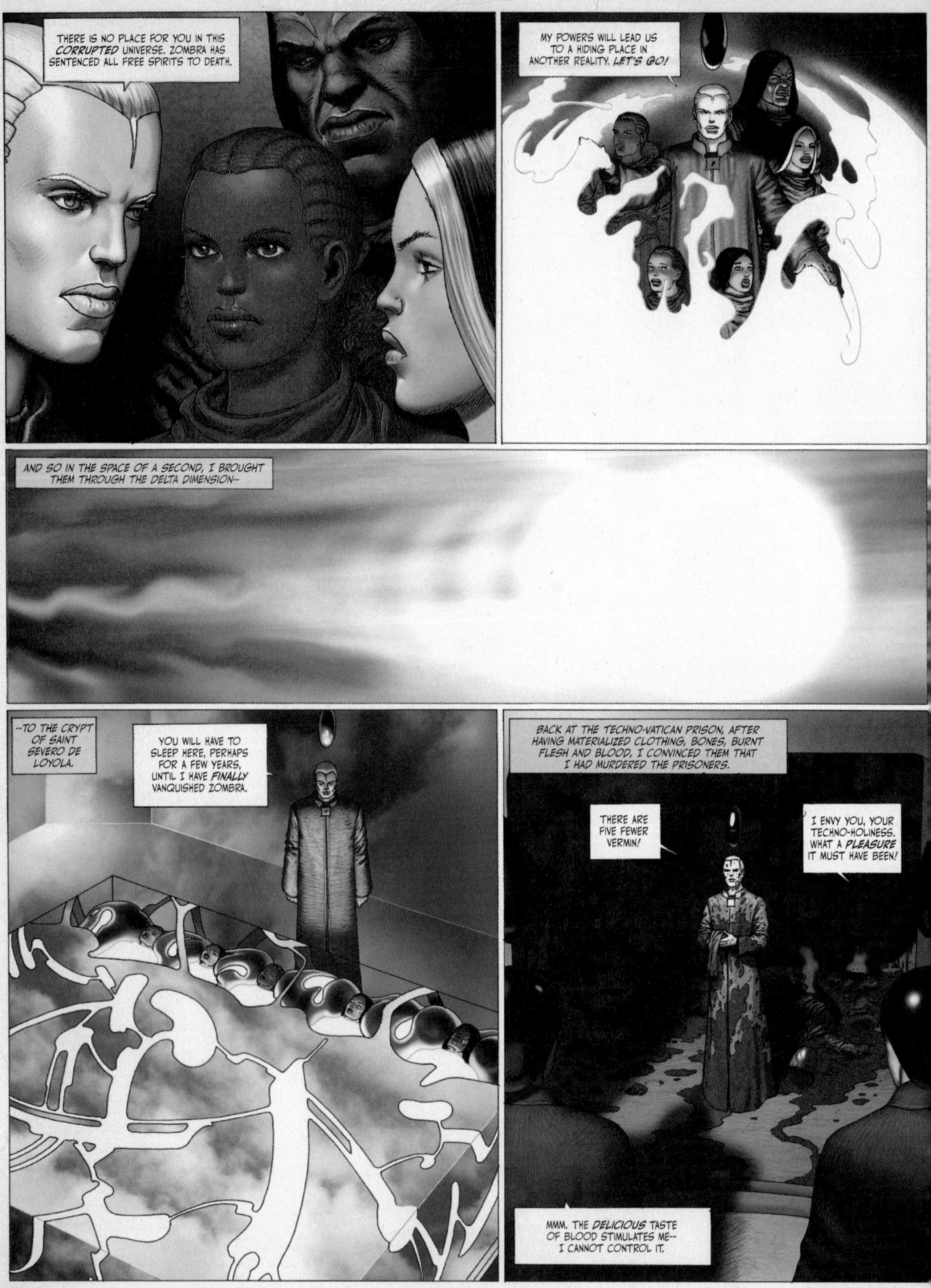

THERE IS NO PLACE FOR YOU IN THIS CORRUPTED UNIVERSE. ZOMBRA HAS SENTENCED ALL FREE SPIRITS TO DEATH.
MY POWERS WILL LEAD US TO A HIDING PLACE IN ANOTHER REALITY. LET'S GO!
AND SO IN THE SPACE OF A SECOND, I BROUGHT THEM THROUGH THE DELTA DIMENSION--
--TO THE CRYPT OF SAINT SEVERO DE LOYOLA.
YOU WILL HAVE TO SLEEP HERE, PERHAPS FOR A FEW YEARS, UNTIL I HAVE FINALLY VANQUISHED ZOMBRA.
BACK AT THE TECHNO-VATICAN PRISON, AFTER HAVING MATERIALIZED CLOTHING, BONES, BURNT FLESH AND BLOOD, I CONVINCED THEM THAT I HAD MURDERED THE PRISONERS.
THERE ARE FIVE FEWER VERMIN!
I ENVY YOU, YOUR TECHNO-HOLINESS. WHAT A PLEASURE IT MUST HAVE BEEN!
MMM. THE DELICIOUS TASTE OF BLOOD STIMULATES ME-- I CANNOT CONTROL IT.

I FELT CALMER, KNOWING THAT MY FAMILY WAS SAFE. THAT CALM WAS SHORT-LIVED.

WHAT DO YOU WANT? HOW *DARE* YOU INTERRUPT MY REST?

A THOUSAND PARDONS, YOUR TECHNO-HOLY EMINENCE. BUT YOU WILL HAVE TO FOLLOW US.

YOUR INITIATION AS THE SUPREME TECHNO-HOLINESS IS NOT FINISHED.

YOU MUST STILL PASS THE GREATEST OF THE TESTS--YOU WILL TRANSFORM INTO AN OPHIDIAN.

IN THE TECHNO-PAPAL SUPER SHIP, THEY TOOK ME TO A SECRET ASTEROID.

THEY UNDRESSED ME AT THE ENTRANCE TO THE HOLY PIT.

YOU WILL BE NAKED FOR THE MUTATION--

--A DEATH--

--AND A REBIRTH.

THEY SHOWERED ME IN THE BLOOD OF SEVEN DECAPITATED VIRGINS.

LET THIS PURE BLOOD BE THE MIRROR OF YOUR SOUL--

--AN IMPLACABLE SOUL THAT HAS NO ROOM FOR PITY--

--WHOSE BEAUTY IS THE AURA OF JUST *FEROCITY.*

I HAD TO FACE THE THREE LEGENDARY SERPENTS--

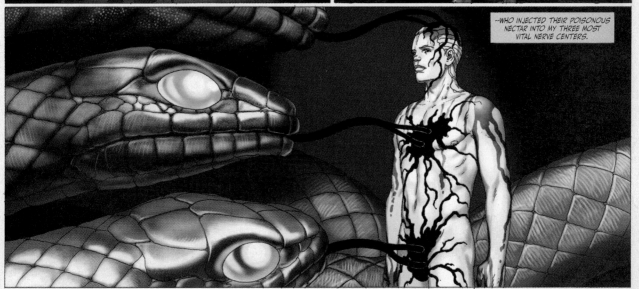

--WHO INJECTED THEIR POISONOUS NECTAR INTO MY THREE MOST VITAL NERVE CENTERS.

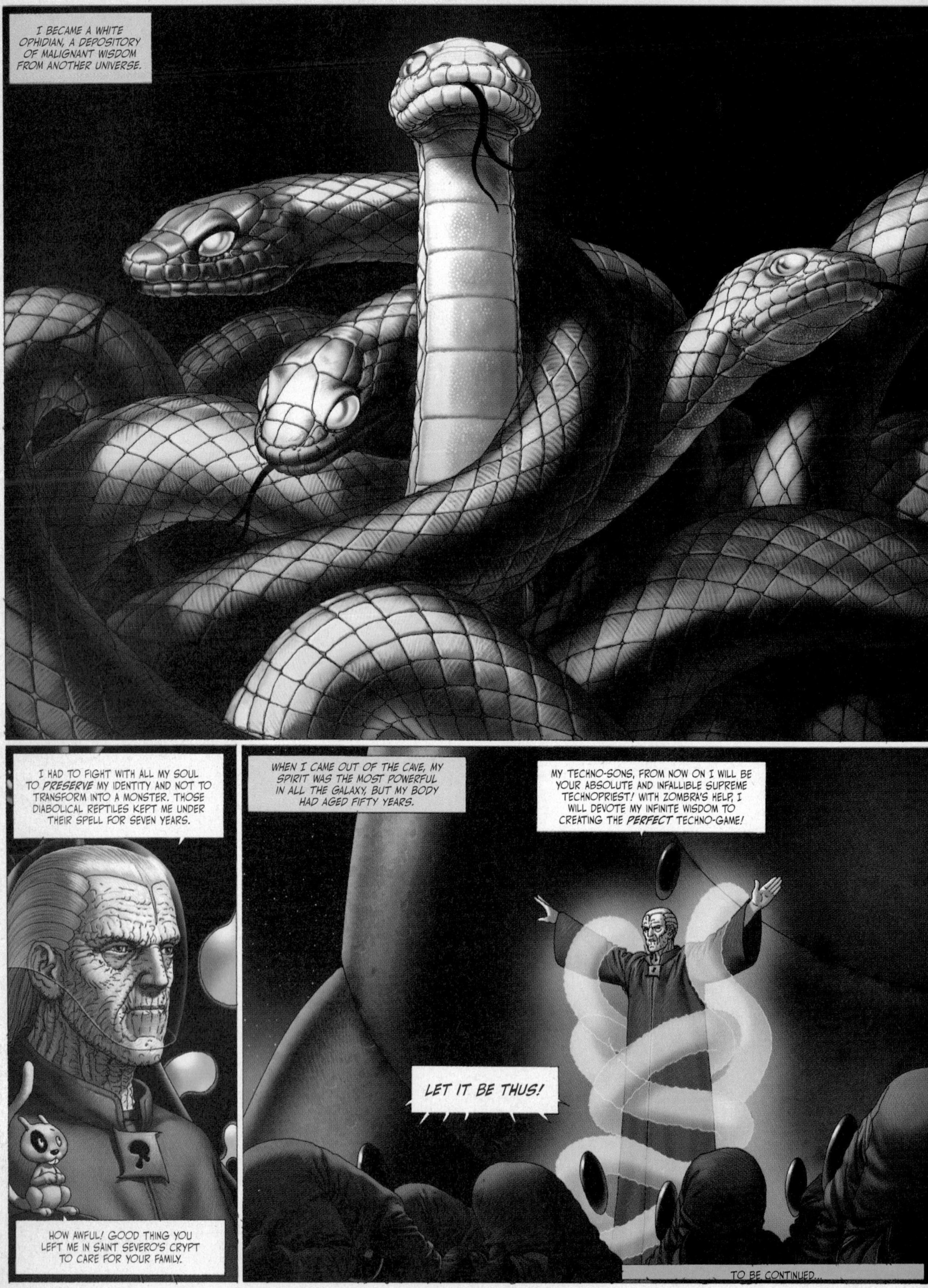
I BECAME A WHITE OPHIDIAN, A DEPOSITORY OF MALIGNANT WISDOM FROM ANOTHER UNIVERSE.
I HAD TO FIGHT WITH ALL MY SOUL TO PRESERVE MY IDENTITY AND NOT TO TRANSFORM INTO A MONSTER. THOSE DIABOLICAL REPTILES KEPT ME UNDER THEIR SPELL FOR SEVEN YEARS.
HOW AWFUL! GOOD THING YOU LEFT ME IN SAINT SEVERO'S CRYPT TO CARE FOR YOUR FAMILY.
WHEN I CAME OUT OF THE CAVE, MY SPIRIT WAS THE MOST POWERFUL IN ALL THE GALAXY, BUT MY BODY HAD AGED FIFTY YEARS.
MY TECHNO-SONS, FROM NOW ON I WILL BE YOUR ABSOLUTE AND INFALLIBLE SUPREME TECHNOPRIEST! WITH ZOMBRA'S HELP, I WILL DEVOTE MY INFINITE WISDOM TO CREATING THE PERFECT TECHNO-GAME!
LET IT BE THUS!
TO BE CONTINUED...

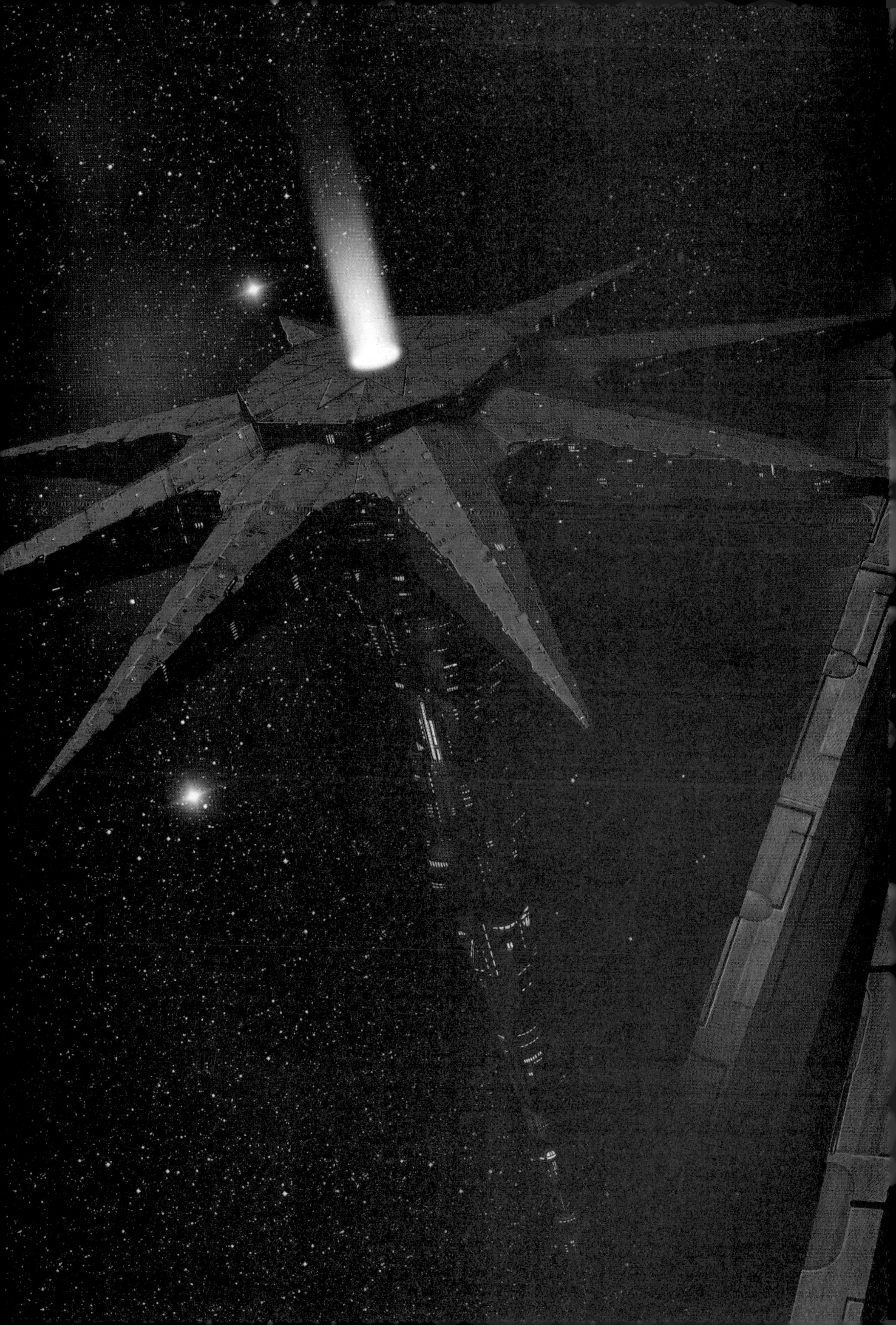

LOOK FOR THESE BOOKS FROM HUMANOIDS/DC COMICS

Alexandro Jodorowsky · Zoran Janjetov · Fred Beltran
THE TECHNOPRIESTS
Book one: Initiation

JODOROWSKY & GIMENEZ
The Metabarons
#1: OTHON & HONORATA
Humanoids / DC Comics

JODOROWSKY & BESS
THE WHITE LAMA
BOOK #1: REINCARNATION

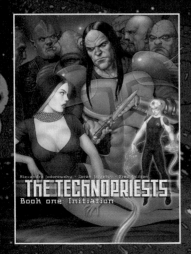

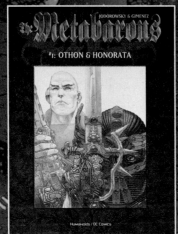

THE TECHNOPRIESTS Vol. 1: INITIATION
Written by Alexandro Jodorowsky with art by Zoran Janjetov and Fred Beltran

THE HORDE
Written and illustrated by Baranko
with colors by Dave Stewart and Charlie Kirchoff

THE BILAL LIBRARY: TOWNSCAPES
Written by Pierre Christin and illustrated by Enki Bilal
with colors by Dan Brown

THE BEAST TRILOGY: CHAPTERS 1 & 2
THE NIKOPOL TRILOGY
By Enki Bilal

THE METABARONS Vol. 1: OTHON & HONORATA
THE METABARONS Vol. 2: AGHNAR & ODA
Written by Alexandro Jodorowsky
and illustrated by Juan Gimenez

DEICIDE Vol. 1: PATH OF THE DEAD
Written by Carlos Portela and
illustrated by Das Pastoras

CHALAND ANTHOLOGY Vol. 1: FREDDY LOMBARD
By Yves Chaland

THE WHITE LAMA BOOK Vol. 1: REINCARNATION
Written by Alexandro Jodorowsky
and illustrated by Georges Bess

SON OF THE GUN Vol. 1: SINNER
Written by Alexandro Jodorowsky
and illustrated by Georges Bess

THE HOLLOW GROUNDS
Written by Luc Schuiten and
illustrated by François Schuiten

BY THE NUMBERS Vol. 1: THE ROAD TO CAO BANG
Written by Laurent Rullier with
art by Stanislas

Call 1-888-COMIC BOOK or visit dccomics.com to locate your nearest comics shop.